D1259598

Design and Production of Multimedia and Simulation-based
Learning Material

Design and Production of Multimedia and Simulation-based Learning Material

Edited by

Ton de Jong
Faculty of Educational Science and Technology,
University of Twente,
Enschede, The Netherlands

and

Luigi Sarti
Istituto per le Tecnologie Didattiche,
Consiglio Nazionale delle Ricerche,
Genova, Italy

This volume is sponsored by the European Commission
in the context of the specific programme:
Telematic Systems of General Interest
Area 4: Flexible and Distance Learning (DELTA).

KLUWER ACADEMIC PUBLISHERS
DORDRECHT / BOSTON / LONDON

A C.I.P. Catalogue record for this book is available from the Library of Congress.

LB
1028.5
T45
1994

ISBN 0-7923-3020-X

Published by Kluwer Academic Publishers,
P.O. Box 17, 3300 AA Dordrecht, The Netherlands.

Kluwer Academic Publishers incorporates
the publishing programmes of
D. Reidel, Martinus Nijhoff, Dr W. Junk and MTP Press.

Sold and distributed in the U.S.A. and Canada
by Kluwer Academic Publishers,
101 Philip Drive, Norwell, MA 02061, U.S.A.

In all other countries, sold and distributed
by Kluwer Academic Publishers Group,
P.O. Box 322, 3300 AH Dordrecht, The Netherlands.

Printed on acid-free paper

Printed in the Netherlands

Table of Contents

Preface

This volume results from a meeting that was held in Barcelona, Spain, April 1993, under the auspices of the DELTA programme of the European Commission. DELTA (Developing European Learning through Technological Advance) is the commission's technology R&D programme that concentrates on "Telematic Systems for Flexible and Distance Learning". The overarching goal of this programme is to contribute through information technology to more efficient and effective design, production, and delivery of learning material. The DELTA programme started its main phase in 1992 with a total of 22 projects and a total budget of 92.4 million ECU. In the meanwhile an extension of the programme has resulted in 8 extensions of existing projects and 8 new projects, bringing the number of projects to 30, with a corresponding total budget of 99.9 million ECU. The programme has three main areas: telecommunication, delivery information systems, and design and production. In the projects, in total 201 organisations (industrial, commercial, and universities) from 12 European Union member states and 5 EFTA countries are represented.

The DELTA programme pays much attention to the exchange of ideas and dissemination of information both between individual DELTA projects and between DELTA projects and other initiatives in the EU. Meetings in which DELTA projects are involved are held several times a year as so-called 'concertation meetings', meetings where also non-DELTA projects participate are called 'concerted actions'. The Barcelona meeting was such a concerted action with as a specific theme: 'Design and production of learning material'. In this specific meeting special emphasis was given to learning material in which multimedia is involved and learning material that is based upon computer simulations. The papers presented at the meeting in Barcelona formed the basis for the present book. Since, however, DELTA (and other) projects are ongoing projects we have requested the authors to update their papers so that the papers reflect the status of their projects at the time of completion of the book, which is spring 1994. All together, the book contains eleven chapters of which eight give descriptions of DELTA projects and three are from outside DELTA.

We think this book gives an excellent impression of the status of European research and development in the area of design and production of computer supported learning. We hope the reader will enjoy reading it as much as we enjoyed reviewing the papers.

It was a pleasure to get the support of a number of different people when preparing this book. Augusto Chioccariello and Teresa del Soldato contributed to the reviewing process. Thyra Kuijpers and Pauline Teppich checked the documents on style and Tim Remmers did a wonderful job in converting different formats of text and in particular graphics into one coherent and consistent format. His efforts made us realise again, how standardisation, one of DELTA's main themes, may alleviate production of material. We certainly also like to thank Guy Weets from the DELTA office who supported this endeavour and organised the funds to make this publication possible.

Ton de Jong & Luigi Sarti

Introduction:
Trends in the Design and Production of
Computer Based Learning Material

Ton de Jong[1] & Luigi Sarti[2]

[1] Faculty of Educational Science and Technology, University of Twente,
The Netherlands; [2] Istituto Tecnologie Didattiche, Italy

Nowadays courseware development is evolving from the status of handicraft activity to that of industrial process: the requirement that quality and cost-effectiveness should be ensured by the adoption of formal models, explicit methods and well-assessed tools is growing stronger and stronger. Software engineering underwent such an evolution years ago: it was a long and complex process that started with the definition of the first software life-cycle models and that is still in progress with the development of modern CASE environments.

Similarly to software, quality and effectiveness of courseware can only be achieved if the development process is modelled so that each activity can be supported at both the conceptual and technical levels. Long and expensive phases need optimisation through the development of proper standards and techniques. Reuse of existing artefacts and collaborative approaches are considered crucial aspects of the authoring activities.

Unfortunately, today's off-the-shelf authoring tools seldom meet the above mentioned needs. Current commercially available authoring systems are most of the times based on a model of the development cycle that is either too generic, incomplete, or simply inadequate; as a consequence, high level design phases are usually neglected; reusability is poorly supported; representation and quality standards are far from being considered.

For these reasons research on better models, methods, and tools for designing and producing courseware is bound to have a crucial impact on tomorrow's authoring systems. All the papers in this book discuss research projects that aim at the development of new ways to support the authoring process. The main focus in the present book is on *design* and *production* of courseware material, which are considered to be two critical activities. For these activities we propose the following two definitions:

- the *design* of the courseware material essentially means the definition of the domain content, context of usage, intended outcomes and instructional strategies for the courseware under development: in short, the 'educational shape' of the learning material;
- the *production* of the material refers to the materialisation of the decisions that have been taken in the design. Here, we can consider a variety of specific

activities, including the actual creation of multimedia material, the synchronisation of time-dependent components, and the organisation of the surface aspects of the learner interaction.

It is sometimes difficult to draw a clear line between these two aspects. For instance, the choice of the media used to present the material is usually related to the production phase, but might as well be considered at design time, given its strong links with such pedagogical aspects as the learner connotation.

Two classifications of papers in this book

Most of the papers in this book have something to say on both design and production, but some have a stronger design emphasis (Grandbastien & Gavignet; Mispelkamp & Sarti; Tait), some accentuate the production (Ulloa; Benamou & Celentano; Busch et al.; Härtel), whilst others (Barker, van Rosmalen, de Jong et al.) pay balanced attention to design and production. Verreck and Weges, finally, take a broader view when they present a general framework (the Common Training Architecture) for describing courseware itself, the design, production and delivery process, and the context in which the courseware should function and in which the distinguished processes take place. In this way, CTA strives towards standardisation that should contribute to a higher level of "interoperability, portability, and ease of use".

A second distinction that runs through this book is the one between 'general' courseware and simulation-based training material. This distinction is based on an essential characteristic of learning material that involves the way in which information on the domain is present. In one class of learning material this domain information is included in a 'non reactive way', and this is traditionally denoted as tutorial. In tutorials domain information is *presented* in some way to the learner (for example in (hyper)text, graphics, or demonstrations); in simulations a model of a domain is present, this model reacts to inputs of the learner, and the learner is expected to *infer* the characteristics of this model. Most of the papers in the book have to do with the more 'tutorial' type of approach, though some of them include simulations as a possible component of courseware (Benamou & Celentano). Four papers (Härtel; Tait; van Rosmalen; de Jong et al.) are specifically dedicated to simulation based learning material. Also here, however, combinations of simulations with direct presentation of information appear (see e.g. de Jong et al.).

Emerging topics on design and production

One 'design topic' that emerges from the papers is the use of 'basic' entities for the design of learning material. These entities are called 'learning units' (Grandbastien) or 'units of learning material' (Mispelkamp & Sarti; Benamou & Celentano). Each unit (or "didactic module" as Benamou & Celentano describe it) has a specific character. Grandbastien and Gavignet give as examples "presentation, exercise, review, and problem". Mispelkamp and Sarti relate the concept of unit of learning material to pedagogical goals for which they distinguish 'knowledge', 'understanding', and 'application'. Benamou and Celentano restrict the use of units of learning material to what they call a 'program oriented paradigm', which in fact is the tutorial approach described above, and, as Mispelkamp and Sarti do, they relate this to the specific goals in which also a well defined part of the domain is included.

In the area of simulation based learning we find a similar approach. Van Rosmalen describes the use of "Instructional Simulation Objects (ISO)", which are "basic educational units". Van Rosmalen distinguishes five different ISOs: demo, task, hypothesis, experiment, and exploration. De Jong et al., following an object oriented approach, describe what they call "basic building blocks". These basic building blocks are the "classes" an author can use for creating a simulation model and for instructional support around the simulation. In the SMISLE system, that is described by de Jong et al, the units, or basic building blocks, are grouped in libraries that are related to different functions in the resulting learning environment.

The choice for the type of units and their linking is a second topic in the design area. Units of material can be linked in many ways and different authors define different sets of relations. Grandbastien and Gavignet distinguish five different types of link between units of learning material which are divided into static links (links in which the learner's evolving knowledge is not considered) and dynamic links (in which the learner's developing skills are taken into consideration, for example whether a learner has passed or failed an exercise assessment). Mispelkamp and Sarti present the most elaborate typology of links by giving 17 types of link (though these links only zoom in on domain concepts).

A typology of links is one of the inputs for the final sequencing of units, which is determined by the instructional, or pedagogical, strategy that is chosen. Grandbastien and Gavignet give three of such strategies (that they label "meta-knowledge"), for example a strategy in which the presentation of information precedes exercises. Benamou and Celentano propose four different educational strategies of which the "program oriented strategies" is one. In this strategy the sequencing of units follows the pattern "presentation, interaction, test, and action". Barker presents an overall instructional paradigm that is supposed to be an "optimum mix" of several other learning paradigms. Barker calls his approach the MAPARI paradigm. This paradigm entails the following stages in the learning process: "mimicry, apprenticeship, practice, assessment, refinement, and improvement". Obviously in each of the stages different basic learning actions will take place. Tait, whose work is in the simulation area, divides the learning process into three phases with associated specific learning process: planning/ prediction, performance/observation, and debriefing/reflection. Van Rosmalen uses what he calls "instructional plans", domain specific descriptions of how to reach a specific educational goal. In de Jong et al. authors are provided with instructional guidelines which help them to decide, for domains and learners with specific characteristics, which instructional support measures should be available to a learner. The author can realise this by attaching so-called "enabling conditions" to instructional support measures.

An important issue in the design area is the level of support for authors. Traditional authoring tools essentially do not provide support that exceeds production techniques which centre around the provision of 'flow charting' support. The introduction of 'units of learning material', or 'building blocks' makes that authors now are supported by abstract (or even domain specific) templates, that they can use for creating their own courseware material. Support in this case therefore moves towards real 'design' support, since authors are offered 'educational' templates. This idea also translates into another new topic in design and production, which is the reuse of existing material. For efficient reuse, it is necessary that existing material is divided into smaller chunks, that have some generality and that are labelled with relevant characteristics, as is done for the above mentioned units of learning material and building blocks.

For both the design and the production of the learning material one of the new and emerging ideas is that of collaborative and distributed authoring. Ulloa's paper pays relevant attention to these aspects, depicting a scenario where a number of authors with different roles and from geographically distributed sites collaborate in the development of courseware. The co-authoring services offered in OSCAR include: collaboration tools, supporting group communication and sharing of information; co-ordination tools, supporting the organisation and management of projects; codecision tools, allowing remote group decision making; reuse tools, fostering the reuse of existing artefacts. Reuse is also a primary concern of the approach proposed both by Grandbastien and Gavignet, and by Mispelkamp and Sarti. Here, a sharp separation is recommended between the conceptual representation of the knowledge to be taught and the actual pieces of learning material the learner will interact with; besides, in both projects a strong distinction is drawn between the contents to be conveyed to the student (i.e., what to teach) and the instructional strategies used (i.e., how to teach). In both cases, the decoupling facilitates the co-operation between different authors and the reuse of existing components. Although not primarily concerned with distributed authoring issues, the emphasis de Jong et al. put on the provision of libraries of building blocks in the SMISLE toolkit constitutes another step towards the adoption of reuse techniques in the courseware development process. A number of aspects in the work of Benamou and Celentano can be related to collaborative authoring: here, authors can play a variety of roles: editor, teacher and course designer; specific tools are provided for such activities as resource management and session management; one of MATHESIS' objectives is to provide an educational server accessed through local area networks and ISDN. The main objective of the COSYS project, described in Busch et al., is to pilot a distributed course production and delivery system. The co-authoring scenario includes such activities as project initiation and management, instructional design, production planning, and material creation, editing and composition; co-authoring is supported through on-line access to a database of raw material and help facilities, and through a variety of communication facilities.

As we indicated above, courseware can be classified according to the nature of the domain that is present: simulation-based or not. Related to this issue are the formal techniques that are chosen in the different projects for describing the domain content of the courseware. Grandbastien and Gavignet propose an associative network where nodes are concepts of the domain subject area and edges represent either hierarchical relationships between concepts or such pedagogical knowledge as pre-requisite links. An interesting point is that the granularity of the network is determined by the assessment activities: the concepts of the network are the most elementary items for which the teacher requires assessment. Mispelkamp and Sarti support the usage of associative networks for a variety of purposes. The domain model, independent of specific learning goals, provides a reusable description of an area of knowledge; nodes are untyped, edges represent relations of various types: hierarchical, aggregational, temporal, spatial, causal, and related to activity. By applying learning goals to the domain model an author derives the content representation, another associative network where the nodes are typed according to a knowledge vs. skill taxonomy, and the edge type set is the same as for the domain analysis, plus the pre-requisite link type. Instructional object types are also organised into a formal hierarchy. In its concern for collaborative authoring and reuse models OSCAR explicitly represents all the actors and objects involved in the courseware development process as a network of classes. The design and production activities can therefore be formally modelled in terms of roles, functions, messages and rules. Strong inheritance hierarchies enhance the retrievability and reusability of artefacts.

The simulation contributions propose the adoption of a variety of specific graphic formalisms for the representation of relevant entities. Tait applies extended bond graphs to represent the functionality of physical systems as energy flows. Van Rosmalen describes a hierarchy where a course is decomposed into learning goals, then into instructional plans and finally into instructional objects; such a hierarchy is explicitly represented in the system, and is used both by the authors in the design phase and by the learners as a navigation tool in the courseware space. SAM also represents a simulation model as a concept network at a variety of abstraction levels; instructional simulation objects are graphically represented as flowcharts. de Jong et al. use bond graphs to model a system in terms of energy flow, and extended petri nets to model both discrete events and operational expertise

A final topic within the production area is the use of existing general applications (such as widely available text processors, or drawing tools) or the development of newly designed and dedicated tools. In the case study described in Barker's contribution existing commercial tools are used in the framework of the proposed methodology. The OSCAR architecture described by Ulloa allows for the integration of external tools in the authoring space: Multimedia Toolbook™, Generic Tutoring

Environment (GTE) and Word for Windows™ are three examples of external applications included in OSCAR which required some customisation work to allow synchronous and asynchronous co-operative activities. Other kinds of tools, such as the Common Information Space Browser, required specific development. Härtel's work lists a number of dedicated tools and final applications that have been developed in the COLOS project; emphasis is also put on the fact that "experience shows a great reluctance of many teachers to the use of software in their teaching, especially if it is a foreign, 'out-of-house' product". As a consequence of this approach, COLOS devotes significant effort to the provision of instruments that let non-programmer authors develop their own simulations. Van Rosmalen's project features a slot-based architecture where authors fill the slots of their SAM environment with either SAM-compatible applications or SAM-developed modules. A specific module is provided, which handles control and communication between individual tools; a package-independent command language is defined, to hide the complexity of platform- and application-dependent technical details. The list of external, SAM-compatible applications includes Authorware™ and Microsoft Excel™. Editing of the material is supported in MATHESIS by a project-specific version of a commercial authoring tool, Apple Media Kit™, as well as by other external graphic and animation editing programs. The integration of external tools is also possible at student-time, to call and use them from within the courseware. The pilot production environments described in Busch et al. implement the Generic COSYS Concept using a wide set of commercial tools and formats, including Lotus Notes™, MS-Access™, FrameMaker™, Ventura Publisher™ and Windows™ Help.

Overview of the papers in this book

We conclude with brief descriptions of each of the chapters in the book.

Barker's work describes an approach to support the design and implementation of courseware systems based on a definition of interactive learning which attempts to mediate across different theories of learning, ranging from behaviourism to constructivism. Barker presents ten basic perspectives of learning design, as formulated in the *ILDIC* project, that each author should consider when creating courseware. The contribution also presents a case study where the proposed model and techniques are applied to the field of foreign language learning; a controlled evaluation study allows for a critical appraisal of the effectiveness of the approach.

ECSA, the generator of learning environments proposed by Grandbastien and Gavignet, consists of a formal model to describe the subject domain and a set of tools which enable the author to associate the elements of the domain structure with existing learning units, characterised by the definition of pre-conditions (elementary items) and post-actions (learner's results). The model also addresses such issues as pedagogical objectives, dynamic evaluation of the learner's performance and instructional strategies.

Mispelkamp and Sarti describe the *DISCourse* approach to courseware design, including those aspects like learner modelling, instructional design and domain representation. Aimed at the systematic support of all the phases of courseware development, DISCourse (Design and Interactive Specification of Courseware) addresses the representation of the subject domain at three levels: domain analysis, learning goal analysis and content analysis. Particular attention is paid to reusability issues. Specific tools supporting the author in these activities are also described.

Benamou and Celentano describe *MATHESIS*, a project aimed at the definition and development of a stand-alone workbench for both the author and the student. The main features of the MATHESIS proposal are its flexible attitude towards educational strategies, its strong support of multimedia and hypermedia functionalities and the independence of its architecture from the underlying hardware platform. External tools can be integrated in the workbench at various levels of binding.

OSCAR (Open System for Collaborative Authoring and Reuse) addresses collaborative and distributed authoring of multimedia training materials. Ulloa sketches an application scenario where authoring resources are distributed over both local and wide areas, with the aim of fulfilling the requirements of uniformity, quality, productivity and reliability for the course development process. OSCAR is based on an open system architecture and provides multimedia communication facilities, a common information space allowing co-operation between different tools and actors, and high level services to support collaboration, co-ordination, codecision and reuse.

The main objective of *COSYS* is to pilot a distributed course production and delivery system. Busch et al. describe that COSYS aims at users such as publishers, producers of courseware, distributors, authors, etc. A central concept in COSYS is that users of course material that is filed in a database should be able to tailor the material to their own needs. COSYS offers a host of services that at the most detailed level translate into for example stylesheets for the presentation of material.

Tait reports on the part of the *DISCourse* project (of which the general part is presented in Mispelkamp and Sarti) that takes care of simulation-based learning environments. In the DISCourse project a systematic methodology is developed for the design and production of a simulation, based on an abstract representation of the model which drives the simulation. For creating the underlying model DISCourse relies on bond as a formalism and also a distinction between a 'pure' domain model (created by a modeller) and a domain model suited for education (created by an author) is made. DISCourse provides additional support to the learner. This support comprises: proposing useful tasks (which can be manipulation or diagnosis tasks), encouraging the stating of hypotheses (a set of propositions) and expectations (represented in graphical form), providing explanations, answering learners' questions, and making suggestions for subsequent investigations The main application area of the DISCourse simulation system is in the field of medicine.

De Jong et al. present the *SMISLE* (System for Multimedia Simulation Learning Environments) project. The aim of this project is to build a general authoring environment for simulations together with instructional support. Four specific types of instructional measures were selected: progressive model implementation, assignments, explanations and hypothesis scratchpads. In SMISLE authors create integrated simulation learning environments by selecting 'building blocks' from libraries and by tailoring these building blocks to their needs through the use of dedicated editors. In this respect the design, (e.g. devising instructional support) and production (e.g. creating this instructional support) are united. Additionally, authors are guided through the authoring process by a methodology and they have access to instructional advice which provides them with ideas on which instructional measures to apply.

The *SAM* (Simulation And Multimedia) project is described by van Rosmalen. The aim of the SAM project is to specify and develop a modelling, authoring and learning framework for simulation-based learning based on external software tools. SAM, therefore, stands for the integration of existing tools, but adds specifically designed SAM tools. At a technical level the integration of existing and developed tools concerns the communication and control between the tools reflected in the creation data exchange protocols. SAM guarantees the conceptual integration through the use of so-called Instructional Simulation Objects (ISO). ISOs are building blocks that allow for different levels of freedom ranging from fully system guided task exercises to learner controlled experiments. With help of a graphical editor the author writes a script both controlling SAM designed functions, e.g. monitoring or exchange of data, and external supplied functions, e.g. running a simulation model or a courseware. To the learner SAM will supply additional tools such as e.g. a multi-media notebook.

Härtel gives insight into the *COLOS* (Conceptual Learning of Science) project. This project builds on a large number of local initiatives and uses as such a bottom-up approach. The common interest of all sites is the use of simulations to help students gain basic concepts in science by reducing the mathematical overload so often characteristic for traditional science instruction, to provide the possibility of easy experimentation with possible change of time scales etc., and to support learners' knowledge acquisition process by offering spatial, 3-dimensional, representations of phenomena. The project develops a core of authoring instruments that allows a non-expert programmer to develop models forming the basis of simulations together with the necessary interaction part. The paper describes this set of tools. Secondly, the project provides authors with 'ready made', but still customasible, applications in specialised fields such as neural nets and integrated circuits. The applications created in COLOS are meant for teachers to be used in their lectures, but may also be given to students directly.

The *CTA* project, finally, as it is presented in the paper by Verreck and Weges has different objectives than the other projects described in this book. CTA is not concerned with developing methods that can be used for design and production, but gives a higher level framework for analyzing and formalising design and production and the methods that are used themselves. The final goal of the CTA project is contribute to harmonisation and standardisation of technologies, systems, and infrastructures for flexible and distance learning.

Designing Interactive Learning

Philip Barker

Interactive Systems Research Group, Human-Computer Interaction Laboratory,
School of Computing and Mathematics, University of Teesside, UK

Abstract

Interactive learning is a necessary and fundamental mechanism for knowledge acquisition and the development of both cognitive and physical skills. Before designing interactive learning resources it is important to understand how interactivity works and the nature of the environments that are needed to support it. The effectiveness of these environments also needs to be examined. This paper discusses the basic nature of interactive learning and describes some models to support the design and fabrication of interactive learning systems. A case study describing the application of these models to the creation of multimedia courseware for interactive language learning is then presented.

1 INTRODUCTION

In his systems map of the universe, Checkland (1972) identified five basic classes of system. The systems he identified were: natural systems; transcendental systems; designed physical systems; designed abstract systems; and systems that involve human-activity. Human-activity systems are important because they involve individuals (or groups of people) 'doing things' either alone, or in conjunction with each other. The activities in which people participate may involve other animate or inanimate objects (such as machines and computers) in order to achieve some particular goal.

One very important class of human-activity system is that which deals with the provision of learning and training opportunities to facilitate the development of an informed society and/or the creation of an effective 'work force'. Systems that fall into this category are often referred to as 'knowledge and skill transfer systems'. Such systems cover a wide spectrum of possibilities. These can be organised into two broad classes: (a) those which depend primarily upon direct human interaction (such as tutoring, group learning and lectures); and (b) those which are in some way mediated by technology. This paper is primarily concerned with this latter class of system.

Systems that use various forms of technology in order to achieve knowledge and skill transfer are now quite commonplace. They can be based either upon the use of static media (such as paper) or dynamic media such as the telephone, interactive compact disc and computer systems. Undoubtedly, computers currently offer one of the most exciting and potentially useful mechanisms for the development and delivery of software to support knowledge and skill transfer. Computers can be

1

T. de Jong and L. Sarti (eds.), Design and Production of Multimedia and Simulation-based Learning Material, 1-30
© 1994 *Kluwer Academic Publishers. Printed in the Netherlands.*

combined with a wide range of other ancillary technologies (such as telecommunications, optical storage, audio facilities, image processing, and so on) in order to create a significant repertoire of possibilities for knowledge, skill and information dissemination within a learning and training context.

For many years people have been exploring and investigating the various ways in which computer-based technology (in its many different forms) might be used to create new types of knowledge transfer system that will provide more cost-effective and more efficient approaches to learning and training. Examples of some of the techniques that have been explored are well-documented in the literature (CACM, 1993; Romiszowski, 1992; Schank, 1993; Harrison, 1991; Piciotto et al, 1989; Latchem et al, 1993; Barker, 1989; 1993a; 1993b). Together these illustrate a wide range of approaches to instruction which between them embed all the different 'theories of learning' - ranging from behaviourism through cognitivism to constructivism.

Currently, our own approach to the development of interactive computer-based learning and training resources is one which is based upon an 'optimum mix' of the learning theories listed above. Obviously, the optimum mix of learning theories will vary from one situation to another depending upon the nature of the learning and training activities that are to be encouraged and promoted. The intent of these can vary enormously. For example, some courseware items will be developed and then used simply in order to alert and inform (that is, create an awareness of an event or a topic). Of course, in other situations the courseware items might be produced in order to develop expert skills or to perform 'just-in-time' training - either in an academic or an industrial setting (Banerji, 1994).

In recent years, a large proportion of the computer-based learning resources that we have been developing in our laboratory has been concerned with the development of 'expert skills' in some particular area of endeavour - such as problem solving, interface design, programming, foreign language learning, and so on. Within this type of learning/training context we have paid considerable attention to: (1) the underlying motivational characteristics of the learners involved; and (2) the subsequent creation of appropriate interactive learning environments to enable them to fulfil their learning ambitions. As a result of the studies that we have made it is our conjecture that the majority of people learn new skills as a consequence of wanting to become an 'expert' within some particular discipline, activity or task. The expertise that people develop may involve intellectual skills, creative activity, organisational ability, communicative competence, manual dexterity, and so on. We believe that the basic learning and training rationale for achieving 'expertise' involves the use of a number of fundamental processes such as observation, mimicry and skill refinement. This basic approach to knowledge and skill acquisition is summarised using a simple six stage schema that we refer to as the 'MAPARI' paradigm.

MAPARI is an acronym for 'Mimicry, Apprenticeship, Practice, Assessment, Refinement and Improvement'. Mimicry involves trying to copy and reproduce a skill that an expert has (for example, a mathematical skill or the correct pronunciation and use of a foreign language). Apprenticeship involves working with a domain expert in order to acquire the skills necessary to gain expert status and achieve expert performance within a particular subject area. In order to realise this status it is necessary for a student or trainee to practice using his/her incipient skills for various purposes - such as problem solving. Within the MAPARI approach the purpose of assessment is to gauge how closely the skills and knowledge of a trainee are approaching those of a relevant expert. The results of a particular assessment phase are used to refine skill development in order to 'fine tune' the developing skills into an appropriate 'region of acceptability'. Once this is achieved learners and trainees have to be encouraged to improve their knowledge and skill levels in order to achieve an optimal performance condition.

Of course, the overall MAPARI process itself is not necessarily a linear one but can involve a range of non-linear activities such as iteration and backtracking in order to achieve a particular learning or training outcome. Obviously, in general, the desired learning outcome is the transition from 'novice' to 'expert' behaviour within a chosen skill domain. This transition is illustrated schematically in Figure 1.

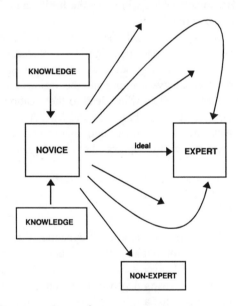

Figure 1 *Learning transitions - from novice to expert*

In this diagram we depict the transition from novice to expert by means of multiple pathways - each one of which denotes a different route to acquiring the expertise associated with the status of being an expert. Different routes therefore require different times and different kinds (and amounts) of resource input.

Two important points emerge from Figure 1. First, not all the transitions that emanate from the novice state will automatically lead to the achievement of expertise in a particular domain; in some cases learning and training activity will fail - leading to the creation of a 'non-expert'. Second, the graph will exhibit a certain number of pathways of least resource requirement (one such traversal in Figure 1 has been labelled 'ideal').

Obviously, the exact meaning of the term ideal is likely to vary from one situation to another. For example, in some cases the ideal transition will be the path of minimum time; in other situations the ideal might be the path of minimum resource, the path of minimum cost or the attainment of a particular level of skill.

The MAPARI paradigm is one which we believe is perfectly general. It is therefore applicable to a wide variety of different learning and training situations. Obviously, it can be used in contexts which do not involve the use of computers. Our own particular interests, however, are oriented towards learning and training situations which depend upon the use of computer-based methods. The purpose of this paper will therefore be to consider the wider issues relating to the way in which the paradigm is implemented within computer-based systems. Naturally, its successful realisation will depend upon the creation of appropriately designed interactive learning environments which will allow the fulfilment of each of the six MAPARI phases that were described above.

In the remainder of this paper we shall discuss the basic factors that must be considered when realising the MAPARI paradigm for the creation of interactive computer-based learning and training resources. Subsequent sections therefore consider the basic nature of interactive learning and the various models of learning design that embed the necessary factors which lead to the creation of a successful learning/training product. A case study based on the MAPARI approach is then presented - this involves the development and assessment of an interactive multimedia learning environment to support the teaching/learning of foreign language skills.

2 THE NATURE OF INTERACTIVE LEARNING

Interaction and interactivity are fundamental to all dynamic systems - particularly, those involving people. So commonplace is the notion of interactivity that Checkland (1972) described the Universe as 'a complex of interacting systems'. Invariably, interaction between systems depends upon some sort of 'flow' taking place between them. This requires that a subset of the outputs from any one system be fed (as inputs) to one or more other systems. Usually, the flow that takes place involves the movement of material, energy or information from one system to another. Obviously, the extent of the flow that takes place between any two systems depends upon the permeability of the boundaries that separate them. A basic consequence of the flow referred to above is that an event (or change of state) taking place in one system can initiate events (changes of state) in the other systems with which it is associated.

The basic principle of interactivity (based upon information flow) is illustrated schematically in Figure 2. This depicts two dynamic processes A and B that interact with each other. The mechanism of interaction is as follows. At some particular instant in time Process B (in state B_1) sends a message to Process A. As a result of receiving this message Process A undergoes a state transition (or change of state) from state A_1 to state A_2. When in state A_2, Process A sends a message to Process B which now moves from state B_1 into state B_2. This process of dynamic interaction through message passing continues until one or other of the processes terminates the interaction - if either is able to do so.

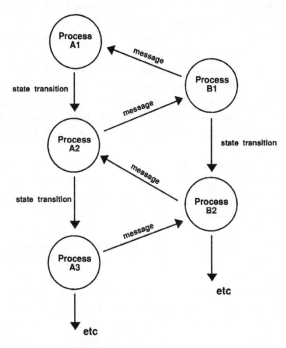

Figure 2 *Basic principle of interactivity*

In many ways the interaction and interactivity that was described above is very similar to the basic mechanisms that underly the paradigm of object orientation that is used in computer systems design and software engineering (Winblad, Edwards, & King, 1990). Here a system is regarded as a collection of reactive objects which are able to pass messages to one another. Objects react to incoming messages by means of the various 'scripts' that are embedded within them; they then interact with other objects by means of further message passing activity.

The simple model of interactivity depicted in Figure 2 can be applied to both human-human interaction and human-computer interaction. In the case of human-human interaction the processes involved are usually of a cognitive nature and message passing (in real-time) most often takes the form of speech acts, gestures and tactile dialogue. The states involved are knowledge states. As a result of a dialogue process, the communicating partners therefore (in principle) learn more about each other or about the topic of discourse.

In the case of human-computer interaction, the processes involved are cognitive and computational, respectively. Message passing in this case usually involves the use of a keyboard and a CRT screen. Of course, if a multimedia personal computer (MPC) is employed then interaction can be based on the use of pointing operations (using a mouse) that are used in conjunction with a suitably designed graphical user interface (GUI). A MPC also allows the use of high-quality sound, static images and motion video to be used for message passing (Jamsa, 1993). Of course, in more sophisticated 'virtual reality' systems, complex tactile and gestural sequences can be employed in order to pass messages between the communicating partners that are involved in dialogue transactions (Rheingold, 1991; Helsel & Roth, 1991; Barker, 1993c). Obviously, if the computational processes involved in human-computer interaction (such as simulations, surrogations and knowledge/information presentation) are designed correctly they can be used to initiate and stimulate cognition, reflection, thinking, creativity and learning within a human dialogue partner.

From what has been said above it is easy to see that the basic model of interactivity depicted in Figure 2 forms the basis of both human tuition and computer-based tuition. The similarities between these two approaches to interactive learning are illustrated schematically in Figure 3 (Barker, 1993b). As can be seen from a comparison of diagrams 3A and 3B there exists an isomorphic relationship between the two types of learning. This is important because knowledge, ideas and experience obtained with one type of system can often be beneficially 'carried across' to the other.

The human tuition depicted in Figure 3A is, of course, an ideal case. It involves a tutor who is participating in a direct one-to-one individualised instructional dialogue with a student/trainee. Because it is so expensive and time demanding to implement, this 1:1 approach is only used in situations that warrant it or in cases where there are sufficient resources available to support it. More often than not, tutorial dialogues of the type depicted in Figure 3A usually involve groups of students in a 1:N situation (where N can be anywhere in the range 5 through 20). Obviously, in this situation many of the advantages of individualisation are lost. However, there are likely to be some gains as a result of the various types of group interaction that can now take place.

The falling cost and widespread availability of computer technology over the last decade has meant that, in principle, many people can afford to have their own personal computer system - and/or a consumer product (such as CD-I) that is capable of delivering interactive learning resources (Hoffos et al, 1992). The development of computer-based tuition for such systems can therefore offer an attractive substitute for 1:1 human tuition. Provided the software is well-designed it should be able to adapt its behaviour to the specific needs of individual users. Furthermore, provided suitable telecommunications facilities and modems are available, this type of tuition can be made totally independent of geographical location; students can receive it wherever they happen to be located - in a college setting, in a public library, at home, on the factory floor or in an office at their place of work. The active research and development currently underway into 'intelligent' tutoring systems and the design of computer-based cognitive tools to support learning attests to the significant potential of this approach to automatic tuition. Examples of the work that is currently underway are documented in Kommers et al (1992) and Lajoie and Derry (1993).

A: Human Tuition

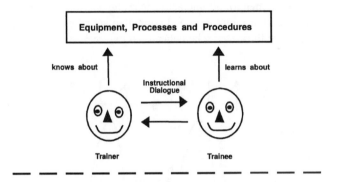

B: Computer-based Tuition

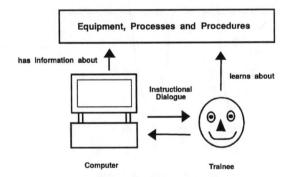

Figure 3 *Examples of interactive learning systems*

Despite their significant potential utility, computer-based learning environments of the sort illustrated in Figure 3B can be difficult and expensive to produce - particularly, if these involve highly professional, 'TV quality', multimedia resources - such as audio narrations, musical accompaniments and significant quantities of full-screen, full-motion video material. Although substantial volumes of audio-visual resources already exist for use in computer-based learning (which could therefore, in principle, reduce production costs), the problems associated with copyright issues are usually quite enormous. Production costs for 'quality' courseware are therefore likely to present a major barrier to the widespread use of computer-based tuition within the foreseeable future.

Fundamental to the instructional dialogues that are depicted in Figures 3A and 3B are the monitoring, feedback and corrective actions that the 'tutor' (human or computer) uses to ensure that the learning/training processes are progressing in the correct way. If learning is not proceeding in the required fashion, appropriate feedback can be given and, if necessary, corrective actions can be taken.

The combination of close monitoring, feedback and corrective action mentioned above is a basic requirement of all interactive learning and training processes. Some typical effects of applying monitoring and corrective activities to a typical learning or training situation are illustrated schematically in Figure 4.

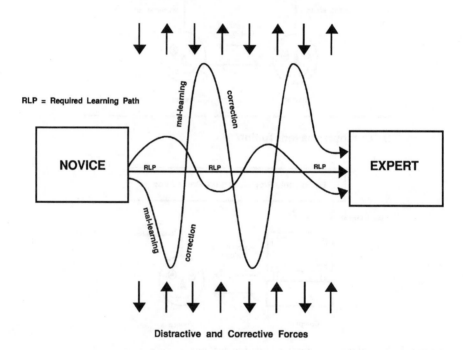

Figure 4 *Interactive learning*

In this figure two types of pathway from novice to expert are shown: an 'ideal' linear transition - the required learning path (denoted by RLP); and various other non-linear transitions which represent departure from ideality. Non-linear transitions are caused as a result of the effects of the various distractive and corrective forces that might influence a learning process. As can be seen in Figure 4, the application of a distractive force causes the learning pathway to go off course and thus depart from the ideal. We refer to this departure from the ideal as 'mal-learning' - that is, learning the wrong things. A simple example of this would be the potential confusion arising between the different meanings of the French words 'poisson' and 'poison' as a result of a student's having unknowingly learned incorrect pronounciations for these words.

In many ways mal-learning is analogous to the creation of cognitive 'bugs' and 'mal-rules' in intelligent tutoring systems (Sleeman & Brown, 1982; Self, 1988). Mal-learning corresponds to the acquisition of the incorrect motor or cognitive skills needed to handle particular situations in which a learner/trainee may find him/herself. For example, it can involve the acquisition of incorrect concepts, models, procedures, facts, principles, theories, actions, and so on. Sometimes, mal-learning can lead to the development of cognitive dissonance, that is, a conceptual conflict between two or more cognitive structures (Gardiner & Christie, 1987).

Of course, provided mal-learning can be detected, corrective action can usually be taken and the learning pathway can then be 'pulled back' towards the ideal. This is illustrated in Figure 4 by the 'turning points' in the learning transitions that are represented by the two curves. Naturally, once learning has been put back on course (as a result of remediation processes) there is nothing to prevent it going off course again. Therefore, at a later stage in the learning pathway some other form of mal-learning may again take place - and again need to be corrected. Naturally, this is where the real and substantial benefits of interactive learning systems are to be found. Their attraction lies in their ability to detect and correct mal-learning (bugs and mal-rules) at a very early stage - thereby, preventing any long-term ill-effects that might arise from it. Undoubtedly, in the future it should, in principle, be possible to design and create interactive learning systems that totally eliminate any form of mal-learning on the part of students and trainees - thereby making learning/training processes more effective and more efficient.

As can be seen from Figure 4, the learning pathways for many transitions between novice and expert are of an 'oscillatory' nature as a result of the application of various types of mal-learning, corrective feedback and compensatory/remedial actions. Naturally, the oscillations involved in any given learning or training process will be multi-dimensional so that the actual transitions between novice and expert will be multi-dimensional surfaces rather than simple linear or curvi-linear transitions as are depicted in Figure 4.

Obviously, the extent of departure from ideality and the magnitude and frequency of the oscillations shown in Figure 4 will depend upon how an interactive learning system is designed and fabricated. The basic rationale underlying the types of system that we design and build is discussed in more detail in the following section.

3 CREATING INTERACTIVE LEARNING

The development of computer-based learning products usually involves a number of quite clearly defined steps. Each of these is well-documented in the literature (Dean & Whitlock, 1992; Harrison, 1991; Giardina, 1992; Criswell, 1989). The conventional development cycle usually involves the following basic steps: needs analysis; requirements specification; learning/instructional design; implementation; and evaluation and testing. Once the requirements specification has been formulated the two most influential factors in determining the final outcome of an interactive learning development project are the learning design and the implementation stages. Because of their importance with respect to creating effective interactive learning these phases are discussed in more detail below. The particular model of learning design that is presented is that derived from the DELTA ILDIC Project 2012 (Integrating Learning Design in Interactive Compact Disc) while the implementation model is based upon the MAPARI paradigm that was described earlier in this paper.

3.1   The ILDIC model of learning design

According to Good, Shanahan, and Shaw (1993), learning design refers to 'the cluster of factors affecting learning which need to be addressed and about which decisions need to be made before and during the process of multimedia learning materials development'. They go on to propose a model of learning design that they suggest can be used as a design tool by designers of interactive multimedia learning products. This model is based upon a set of guidelines the intention of which is to lead designers through a number of structured 'thinking tools', ideas and metaphors that are intended to put learning 'into focus'.

The model (which is extensible) covers a number of dimensions or 'perspectives' which place the activity of learning 'at the centre of things'. Currently, there are ten perspectives in all. These perspectives represent the major factors that designers should take into account as they work through the development processes associated with the creation of a learning product. The ten perspectives covered by the model are listed in Table 1. Each one of these is discussed in more detail in the remainder of this section.

Table 1 *The basic perspectives of learning design*

1.   learning theory mix;
2.   instructional position mix;
3.   machine character mix;
4.   environmental factors;
5.   mode of use;
6.   locus of control;
7.   extent of intervention;
8.   aesthetic features;
9.   content;
10. role of technology.

People learn in a variety of different ways using a broad range of different tools, techniques, styles and strategies. When designing a learning product it is important to consider the nature of the '*learning theory mix*' that will underpin the design of any given product. The three fundamental learning theories that were found to be most important in the formulation of the learning design model were those based upon behaviourism, cognitivism and constructivism.

All learning products, in some way or another, act as an instructional resource. Frequently, it is possible to embed different modes of instruction to various extents within a given learning product. The perspective of '*instructional position mix*' therefore describes the different instructional roles that a given learning product can fulfil. These roles will depend upon the basic intention of the particular product concerned - such as, the provision of information, tutoring, remediation, reflection, experience, counselling, and so on.

The perspective of '*machine character mix*' refers to the basic way(s) in which a learning product presents itself (or appears) to its end-user population. Typical examples include: tutor; instructor; coach; assistant; book; toolkit; tester; simulator; database; and toy. Many learning products will be able to fulfil several different roles - depending upon the particular needs of each individual user at any given instant in time.

Another important perspective that the model deals with is that concerning the importance of '*environmental factors*'. Broadly, this perspective is concerned with the physical setting in which learning takes place - for example, a home environment, a workplace setting, an open learning centre, a conventional classroom, an electronic classroom, a virtual classroom, a conferencing situation, and so on. Obviously, if learning is to be encouraged it is important to consider all those ergonomic and human factors issues that will help make using the learning product (within a given environment) a pleasant and motivating experience.

The '*mode of use*' of a learning product is often a perspective over which designers have only limited control. While it is possible to prescribe that a product should be used in a particular way there is often no guarantee that it will be used in that fashion. In order to achieve maximum flexibility of use it is therefore important for designers to consider as broad a range of potential modes of use as is consistent with the overall objectives of the learning product concerned.

An important aspect of interactive learning product design is the '*locus of control*'. That is, the way in which control of learning activity lies either in the hands of the learner, the learning product, or both of these agents. Fundamental to any consideration of interactive control will be the frequency with which control changes hands and the conditions under which these changes take place. Within the learning design model four 'touchstones' are provided which help designers to make decisions relating to these matters.

Another important aspect of the design of an interactive learning product is the '*extent of intervention*' that it will exhibit with respect to the underlying learning processes that it is intended to initiate and foster. Truly interactive learning involves a very close coupling between the states of the learning product and the cognitive and psychomotor states of the learner. This perspective is therefore concerned with the level, type, quality and quantity of help and feedback that is either made available or which is accessible to the user of a learning product.

The '*aesthetic*' perspective refers to the nature of the visual, tactile and aural frameworks that are used by a designer in order to improve and enhance the overall quality of a learning product. Primarily, aesthetic factors are used to improve the 'look and feel' of a learning product thereby making it more appealing to its intended end-user population. Through the appropriate use of aesthetics, a designer can make the use of a particular product become both a pleasurable and an enjoyable experience - thereby making it more engaging and motivating.

The '*content*' perspective is obviously a very important one since it is this which will ultimately dictate what a user learns and the extent to which learning can take place. Of course, in most situations the basic content of a learning product will usually be specified by a 'subject matter expert'. The designer therefore has less of a role to play with respect to this perspective of learning design. However, three important issues which designers will need to consider in the context of content will be: the way in which the content is structured (based upon the use of linear and/or non-linear information structures); the types of learning strategy that are embedded within the content; and the best way of using the available resources in relation to the subject matter that is to be contained within the learning product under consideration.

The final perspective in the learning design model, the '*role of technology*', is of paramount importance because it is technology (along with cost considerations) that will ultimately determine the type (and characteristics) of the delivery mechanism that any particular learning product might employ. For sophisticated learning products a range of different types of delivery platform currently exist - such as CD-I, CDTV, CD-ROM XA, DVI, MPC, and so on. Each of these is able to provide (in different ways and using specialised techniques) a multimedia mix that can embed text, sound, static pictures, animations and motion video. Obviously, in choosing a suitable delivery platform for a learning product it is important to bear in mind the maxim 'choose the medium that is most appropriate for the message'. An important aspect of design (in the context of technology) will therefore be choosing the optimum combination of resources needed for a given learning product within a specified set of cost constraints.

In any given learning design situation the ten perspectives listed in Table 1 will each play a role - but to varying extents. Obviously, the relative importance of each individual design perspective within the learning design activity will depend upon the particular circumstances within which the model is applied. In many situations some early indications of which will be the most important perspectives to consider will usually be obtained from the 'needs analysis' that normally precedes the design of a learning product (Dean & Whitlock, 1992).

3.2 The MAPARI implementation model

Models of learning design similar to that described in the previous section can be used in both a coarse-grained and a fine-grained way in order to identify important design decisions during the initial phases of development of an interactive multimedia learning product. We have used models such as this in order to add detailed fine-structure to the implementation model that we have produced in order to facilitate the realisation of the MAPARI paradigm which was described earlier in this paper. The important features of this implementation model and the relationships between them are illustrated schematically in Figure 5 (Barker, 1990a).

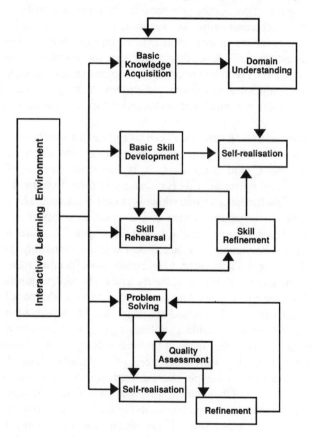

Figure 5 *Functional requirements of an interactive learning environment*

We believe that any implementation of an interactive learning environment (ILE) according to the MAPARI model must accommodate an appropriate subset of the following five basic functions: knowledge acquisition; skill development; skill rehearsal; problem solving; and self-realisation.

Obviously, the two most fundamental functions that an ILE must foster are: (a) the need for students and trainees to achieve a basic knowledge and understanding of their domain of interest through the provision of support for various types of knowledge acquisition process; and (b) the development of those skills that are necessary and appropriate to the activities that students will undertake within that domain. Knowledge acquisition and skill development could be based upon the provision of conventional computer-based training or computer-assisted learning (Dean & Whitlock, 1992; Barker, 1989). These processes might also involve the use of interactive learning support environments similar to those described by Barker (1994) and Lim (1994).

The 'stopping condition' for the processes involved within activities (a) and (b) is determined by a mechanism called 'self-realisation'. Self-realisation, in the contexts referred to here, generates an awareness that an adequate stock of knowledge has been acquired and that skill development has been successfully accomplished (for the particular tasks that are to be undertaken). Stopping conditions such as these are extremely important in situations where 'just-in-time' training is being used - as, for example, is the situation in electronic performance support systems (Banerji, 1994; Gery, 1991).

The acquisition of basic levels of skill can take place in a variety of different ways (such as the use of simulators, simulations, role playing, and so on). In addition to the support of basic skill acquisition, it is important that an ILE provides opportunities for skill rehearsal. This is necessary in order to achieve either a pre-specified level of performance or one which is innately determined by the particular characteristics of a given student or trainee. The processes involved in skill rehearsal are closely bound to those associated with skill refinement. This latter mechanism is concerned with the fine tuning of acquired coarse-grained (possibly, generic) skills in order to achieve the skills necessary to undertake more specific tasks.

Within a given domain of discourse, the motivation for skill acquisition is usually provided by the need for students, trainees and experts to be able to solve problems within that domain in an effective and efficient way. The learning/training facility that is used must therefore provide a problem solving environment which can be used in order to 'exercise' the incipient problem solving skills. Obviously, a wide range of problems having various degrees of complexity must be available. Appropriate mechanisms for mapping the problem set onto users' abilities must also exist - if the real benefits of the problem solving approach are to be fully realised.

Two important aspects of the problem solving facility that is provided in an ILE are: quality assessment (QA) and self-realisation. The QA facility is used as a 'mirror' that enables users to see the relative quality of the problem solutions that they formulate. Obviously, through various refinement processes the quality of any given problem solution can be improved and, if necessary, optimised with respect to the constraints imposed by the framework within which problem solving is taking place. As was the case in the basic knowledge acquisition and skill development processes described above, the self-realisation associated with problem solving activity acts as a stopping condition. This can be used for two purposes. First, it can be is used to decide whether or not a student, trainee or expert has the necessary skills to solve a particular problem; second, it can act as a balance which trades off the quality of the solution that can be achieved against the level of skills needed.

Various types of computer-based interactive learning environment currently exist. These range in complexity and capability from basic 'drill and practice' facilities through sophisticated intelligent tutoring systems to the expensive, 'immersive' learning environments that are to be found in virtual reality environments. We believe that the model depicted in Figure 5 acts as a useful basic conceptual architecture for all of these types of system. In the following section a description will be given of how this model has been used to create prototype interactive learning environments to support the teaching of foreign languages.

4 A CASE STUDY - LANGUAGE LEARNING

The case study presented in this section describes an interactive language learning project (ILLP) that has recently been undertaken in our research laboratory (Barker et al, 1993). The material that follows summarises the work that was undertaken and is organised into six basic sub-sections that describe: the background to the project; the rationale underlying its realisation; courseware development; multimedia resource production; the evaluation results; and a summary conclusion.

4.1 **Background**

Increasingly, as people become more internationally mobile there is a growing demand for tuition in modern 'spoken' languages such as French, German, Dutch and Italian. In order to cope with this demand language instructors are now turning to the use of computer-assisted language learning (CALL) techniques based upon the use of interactive computer-based workstations (Cameron, 1989; Chesters, 1990; Pollard & Yazdani, 1991; Ingraham and Emery, 1991). In the past the use of CALL techniques was severely hampered because of the limitations imposed by the delivery stations and the courseware which had to be used; these were mainly text-based and there was only very limited end-user interaction and participation. Currently available technology now enables markedly improved CALL environments to be developed based upon the use of high-quality pictures, sound input and output, and moving images. These multimedia resources can be organised in either a linear or non-linear (hypermedia) fashion depending upon the objectives to be realised (Barker, Fox & Emery, 1992; Barker et al, 1992).

Some time ago we embarked upon an exploration of the potential of reactive pictures and multilingual audio resources as a means of augmenting the teaching of foreign languages using CALL methods (Barker, 1990b). This work was based upon an electronic book metaphor (Barker, 1991). That project, which was called SPBAN (an acronym for Static Picture Books with Audio Narration), used high-quality static pictures and audio recordings organised in the form of a highly adaptable electronic book that users could tailor to their own particular requirements (Giller, 1992).

Although the research described above only involved creating experimental prototypes, commercial products embedding these ideas are now available at relatively low-cost. One extremely good example of a product range that embeds the electronic book metaphor is the 'talking electronic books' series produced by the Discis corporation (Discis Knowledge Research, 1991). The electronic books that make up this product line are essentially multilingual, multimedia story books for children. They are published on compact disc read-only-memory (CD-ROM) for delivery (primarily) in an Apple Macintosh PC environment - although some of the books are also available for use with Commodore's Dynamic Total Vision (CDTV) system. Fundamental to the success of these books is their use of high-quality reactive pictures and text and, of course, their incorporation of multilingual digital sound.

Undoubtedly, within a learning and training environment the use of interactive multimedia and hypermedia techniques for CALL can lead to substantial improvements in the quality of linguistic experience that can be provided for students (Fox et al, 1990). Obviously, the relatively low cost of producing and mastering digital optical compact discs (CDs) now means that this type of storage technology can be employed in various ways to develop and distribute CALL resources and, in so doing, improve the quality of the training experience to which students are exposed. Because of the potential future importance of interactive computer-based technologies for the support of foreign language learning the remainder of this section describes the evaluative multimedia development project (ILLP) in which we have recently been involved - the intention of which was to assess the potential of emerging interactive multimedia technologies for language teaching.

4.2 Rationale and scope of ILLP

The Interactive Language Learning Project was funded by the United Kingdom's Learning Technology Unit. The project commenced in late 1991; its intent was to investigate and evaluate the potential of various digital optical storage technologies (based upon CD-ROM) for the dissemination and delivery of CALL resources. This project was run in conjunction with the UK's National Council for Educational Technology (NCET).

CD-ROM offers a high capacity integrated storage medium for the storage and dissemination of learning resources for use in many learning situations. This technology is particularly useful for the support of distance learning, open learning, and use in the home. Conventional CD-ROM allows the storage of significant quantities of text, multilingual sound, high quality pictures and cartoon animation. Extensions to the basic CD-ROM facility enable TV quality motion video pictures to be utilised. The ILLP project was therefore intended to explore the ways in which these digital resources might be used for the creation of interactive learning environments to facilitate foreign language acquisition and study.

When the project started there were five basic approaches to using digital optical storage media on a low-cost PC: (1) applications of conventional CD-ROM; (2) use of CD-ROM extended architecture (CD-ROM XA); (3) use of Commodore's Dynamic Total Vision system (CDTV); (4) applications of CD-I (compact disc - interactive); and (5) use of digital video interactive (DVI). When the project commenced we thought that the latter two technologies are not sufficiently widespread within schools and colleges to warrant their use in the project. We therefore chose to explore the potential of conventional CD-ROM, CDTV and CD-ROM XA because equipment to support these technologies could be purchased commercially at relatively low cost.

The major advantages of using CD-ROM technology for instructional systems stem from the potential portability that this medium offers and the low-cost development and delivery stations that can be produced - based on existing computer workstations (CD-ROM and CD-ROM XA) or equipment that is available in the consumer marketplace (CDTV).

Bearing in mind what was said above, the major objectives of the project were: (1) to create three demonstrator systems that could be used to compare the relative merits of CD-ROM, CDTV and CD-ROM XA as media for the storage and distribution of interactive instructional material; and (2) to evaluate the potential utility of these technologies for the delivery of instructional materials related to the teaching of foreign languages - particular emphasis being given to French.

Unfortunately, as the project progressed we began to realise that the creation of three demonstration systems had been an over-ambitious aim - in view of the resources that were available to us. Furthermore, a considerable number of developments in technology had taken place between the time the project was proposed and the time it actually commenced. As a result of these factors the project objectives were reviewed and re-drafted so as to necessitate the creation of just two demonstration workstations - both based on CD-ROM. One of these would use basic CD-ROM involving text, sound and static pictures while the other would also incorporate motion video based upon Intel's DVI technology.

Following this decision the next important part of the project was the preparation of a short (30 minute) instructional unit based upon a series of situation scenarios (Pollard & Yazdani, 1991). The courseware for this experimental lesson was developed using Authorware Professional. This software was chosen to run within a Windows (3.1) environment for delivery using an IBM PC compatible (Person & Rose, 1992). When the courseware was complete it was published (in two versions) on CD-ROM and evaluated in a number of colleges.

The evaluation phase of the ILLP project had two main objectives.

First, to try and measure skill acquisition across the four generic language skills: speaking; reading; listening and writing. It was intended that learner skill acquisition using the two platforms should be compared to that of a control group which received normal teaching with conventional materials. Data gathering on this was accomplished using a post-test constructed to examine mastery of the courseware content.

The second objective was to compare the platforms against each other. Measurements here were to include: the usability of the systems; attitudes and motivation; individual or groupwork preferences; learning styles; and feedback on the role of the tutor. The techniques used for these measurements involved the use of: observations; interviews and questionnaires that were refined as a result of a pilot study.

The second evaluation objective meant that in the evaluation, groups of learners would need to have access to each of the two hardware platforms after completing the post-test following their work on one system.

Resources of people and time were strictly limited on the project, therefore, evaluation of the systems took place in only three or four centres. These included a university with post-18 students, a further education college with students in the 16-19 age range, and a group of adults on a company language training programme. It was assumed that learner entry competence approximated to levels 6 or 7 of the National Curriculum Key Stage 4 in French (that is, someone who had obtained the equivalent of a grade C at GCSE). The material was therefore not aimed at ab initio learners, but at students wishing to continue with their language studies either for interest as part of a core entitlement, or for vocational/academic purposes.

Unfortunately, the timetable of the project only allowed for the evaluation centres to have the systems for a couple of weeks each, during which time the unit of work had to be covered, observations taken, questionnaires filled in, the post-test completed and interviews conducted. Some of the key questions to which we were seeking answers were: does the courseware presented on these systems allow greater skill acquisition faster than the materials presented in the normal way; is there more of a pay off in one of the language skills than the others; do the technologies and the material facilitate group interaction or individual study; what are the attractive features of the media; what are the preferred learning styles; is there a difference in usability between the different platforms; is there an increase in motivation; what is the role of the tutor when using interactive technologies with groups of learners?

Obviously, not all of the above questions could be answered within the confines of a relatively small-scale investigation as is described here. However, we believe that the project was extremely successful in what it was able to tell us about the potential of interactive multimedia for foreign language learning.

4.3 Courseware development

The creation of the courseware involved a number of key phases: agreement on lesson content; lesson design; programming; creation of multimedia resources; and system integration and testing. The overall production time available for the realisation of the key phases listed above was about nine months. A very tight schedule was forced onto the project by the creation of an 'evaluation timetable'.

This imposed deadlines that would need to be met if the arrangements that were being made with the evaluation sites were to be honoured.

It was intended to include the courseware module as a lesson element within an existing traditional French course. It was therefore necessary to choose a subject area which had not been previously covered during the course and which would build upon users' existing knowledge of the subject. The basic design for the courseware unit was therefore based upon a video film of an actual 'live' 1 hour language lesson. This was analysed to identify the lesson objectives and teaching points. These were then converted into discrete descriptions for each linked learning activity. A vocabulary list was also drawn up at this point.

It was anticipated that users would have a wide range of abilities in computer use. Consequently, although the software was designed to run in a Windows environment, it was developed using a 'clean screen' interface so that users who were not familiar with Windows would not have to waste time in learning how to use it.

Once the details of the lesson had been agreed they were developed into appropriate sections which could be transformed into interactive user activities based upon the objectives and teaching points from the traditional lesson. At this stage, an outline plan of the courseware was produced, along with written descriptions of suggested pictorial material - graphics and video.

The two versions of the courseware unit each consisted of a number of different parts: the introduction; an optional mouse practice session; information on how to use the system; and the main option area from which users could select, in any order, the exercises of their choice. There were four lesson exercises. These were:

1. *'Teacher'* - a simulated linear lesson based on the original video;
2. *'Camera'* - a vocabulary exercise which allowed users to select and listen to the basic items linked to descriptions (colour, hair style, fabric patterns and clothing);
3. *'Photo Album'* - a listening exercise showing a series of still video images of people linked to an audio description of one which should be selected before continuing;
4. *'TV'* - three comprehension exercises each presenting a short scenario followed by some simple questions.

Scripts for each of the four exercises were produced. These were supplemented with written details of the multimedia components needed for each of the exercises. At this stage the basic screen layout and interface was also defined.

It was intended that the courseware module should present itself entirely in French. End-user interaction was therefore facilitated through the use of a graphical user interface - in order to eliminate the necessity for textual menus. This fulfilled three criteria. First, users were able to use interactive choices without having any knowledge of the French language specific to a menu-driven program. Second, research has proved that the majority of computer users are able to identify more quickly with graphic-based cues, such as icons, thus making the program more efficient. Third, it would be possible to translate the base language (that is the native language of users) to any other European language easily and relatively quickly if the need ever arose.

4.4 Multimedia resource production

The multimedia resources used in the ILLP project consisted mainly of text, graphics, moving video images, static video images and sound.

Unlike interactive video (where filming is delayed until the final stages of production), it was an essential part of the program development to produce the moving video at an earlier phase. Although the moving video element was not to be incorporated into the second version of the program until late in the project life cycle, it was to be used to provide sound and static video images for the first version.

All the resource elements were produced in-house with the exception of the moving video images. The development of each of the elements is described below.

Text

It was inevitable that there would be a considerable amount of text displayed on the screen. Since this was to be in the most part in the form of French language, it was important that text should be displayed in the correct format. Having produced a basic script for each element within the program, the whole text was then translated into French by a subject specialist.

At this point the computer keyboard was configured to include French character notations. This proved to be a simple task using the Windows keyboard configuration set-up. The new configuration was automatically accessed by Authorware which defaults to the settings within Windows. It was at this point that the default font was also chosen - using the same principle.

Graphics

Several graphics development packages were considered these included: PC Paint; Microsoft Windows Paintbrush; and CorelDRAW. Although it was possible to import most of the graphic files produced using these systems into Authorware, the most satisfactory results were obtained using CorelDRAW to produce the graphics and then saving the results in Windows Metafile (WMF) format. Graphics imported into Authorware were then more easily manipulated within the presentation screens.

A basic list of the graphics to be used in each section of the courseware was produced and example sketches were drawn up by hand. Because of the nature of the subject area, the program contained a large number of human features. To facilitate the graphics production, a basic human figure (named 'Fred') was constructed within CorelDRAW. This figure was composed of a series of component parts which could be manipulated on-screen to form a variety of different poses.

The main 'menu' for the program is a picture of a classroom incorporating the elements of the lesson each represented by a relevant graphical item. All the graphical components were first developed individually in CorelDRAW and then imported into the main screen within Authorware.

Motion video

Three video scripts for the 'TV' exercise were produced by one of the subject specialists. Storyboards were then drawn up to accompany the scripts in preparation for filming.

The three video scripts were filmed by a professional film crew. In order to achieve the best possible quality video, the film was produced in broadcast quality Umatic format. Three French 'actors' were used to play the characters.

During the final stages of programming, this film was converted into compressed digital format using a Umatic tape drive linked to a PC with a DVI capture board. Two versions of the video files were produced. The first version was presented in linear style in which users could only view each of the three video sequences as a whole. After a considerable amount of experimentation, the second version was produced as an interactive video sequence in which users could control the presentation to allow for short clips of each sequence to be viewed in succession. This second version allowed users to access translation, transcripts and replay options for each short clip.

A second Umatic film was also produced in-house at the University of Teesside. This film was intended only as a source of still video images to be used in the 'Photo Album' exercise that was embedded within the courseware unit.

Static video images

The basic CD-ROM version of the courseware contained still video images captured from both the 'TV' film and from the 'Photo Album' film. These images were captured, digitised and manipulated on a PC using a digital capture board called 'Screen Machine'. The resulting images were saved in PCX format in preparation for importing into the Authorware screens.

Sound

Several sources of sound were used in the development of the courseware module. Each of these is briefly described below.

First, a non-copyright introductory piece of music was captured by linking the microphone input socket on the Sound Blaster board in the PC directly to the headphones socket of a personal stereo unit.

Second, sound cues (or earcons) were copied directly from the existing Windows and Sound Blaster libraries of sound files into the Authorware subdirectory.

Third, the scripts produced for the program exercises called for a female narrator and a male voice. Each sound item throughout the script was given a unique reference code prefixed by 'f' for female or 'm' for male. This reference code was also given to the relevant sound file. This code referred to both the French and English versions of the written script in order to facilitate the incorporation of the resulting sound files into the courseware. The scripts were then recorded directly by microphone linked to the Sound Blaster socket.

Fourth, the sound tracks of the three video scenarios were captured by connecting the sound output socket on the Umatic player directly to the microphone input socket on the Sound Blaster board.

All of the resulting sound files were edited using the Windows sound editing facilities. The results of all these capturing techniques were extremely good when delivered through the Windows play-back option, but became slightly distorted when delivered through Authorware. This effect was evident throughout all the sound samples used.

Two versions of sound were used. The basic CD-ROM program contained sound produced in Sound Blaster (WAV) format and are described above. The resulting sound files were then captured and converted using DVI utilities for the second version of the courseware. This was accomplished by running two MPCs in parallel and linking the Sound Blaster output socket on the first directly to the DVI input socket on the second. All the WAV files were then re-recorded individually and saved in DVI format. Unfortunately, the resulting sound quality was severely impaired.

System integration and testing

During the development of the project a substantial quantity of resources was produced. Initially, these existed in two different formats: analogue (mainly video material) and digital. Obviously, prior to creating the final courseware product on CD-ROM, all these resources had to be converted into a common digital format and then brought together to form the final application.

The different resources that were developed (even after conversion to digital format) were distributed on a number of different MPC workstations within the development laboratory. The various MPCs that were used during the development phase therefore had to be connected together and the different resources then all transferred to the main authoring station. The storage requirements for the motion video were quite substantial (about 10 Mbytes per minute) and so a second hard disc unit had to be fitted to the authoring station. This extra storage space was also needed in order to build 'mock-up' disc images of the final CD-ROM discs that were to be produced.

As was mentioned earlier, two CD-ROMs were to be produced. Each one would be identical apart from the motion video material that would be embedded in the second of the two discs. Once a disc image of the first CD-ROM disc had been created it was transferred to a re-writable magneto-optical CD for testing purposes. An exhaustive period of testing and critical appraisal then followed. Any final amendments needed to the courseware were then undertaken. Finally, after the testing and revision was complete, the material on the re-writable CD was transferred to tape-streamer and then dispatched to Nimbus Information Systems (Nimbus, 1993) for mastering and replication (as CD-DISC-01). Fifty copies of the CD were produced. When the discs came back to our laboratory the final stages of 'testing and tuning' were undertaken for this disc using the actual delivery station that would be employed in the evaluation phase of the project.

While the testing and fine tuning of the first CD was well underway the motion video clips and sound (in DVI format) were added to the basic courseware lesson in order to initiate the final production of the second deliverable. A second disc image on re-writable CD was then created and tested. On completion of its testing and amendment this second disc image was transferred from re-writable CD onto tape-streamer and then dispatched to Nimbus Information Systems for mastering and replication (as CD-DISC-02). Again, fifty copies of the disc were produced. When the 50 copies of the second CD came back its final stages of testing and fine tuning were undertaken using the host delivery station that would be used in the evaluation phase of the project.

The two interactive delivery stations, each with their individual CD-based courseware, were finally tested and tuned and ready for shipment to the evaluation sites by mid-January, 1993. The evaluation phase of the project and the results obtained are briefly discussed in the following section.

4.5 Evaluation results

From the start of the project, the evaluation phase was conceived as an integral element. In practice, the balance of responsibility for this was given to NCET, whereas the main responsibility for the materials development was with the Interactive Systems Research Group within the Human-Computer Interaction Laboratory at the University of Teesside. Staff from both organisations attended all development group meetings, ensuring cross-fertilisation of ideas and good communication between different phases of the project. Particularly valuable was the involvement of teaching staff from the trialling institutions at an early stage in content and design of courseware and developing the evaluation strategy.

The evaluation was designed to identify the educational effectiveness of the systems and courseware based on trialling carried out in a small number of colleges with groups of post-16 language learners. More specifically, the project was designed to evaluate the potential utility of the selected technologies for the delivery of learning materials related to the teaching of foreign languages generally.

In the initial stages of the evaluation design, the evaluation activities were identified as summative in nature, in that the project would collect and summarise information about the systems and their value for modern language learning. As the project developed and as meetings took place with teaching staff from the trialling institutions, the objectives of the evaluation were refined to two principle ones.

First, to measure skill acquisition across three of the four generic language skills: speaking, reading and listening. It was intended that learner skill acquisition using the two platforms would be compared to that of a control group who would receive usual class teaching with conventional materials.

Second, to compare the platforms against each other. Measurements here would include: usability of the system; attitudes and motivation; individual or group work preference; learning styles, and feedback on the role of the tutor.

Trialling of the systems was arranged to take place with three different groups of learners: 16-19 year old full-time learners in a Further Education (FE) college; post-18 full-time Higher Education (HE) students; and adult part-time learners in college. These groups of learners were chosen to reflect a spread of the post-school population, from FE through adult education to HE. Actual institutions were chosen for their typicality within these categories: North Warwickshire College, a medium to large sized college of further education; Lancashire College, an adult residential college specialising in modern language work; and the University of Teesside one of the 'new' universities with a large undergraduate population.

Discussions were held with tutors from the three centres, regarding the practicalities for the trialling, and a timetable was agreed. Thereafter, tutors were responsible for selecting groups of learners, and making arrangements for testing and use of the systems within lesson schedules.

The pre- and post-tests were written only with reference to the defined content and skills, and no account was taken of the teaching materials actually devised for the control and experimental groups; thus, a degree of objectivity was maintained. The tests were designed to fit in with current practice and resemble GCSE papers, for example, the target language was used as far as possible, and communicative, meaningful, and relevant tasks were set. Tests covered listening (students listened to a tape and provided details of a person described), reading (students read a letter and provided a description), and speaking (students were asked six questions about a picture of a family).

The two interactive learning systems were taken to the centres for the trialling to be carried out and arrangements were made with the tutors for students to have access.

An evaluation protocol was written to be followed by tutors at the three centres. Two evaluation questionnaires were developed, with reference to the literature on evaluation of CALL. The first was to ask specific questions of the learners using the systems, and to enable the researchers to answer the evaluation questions of the project. The second was designed to ask tutors their opinion regarding the potential utility of the systems and how it might affect their role. An observation schedule was developed to note how the systems were used by the learners.

Each student was required to attend for the pre-test, and either the lesson with the tutor or a computer-based lesson, and for the post-test. Students who missed one of these were excluded from the trial. Due to the timetabling differences at the three centres, the trialling process differed from centre to centre. For example, the adult learners were only present for the trialling over a weekend, while trialling with the FE students took place over one week. For these reasons, results of the tests at the three centres were not compared with each other.

The results of the pre-test were analysed and compared for each of the three groups (CD-ROM, DVI and Control) in each of the three centres. There were no significant differences between any of them, therefore it is safe to assume that the randomisation was successful.

The mean and standard deviation scores for the pre-tests and post-tests for each centre are shown below in Tables 2, 3 and 4, together with the actual and percentage gain in scores for each language skill.

For each of the language skills, a comparison of post-test scores was made between the DVI, CD-ROM and Control groups using an Analysis of Variance test (ANOVA).

A detailed analysis and discussion of the results of the evaluations is presented elsewhere (Barker et al, 1993). In the following section some of the main findings from the work are summarised.

4.6 Summary of findings

Because of the small number of students involved in these trials, it is only possible to draw tentative rather than firm conclusions. The major conclusions that can be drawn from the trialling of these systems with these students are listed below:

1. Virtually all students enjoyed using the systems and found the material easy to use.

Table 2 *Mean and SD for pre-test and post-test scores, actual and percentage gains in each language for adult students*

Group	N	Mean Pre-test Score	SD	Mean Post-test Score	SD	Actual Mean Increase	% Increase
LISTENING							
CD-ROM	4	8.00	3.37	9.00	1.77	1.00	12.5
DVI	4	7.00	2.94	9.75	2.06	2.75	39.0
Control	4	6.00	2.45	8.25	1.89	2.25	37.5
READING							
CD-ROM	4	7.25	3.30	11.25	0.95	4.00	55.0
DVI	4	6.75	0.95	11.00	0.82	4.25	63.0
Control	4	7.50	0.58	9.00	2.00	1.50	20.0
SPEAKING							
CD-ROM	4	8.75	3.30	11.00	0.82	2.25	26.0
DVI	4	8.25	1.50	11.25	0.50	3.00	36.0
Control	4	7.50	3.70	8.00	2.58	0.50	7.0

Table 3 *Mean and SD for pre-test and post-test scores, actual and percentage gains in each language for HE students*

Group	N	Mean Pre-test Score	SD	Mean Post-test Score	SD	Actual Mean Increase	% Increase
LISTENING							
CD-ROM	5	6.2	2.17	8.4	2.19	2.2	36.0
DVI	5	7.6	2.51	9.4	2.07	1.8	24.0
Control	3	7.7	1.52	10.0	1.00	2.3	30.0
READING							
CD-ROM	5	5.6	2.07	7.4	0.89	1.8	32.0
DVI	5	6.6	1.82	8.2	1.30	1.6	24.0
Control	3	7.3	0.58	9.3	0.58	2.0	27.0
SPEAKING							
CD-ROM	5	8.4	2.61	9.4	1.52	1.0	12.0
DVI	5	7.6	4.28	9.0	2.92	1.4	18.0
Control	3	10.3	0.58	9.7	2.52	-0.6	-6.0

Table 4 *Mean and SD for pre-test and post-test scores, actual and percentage gains in each language for FE students*

Group	N	Mean Pre-test Score	SD	Mean Post-test Score	SD	Actual Mean Increase	% Increase
LISTENING							
CD-ROM	5	2.0	1.41	3.8	2.17	1.8	90.0
DVI	5	2.4	1.52	4.4	2.19	2.0	83.0
Control	4	3.8	2.35	4.8	4.08	1.0	26.0
READING							
CD-ROM	5	1.6	1.34	2.4	1.52	0.8	50.0
DVI	5	3.0	2.12	5.0	2.30	2.0	67.0
Control	4	3.4	2.75	5.0	3.32	1.6	47.0
SPEAKING							
CD-ROM	5	4.4	4.16	6.6	3.85	2.2	50.0
DVI	5	4.8	1.92	5.6	2.79	0.8	16.0
Control	4	5.2	3.11	5.8	1.89	0.6	11.5

2. Relative improvements in skill acquisition by students in the experimental groups in the three language areas over the control group were demonstrated to varying degrees.

3. There was more of a benefit in some language skills than others, however, this was different at each centre. With the HE students, the experimental group gains over control were more pronounced in speaking. For the adults clear gains were evident in speaking and reading, whereas with the FE students, the gains were demonstrated in speaking and listening.

4. The greatest gains were shown by students with lower entry competence in all three language skills, although some higher ability students felt they might benefit with materials of a higher level of difficulty.

5. Learning styles with the technology varied; some students said they would have preferred working in groups, whereas others preferred working singly. However, most students commented favourably on the greater control over the pace of their learning provided by the computer systems.

6. In terms of usability, the majority of adult and FE students using the DVI system commented on slowness of the system. HE students were also critical of the slowness of the CD-ROM system too.

7. Many students agreed that more on screen help was needed. Clearer instructions for working through the courseware would have been appreciated.

8. Teachers agreed that such systems have good educational potential and can improve student motivation and confidence.

9. If such systems were generally available, the teachers considered that their role would change. More emphasis would be needed on support and supervision rather than on didactic content teaching. Concern was expressed that lesson planning would be more time-consuming and tutors would need improved IT skills.

10. Students and tutors alike were keen to see more of such materials developed to run on similar platforms.

5 CONCLUSION

Interactive learning based upon the use of computer-based technologies is rapidly becoming an important mechanism of knowledge and skill transfer within many different areas of human activity. However, if it is to be optimally effective it has to be extremely well-designed. That is, the principles underlying its mechanisms of operation have to be understood and these have to be incorporated into an appropriate technological framework. In this paper the principles of interactive learning have been discussed and some models to support its effective utilisation have been outlined. The basic techniques involved have been illustrated by means of a case study involving foreign language learning. The results of a controlled evaluative investigation provide some support for the effectiveness of computer-based interactive learning environments.

REFERENCES

Banerji, A.K. (1994). *Designing Electronic Performance Support Systems*. Draft PhD Thesis. Middlesbrough: The University of Teesside.

Barker, P.G. (1989). *Multimedia Computer-Assisted Learning*. London: Kogan Page.

Barker, P.G. (1990a). Designing Interactive Learning Systems. *Educational and Training Technology International, 27(2)*, 125-145.

Barker, P.G. (1990b). Human-Computer Interface Design for Electronic Books: a Case Study in Foreign Language Learning. In *Proceedings of CD-ROM Europe '90*. London: Agestream Ltd.

Barker, P.G. (1991). Interactive Electronic Books. *Interactive Multimedia, 2(1)*, 11-28.

Barker, P.G. (1993a). *Exploring Hypermedia*. London: Kogan Page.

Barker, P.G. (1993b). Introducing Computer-Based Training. In J.M. Brittain & W. Abbott (Eds.). *Guide to Education and Training* (pp. 160-171). London: Taylor Graham.

Barker, P.G. (1993c). Virtual Reality: Theoretical Basis, Practical Applications. *Journal of the Association of Learning Technology, 1(1)*, 15-25.

Barker, P.G. (1994). *Designing Interactive Learning Support Environments*. Paper presented at AETT International Conference. Edinburgh: Napier University.

Barker, P.G., Fox, P. & Emery, C. (1992). *Multimedia Support for CALL*. In Volume 1 of Proceedings of the Ninth International Conference on Technology and Education - Education 'Sans Frontiers' (pp. 369-371). Austin: University of Texas.

Barker, P.G., Giller, S., Morgan, J. & Glover, L. (1992). *Interactive Technologies for Language Learning*. Proceedings of CD-ROM Europe '92. London: Agestream Ltd.

Barker, P.G., Giller, S., Morgan, J. Glover, L. & Blamire, R. (1993). *Interactive Technologies for Language Learning*. Final Report of a One Year Project. Sheffield: The Learning Technology Unit of the UK's Department of Employment.

CACM, (1993). Technology in Education. Special edition of *Communications of the ACM*, 36(5), 28-91.

Cameron, K. (1989). *Computer Assisted Language Learning*. Oxford: Intellect Books.

Checkland, P.B. (1972). A Systems Map of the Universe. In J. Beishon & G. Peters (Eds.), *Systems Behaviour* (pp. 50-55). London: Harper and Row.

Chesters, G. (1990). *ReCALL Software Guide (Issue 2)*. Hull: The CTI Centre for Modern Languages, University of Hull.

Criswell, E.L. (1989). *The Design of Computer-Based Instruction*. New York: Macmillan Publishing Company.

Dean, C., & Whitlock, Q. (1992). *A Handbook of Computer-Based Training*. Third Edition. London: Kogan Page.

Discis Knowledge Research Inc. (1991). 45 Sheppard Avenue East, Suite 410, Toronto, Ontario, Canada, GU1 3UW.

Fox, J., et alia. (1990). *Educational Technology in Modern Language Learning.* Sheffield: Learning Technology Unit, Training, Enterprise and Education Directorate, Department of Employment.

Gardiner, M.M., & Christie, B., (1987). *Applying Cognitive Psychology to User-Interface Design,* Chichester: John Wiley & Sons Ltd.

Gerry, G.J. (1991). *Electronic Performance Support Systems - How and Why to Remake the Workplace Through the Strategic Application of Technology.* Boston: Weingarten Publications.

Giardina, M. (1992). *Interactive Multimedia Learning Environments - Human Factors and Technical Considerations on Design Issues.* NATO ASI Series, (Series F: Computer and Systems Sciences, Volume 93). Germany: Springer-Verlag.

Giller, S. (1992). *Design Guidelines for Electronic Book Production.* MPhil Dissertation. Middlesbrough: The University of Teesside.

Good, M., Shanahan, L., & Shaw, S. (1993). *Final Specification for a Demonstrator Model.* Deliverable 4, Workpackage 1, DELTA Project D2012 (ILDIC). Cambridge: Cambridge Training and Development.

Harrison, N. (1991). *How to Design Effective Computer-based Training.* London: McGraw-Hill.

Helsel, S.K. & Roth, J.P. (1991). *Virtual Reality - Theory, Practice and Promise.* Westport: Meckler.

Hoffos, S., Sharpless, G., Smith, P., & Lewis, N. (1992). *CD-I Designer's Guide.* Maidenhead: McGraw-Hill Book Company.

Ingraham, B., & Emery, C. (1991). 'France InterActive': a Hypermedia Approach to Language Training. *Educational and Training Technology International, 28(4),* 321-333.

Jamsa, K.A. (1993). *Instant Multimedia for Windows 3.1.* New York: John Wiley & Sons.

Kommers, P.A.M., Jonassen, D.H., & Mayes, T.J. (1992). *Cognitive Tools for Learning.* Proceedings of the NATO Advanced Study Institute on 'Mindtools: Cognitive Technologies for Modelling Knowledge' held in Enschede, The Netherlands, July 4-10, 1990, Volume 81 in Series F: Computer and Systems Sciences. Germany: Springer-Verlag.

Lajoie, S.P., & Derry, S.J. (1993). *Computers as Cognitive Tools.* Hillsdale: Lawrence Erlbaum Associates.

Latchem, C., Williamson, J., & Henderson-Lancett, L. (1993). *Interactive Multimedia - Practice and Promise,* London: Kogan Page.

Lim, J.T. (1994). *An Interactive Learning Support Environment for HCI.* BSc Dissertation. Middlesbrough: The University of Teesside.

Nimbus. (1993). Nimbus Information Systems, Raglan House, Llantarnam Park, Cwmbran, Gwent, NP44 3AB, UK.

Person, R., & Rose, K. (1992). *Using Windows 3.1 - Special Edition*. Carmel: Que Corporation.

Piccioto, M., Robertson, I., & Colley, R. (1989). *Interactivity - Designing and Using Interactive Video*. London: Kogan Page.

Pollard, D., & Yazdani, M. (1991). A Multilingual Multimedia Restaurant Scenario. *Interactive Multimedia, 2(4)*, 43-51.

Rheingold, H. (1991). *Virtual Reality*. London: Secker and Warburg,.

Romiszowski, A.J. (1992). *Developing Auto-Instructional Materials - From Programmed Texts to CAL and Interactive Video*. London: Kogan Page.

Schank, R.C. (1993). Learning via Multimedia Computers. *Communications of the ACM, 36(5)*, 54-56.

Self, J. (1988). *Artificial Intelligence and Human Learning - Intelligent Computer-Aided Instruction*. London: Chapman and Hall.

Sleeman, D.,& Brown, J.S. (1982). *Intelligent Tutoring Systems*. London: Academic Press.

Winblad, A.L., Edwards, S.D., & King, D.R. (1990). *Object-Oriented Software*. Reading: Addison-Wesley Publishing Company.

ECSA: An Environment to Design and Instantiate Learning Material

Monique Grandbastien[1] & Elisabeth Gavignet[2]

[1] C.R.I.N., University of Nancy 1, France;
[2] I.U.F.M. de Bourgogne, University of Dijon, France.

Abstract

This paper describes a generator of learning environments called ECSA. It consists on one hand of a formal model to describe the subject matter to be taught and on the other hand of tools allowing authors to instantiate their frame with existing pieces of software called 'learning units'. These units are dynamically linked by the system to built a courseware program. The domain knowledge is modelled through concepts associated with elementary items. The runnable pieces of software are described as learning units characterised by pre-conditions and post-actions expressed in terms of elementary items and learner's results. Other parts of the model include pedagogical objectives, learner's performance dynamically updated and knowledge about decision making to build a complete learning material from a set of existing modules, a learning goal and information gathered through interaction with the user.

1 INTRODUCTION

After years of research and prototyping in the field of Intelligent Tutoring Systems (ITS), no authoring environment seems to be widely accepted and even available. Other papers have commented this failure in the past two years (Major & Reichgelt, 1991) and have tried to point out many reasons for that. We summarize in this introductory section three main reasons from our viewpoint. Existing authoring languages are well suited to create sequences of screens presenting the subject matter, providing questions or exercises with pre-recorded solutions; learning sessions are not identical, they depend on the learner's answers, but this dependence is according to a number of pre-defined paths. They never include any problem-solving abilities, nor error diagnoses or flexible teaching strategies. In the last decade several ITS have been proved successful for accelerating the rate of skill acquisition among students (Anderson, 1992). But the development of most existing ITS prototypes has been conducted in computer science laboratories with general programming languages, and it is often impossible to modify them without the help of a software engineer, even without the help of the designer of the system. Of course, this is not in favour of a dissemination of those systems among teachers and trainers. So, despite several attempts to allow teachers to build ITS, such as IDE (Russel, Moran, & Jordan, 1988), and GTE (Van Marcke, 1990), one research way

T. de Jong and L. Sarti (eds.), Design and Production of Multimedia and Simulation-based Learning Material, 31-44

could be the design of authoring environments allowing the design of ITS-like systems.

We would not immediately recommend such a research direction for the following reason. There is a shift of interest from the concept of ITS (mostly devoted to a specific activity in a narrow domain) to the idea of Interactive Learning Environments (ILEs) including the many kinds of activities involved in learning, self-discovery as well as guided sessions, knowledge presentation, as well as problem solving or assessment. Most existing ITS prototypes do not provide any authoring environment and none of them succeed in giving birth to a widely spread ITS shell. So it is necessary to widen the aims and to think about the authoring environments directly in terms of ILEs, including ITS as particular schemes.

Finally, most ITS were built from nothing, that is without reusing any existing material, except previous ideas or experiences. Professionals, training centers and companies own pieces of educational software; they underline the necessity to reuse existing material, at least partly, when moving to more sophisticated learning systems including some kind of intelligence. This is another strong requirement for future work.

To take all these requirements into account in the design of authoring environments, we think that we must find the proper level of abstraction to describe the universe. This objective is a long term one and needs the collaboration of many people in the field. The work that we present in this paper is a contribution towards this objective. Other contributions can be found in the proceedings of ITS'92 (Murray & Woolf, 1992) (Brusilovsky, 1992) and among the DELTA projects for instance in AAT (DELTA AAT, 1991). We propose a formal model for the description of teaching material and a knowledge-based system using this model. The system provides teachers with an authoring interface allowing to describe learning units and learners with dynamically built learning sequences.

The organisation of the paper is as follows: Section 2 describes the formal model. Section 3 is about the metaknowledge included in the system which is used to create links between the units and to select the next unit in a sequence. Then, we present the existing prototype running on a Sun workstation and we conclude with unsolved problems, comparisons on related work, and future developments.

2 DESCRIPTION OF THE MODEL

2.1 Basic hypothesis

In order to fulfil the aim of describing existing pieces of software as well as new ones, we make the hypothesis that we are working with a physical database of learning units. Our system dynamically links some of those units to build a piece of courseware according to the learner's needs. To describe such units in an abstract model, we have to answer the following question: What are the features of a learning unit that we need to describe in order to formalize pedagogical objectives and choices related to the use of these units? Many features can be taken into account, depending on different points of view. For instance it can be important to know if the unit needs a colour screen or a microphone to be run, from the point of view of technical requirements. Others can be interested by the duration of the unit if they are to plan a training activity within a limited amount of time. We focus our attention on features from the domain model, but the formal model is open and can be enriched.

As in many other models (Lesgold, 1988; Merrill, Li, & Jones, 1990) the pedagogical objectives are mainly expressed in terms of concepts or know-how in the domain that have to be mastered by the learner. So our second hypothesis is that the author is able to describe the domain to be taught with a network of concepts. When describing the concepts of a domain, the problem of choosing the good level of granularity often arises. If too many concepts are included into the network, the domain model becomes unusable, there are too many details; on the other hand, a poor model does not allow one to express the knowledge needed to solve problems. In our model, the size of the number of concepts is guided by the assessment activities, the subject to be taught is divided into 'evaluation items' which are the smallest elementary concepts of the domain for which the teacher wants an assessment.

Semantic links exist between evaluation items, some come from the hierarchical organisation of the domain, others represent pedagogical knowledge. These links may or may not result into links between the learning units, according to teacher's specific requirements and to pedagogical decisions made by the system from its embedded knowledge. Figure 1 summarises these first hypotheses for the model.

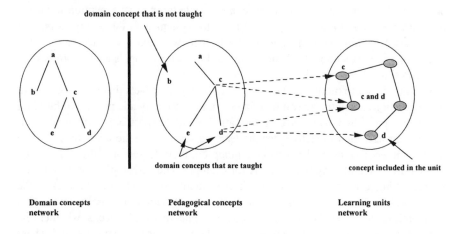

Figure 1 *Domain concepts model*

2.2 The learning units

Each learning unit of the data base is represented by a formal unit in the model. A unit corresponds to one of the many pedagogical activities offered to the learner. For a given part of a domain there exists a determined set of concepts (knowledge and know-how) that can be approached by the learner during the learning session. These important concepts are, very often, involved in a presentation followed or not followed by more or less difficult exercises. They can also be reminded later on, and a synthesis may result. Thus, a first feature of a learning unit is its nature (presentation, exercise, review, problem, other).

Then, since each activity refers to one or several concepts, it seems logical to differentiate the units according to the most important concepts about which they are. Finally, the difference of complexity between each activity and the non-linear aspect of the acquisition of concepts lead us to ask the teacher to define its prerequisites for a unit. This is done through a filter which enables the selection and the control of access to the various activities in relation with the learner's skills.

In short we can say that a unit is characterised by two main elements: its filter and its content, the content being divided into the nature of the activity and the set of concepts involved in the activity. A third element, the post-actions, completes this description, it helps to provide data related to the execution of the unit. Such data is used to model the learner's skills within the system and to determine the next learning unit to run.

2.3 Learner's skills: definition and features

We defined a unit as a compound structure capable through its execution to enrich the learner's skills. In order to provide the tutor system with the ability to build a sequence of learning units adapted to the learner, we need a way to measure the effects of a unit execution upon the learner's skills. This compels us to represent the learner's skills in our model.

Our aim is not to model the learner, but only to gather facts that are necessary to make decisions about the activation of a next unit in the dynamic process of building a learning path. Some pieces of information about learners are permanent, their name, their age, their objectives for the learning session and the items they already master. Others change as the session is going on, their degree of ability on a given know-how or the already visited units for example. The pedagogical objectives are expressed in terms of evaluation items in our model. So, we choose to represent the learner's skills by sets of triples (idf, static-measure, dynamic-measure) where '*idf*' is an identifier for a evaluation item, where '*static-measure*' checks whether the concept has been or has not been dealt with during a learning sequence and where '*dynamic-measure*' estimates memorizing and reusability capabilities of the concept by the learner.

The static-measure can take one of the four following values: unknown (never learnt), acquired (learnt before using the system), started (acquisition during the current session) and seen (acquisition during previous learning sessions). These fours values are useful to locate the acquisition of concepts in time. The values acquired, started and seen are significant to determine whether to give explanatory teaching or summarising, but they are considered as equivalent for an assessment.

The dynamic-measure evaluates the learner's ability on an item with tokens. These tokens are won or lost during the running of a unit. Each time the learner's answer is correct, he or she gets a number of tokens, more or less according to the difficulty of the exercise. The more complex is the exercise, the more significant is the number of tokens. Thus, when setting up the token rules of an activity the teacher defines his or her own scale of difficulty for this task.

For instance, if the learner's skill for the concept number 3 is represented by (3, started, 5), it means that the learner had a presentation of concept number 3 during the current session, that some exercises on this concept were proposed to him or her and that now he or she owns five tokens for concept number 3.

The learner's skills are a significant part of our model. They are used in the filter in order to limit the access to a unit. They are also useful to describe the pedagogical objectives the learner has to reach through the learning process. They provide a view of the learner's abilities on each main concept that the teacher determined. At the end of each unit execution, the learner's skills are automatically brought up to date. So, the tutor system is able to take the last knowledge acquisition of the learner into account.

For instance, let us look at the unit represented in Figure 2. In this figure, the unit is represented by a box made of three parts containing respectively the filter, the nature of the unit and the concepts referred to in it, and the knowledge inputs after the execution of the unit. This unit is an exercise about the concept number 5. The filter indicates that for activating this unit the learner's skills about the concept number 5 must be equal or greater than (started, 0). If the learner's skills are the following, (2, seen, 1), (3, unknown, 0) and (5, started, 3), then the tutor can activate the unit because for concept 5 three is greater than zero. From the assessment point of view, the comparison is based on the number of tokens. Success inside this unit gives the student 2 more tokens for the concept number 5 and the set of learner's skills becomes equal to (2, seen, 1), (3, unknown, 0) and (5, started, 5).

Item 5 started tokens = 1	Exercise unit Concept = 5	Item 5 started tokens + 2

Figure 2 *An example of a learning unit*

2.4 The learning universe

The previously defined learning units constitute the nodes of an oriented semantical network. The links in this network are created by the tutor system to make up what we call the '*learning universe*'. This universe models the different activities that can be used by a teacher for a subject matter and the relations existing between them. A particular path in this network represents a sequence of units inside the universe and defines a piece of courseware for a given student.

The links represent many possible relations between the units. For instance, there is an arrow from unit U1 to unit U2, if unit U2 can be proposed to the learner directly after unit U1. This situation happens when the contents of U2 enriches the learner's skills: that is to say, when the content of U2 is, from a pedagogical point of view, similar to that of unit U1 or if unit U2 provides the learner with added knowledge.

The teaching process is, by nature, a complex activity and the model described in this paper does not claim to simulate the teacher's behaviour. Simply it tries to reproduce the most typical situations. For instance, if the learner has not well understood a concept, a unit discussing the same concepts but using another medium will be considered. On the other hand, if the learner follows approximately the evolution foreseen by the teacher, a new concept or a more difficult exercise will be proposed to him or her. Finally, if the initial learner's abilities are higher than those expected by the teacher, the learner will be immediately confronted to more complex problems which use several concepts together.

We need links to model such relations between units. But how many kinds of links? Another strong requirement for our model is to remain general and open to many domains of application, even if the sequences built are not very sophisticated concerning the pedagogical strategies implied. In order to reach this objective we propose only two kinds of links that are detailed below. We have defined five links. Other links or classes can be added to this current state of the model.

2.4.1   *The static links*

A link 'direct-access-to' expresses a selected relation between two units. It allows the teacher to link two units the contents of which must be successively presented whatever the situation of the learner is. The only link expressly defined by the teacher is this one; other relations have to be indirectly expressed through the filters of the units.

A link 'same as' expresses a relation of substitution between two units. The content of each unit allows to present or to test the same content but different ways are used.

A link 'logically-to' expresses that the post-actions of one unit satisfy the pre-conditions of another one. U1 is followed by U2 if the knowledge missing for having access to U2 has just been learnt in unit U1.

These three kinds of links do not take into account the learner's skills. They are the same, regardless of who the learner is. It is why we call them 'static links'. They can be created only once since they operate on permanent information.

Figure 3 illustrates these three static links. Unit U1 is the same as unit U2, differences are to be found in the texts, figures and questions provided to the learner during the execution of the unit. Unit U2 must-consider unit U3 because after having performed U2 the learner has started concept number 7 with 0 token, which is the exact pre-requisite for unit U3; for the same reason, U3 must-consider U4.

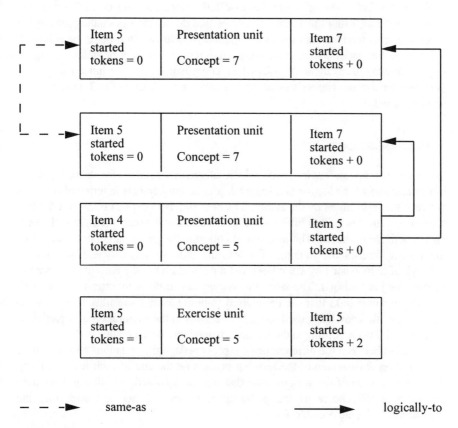

Figure 3 *Example of static links*

2.4.2 *The dynamic links*

This second group of links takes into account the permanent evolution of the learner's skills. We give an example of an exercise where the learner gets tokens but if his or her answer is wrong he or she can also loose some of them. Before explaining in detail these links, let us define two such links included in our model.

The 'equivalent-to' link is similar to the static 'same-as' link. It connects two learning units which have the same knowledge contents, but not in the same context, for instance units having different filters.

The 'must-consider' link relates two units, still unconnected, that could be presented one after the other because the second one gives the learner added knowledge and also because the learner's skills are high enough to satisfy the conditions expressed in the filter of the second unit. Compared to the 'logically-to' link seen before, this link is more interesting. Its widens the research and takes into account the learner's latest skills.

These two links belong to the dynamic links since they are created during the learning process, using the learner's abilities that do not stop evaluating during the session. The different kinds of links are mutually-exclusive. In order to be coherent, a link cannot replace another and it is crucial to respect the order of inclusion. Figure 4 gives an example of dynamic links which complement the static links of Figure 3. We consider that the learner's skills are the following: (2, seen, 1), (3, unknown, 0) and (5, started, 3).

3 META-KNOWLEDGE

We have set up an environment which allows us to describe learning units, information about the learner and some additional requirements in terms of relations between the units given by the author. The next step is to explain on what criteria a sequence of units is built to fulfil a set of given aims, or in other words, how the next unit to activate is chosen. The problem of choosing the next unit happens each time the learner finishes the running of a learning unit. At this moment, we have a network of units related by static links and a particular unit, the current unit, that the learner has just finished. The work the system has to do is to extend the network with the dynamic links that can be inferred from the learner's results. Then it has to use the specific knowledge used to make decisions in the elaboration of a particular sequence of units according to the learner's behaviour and capabilities.

The links between the different units express pedagogical relations and are called into question at each step of the learning process (at the end of each learning unit). The determination of the various units that will be activated, is split into two main phases: first the choice of the pedagogical strategy to set and after that the organization of some possible activities.

3.1 The pedagogical strategies

The pedagogical strategies are processes that use a large variety of information, and of course which are not easy to formalize. Our objective is not to build an ad hoc system, it seems more reasonable to give the teacher the opportunity to describe the strategies he or she wants to see used. In these conditions and in order to allow the reproduction of our model in many domains of application, we choose to define inside our system a set of strategies founded on general principles.

Few implemented systems give this opportunity: COCA (Major & Reichgelt, 1992), a CO-operative Classroom Assistant, is a system developed specifically to allow for authoring both the domain to be taught and the way in which the material

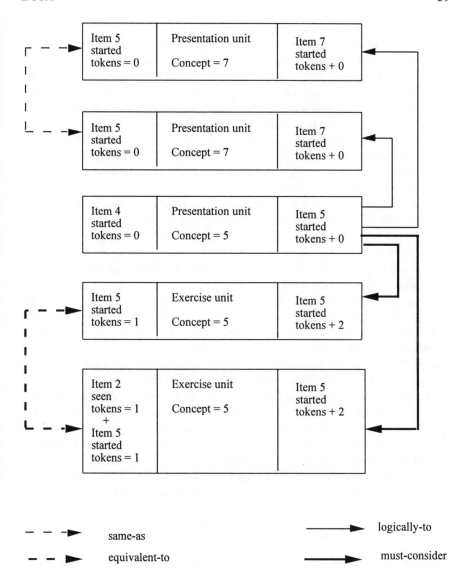

Figure 4 *Example of dynamic links*

is taught. In COCA, the strategy rules are partitioned in four sets. Each set corresponds to a separate heuristic decision: the next concept to use, the nature of the next interaction, the content of the next interaction, the response to student. As in COCA, ECSA calls its meta-strategy after the execution of a unit. The features of the learning units provide the tutoring system with similar elements to determine the next material.

The three existing strategies in the first release refer to the different ways in which the next material is chosen. Each selects the nature of the next interaction (teach, test or summarise) and the specific set of evaluating items to concentrate on.

In the first strategy, the presentation of the knowledge is given before the exercises. This solution seems perfectly adapted to certain domains of application that require a lot of practice and only few pieces of factual knowledge. The polynomial factorization is a good example because there is only few factual knowledge and the exercises are necessary to acquire the practice (Nicaud, Nguyen-Xuan, Saidi, Aubertin, & Wach, 1990). One advantage of this method is to increase significantly the set of exercises which are considered because all the basic elements are known when the practice begins.

In the second strategy the application of a concept follows more or less systematically its presentation to the learner, and finally some more difficult exercises are proposed. This solution provides a way to have a progressive approach of a specific concept and, if necessary, 'close' concepts of the last one through synthesis. A close concept is a concept discussed in a learning unit which is related to the previous one by a static link.

These two strategies deal with two different tree searches. The first one corresponds to width-first search, where all the concepts are presented and then evaluated, when the second one corresponds to in depth-first search where all the activities about a same subject are run before starting with another topic. The last strategy is based on the second one. A depth-first exploration of the tree nodes is used but the order of the different nodes depends on the objectives.

The goals for the student are given by the teacher. They represent, for each evaluation item, the skills the learner has to master. With the last strategy, defined above, the order defined on the objectives is significant. It can be an order of importance: the teacher wants the learner to start with the main concepts in order to practice a lot. It seems obvious that they could not be learned if the pre-requisites are not known. Nevertheless this order is important for the choice of the units. We will now give more details about the way the learning units are selected.

3.2 The selection of a learning unit

Choosing the best unit for a given learner is not an easy task. From our point of view, knowing if the choice is effectively the best one or not, is something impossible to judge using formal criteria. So we choose by a process of elimination. Starting from a set of constraints we pay particular attention to choose among the units belonging to the learning universe those which meet the fixed conditions.

Let's remember that in the learning universe there are static links created once and a specific unit, called current unit, which is the last unit the learner comes through. At the end of each execution of a unit, the learner's skills are brought up to date and the selection of the next unit can start. This selection is done by successive cutting, considering that the unit is partially determined by its nature (presentation, exercise, problem, recall), and its content.

At a given moment in the learning process, all the units belonging to the learning universe could not all be proposed to learners because they does not have enough skills to access them. Only the units accessible from the current unit can participate to the selection. At this step only the learner's skills are taken into account. A unit U2 is called accessible from a unit U1, if there is a link (static or dynamic) between U1 and U2. It is for establishing this sequence of accessible units that the dynamic links are created from the current unit. The dynamic links starting from the other units are not created.

So, for a given student and at a specific moment, the tutor system has a set of accessible units (Figure 5). Among the accessible units from the current unit U, some of them do not agree with the criteria (about nature and content) given by the pedagogical strategy. Of course, this last one gives exactly the nature and sometimes the content of the unit the tutor system is looking for.

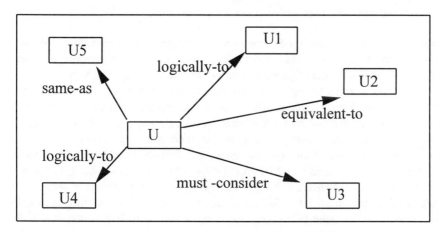

Figure 5 *The accessible units form the current unit*

The second phase of the selection consists in excluding from the accessible units all the units which have a nature or a content different from those expected. The remaining units after this cleansing are the candidate units and one of them will be the next unit executed.

The next step is useful for arranging the set of the candidate units taking account of the nature of the link relating each unit to the current unit U. Those with a link 'direct-access-to' come first, second those with a dynamic link and lastly those with a static link except 'direct-access-to'. So the wish of the teacher, using the link 'direct-access-to', is always be chosen.

For a given kind of link, if there are still several candidate units after this step, the choice could be more precise. But, in the existing prototype the first unit of the sequence is chosen. The learner's profile could be used, as many studies pointed out that some pupils do not always have the same facilities with all the different physical supports. Graphics are often best adapted to specific domains such as geometry and chemistry.

If there are several possibilities for the presentation of the same concept, it would be of interest to have the information to know how to increase the efficiency of the learning process. Some technical aspects can constrain the tutor system to choose a solution instead of another one. For instance, during initial studies it is not always possible to choose one's pace. The selection of the learning units can depend on the time the learner has for learning activities. Among many candidate units the system should be able to choose the one that allows the more quickly learning process.

Finally, if all the sequences are empty, and of course no unit can be found, another strategy will be chosen and a second search begins. The learning process stops as soon as the goals are reached or as soon as no unit is available.

4 IMPLEMENTATION, PROTOTYPING AND RELATED WORK

The previously described model has been implemented in an interactive authoring environment running on a Sun workstation. The kernel of the application is written in C to ensure easy portability, the interfaces were built through Sun Views.

An author is asked to describe a learning universe through a sequence of screens providing user-friendly menus. The available functionalities allow the author to focus his or her attention on the specification of the current unit; at any step of the design process, it is possible to simulate the execution of a learning session and consequently to check if the units that are already described lead to what is expected by the author. Compared with SHIVA (SHIVA, 1991), ECSA has not yet editors as powerful as those of ORGUE, but it keeps a larger part of the design work by itself, namely the creation of links. The visualisation of the links created among units by the system allows rapid corrections, for instance on the filter part of a unit if the network does not satisfy the author.

This environment provides a pre-defined framework which facilitates the author's task together with functionalities that allow him or her to enrich or modify the courseware being generated by the system. The prototype has been tested on chemistry lessons and those tests have permitted us to overcome some problems. In such a framework teachers can benefit of existing units (especially units that are difficult to create by oneself), they can arrange them according to their own way of teaching and they can add very simply some units that they do not found in the existing data base of units. In order to become a ready to use product it needs to be enriched by many missing functionalities and to be written for a Windows interface on PCs.

Other contributions are currently developed in the research community. The idea of a database of existing or half-fabricated materials has been formulated and implemented in several DELTA projects such as OSCAR and DISCOURSE. In other environments, such as COCA and GTE, the domain knowledge or the instructional knowledge has to be structured into predefined hierarchical levels, whereas ECSA model gives more freedom to the designer.

5 CONCLUSION AND FUTURE TRENDS

The development of creation environments for learning systems is a relevant aspect for ILEs. The model we proposed through ECSA is a first step. Its main interesting features seem to be the following: Concerning the resulting learning sessions, the automatic generation of links and learning paths is somewhere an idea that allows to have a dynamic building of a sequence. The use of information about the learner's skills to choose the next activities to present him or her gives a good adaptation to the learner, even if it is certainly possible to take more precise criteria into account. Concerning the authoring point of view, ECSA provides a user-friendly interface that minimises the task of the author, it is easy to create a learning environment, it is also easy to modify it. But, of course, the functionalities available in our model need to be enriched.

A first extension we are working on is to complement the set of pedagogical strategies. We provide the authors with new functionalities to describe their own strategies, starting from 'pieces of strategy' and using a rule based language. A second one would be to allow an author to add other features to the unit description. It could be interesting to check whether an object-oriented representation with a precise semantic is adapted to attain this objective. Finally, when the execution of a learning unit uses a knowledge based system to solve problems and to provide explanations to the learner, it would be necessary to create links between the concept network of this unit and the general concept network of the learning environment.

Moreover the involvement of partners from other subjects will serve to evaluate the effectiveness of the prototype and to suggest future improvements.

REFERENCES

Anderson, J.R. (1992). Intelligent Tutoring and High School Mathematics. In C. Frasson, G. Gauthier & G.I. McCalla (Eds.) *Proceedings of the 2nd international conference ITS'92* (pp. 1-10). Berlin: Springer-Verlag.

Brusilovsky, P. (1992). A Framework for Intelligent Knowledge Sequencing and Task Sequencing. In C. Frasson, G. Gauthier & G.I. McCalla (Eds.), *Proceedings of the 2nd international conference ITS'92* (pp. 499-506). Berlin: Springer-Verlag.

DELTA AAT. (1991). *Advanced Authoring Tools*. Final report of the DELTA project D1010.

Lesgold, A. (1988). Toward a theory of curriculum for use in designing intelligent instructional systems. In H. Mandl & A. Lesgold (Eds.), *Learning Issues for Intelligent Tutoring Systems* (pp. 114-137). New York: Springer Verlag.

Major, N.P., & Reichgelt, H. (1991). Using COCA to build an intelligent tutoring system in simple algebra. *Intelligent Tutoring Media, 2,* 150-169.

Major, N.P., & Reichgelt, H. (1992). COCA: A shell for Intelligent Tutoring Systems. In C. Frasson, G. Gauthier & G.I. McCalla (Eds.), *Proceedings of the 2nd international conference ITS'92* (pp. 66-73). Berlin: Springer-Verlag.

Marcke, K. van (1990). A generic tutoring environment. In L. Carlucci Aiello (Ed.), *Proceedings of ECAI'90* (pp. 655-660). London: Pitman.

Merrill, M.D., Li, Z., & Jones, M.K. (1990). Second generation instructional design, *Educational Technology, 30,* 7-12.

Murray, T., & Woolf, B. (1992). Tools for Teacher Participation in ITS Design. In C. Frasson, G. Gauthier & G.I. McCalla (Eds.), *Proceedings of the 2nd international conference ITS'92* (pp. 593-600). Berlin: Springer-Verlag.

Nicaud, J.F., Nguyen-Xuan, A., Saidi, M., Aubertin, C., & Wach, P. (1990). APLUSIX: a learning environment for acquiring problem solving abilities. In *Proceedings of Cognitiva 90.*

Russell, D.M., Moran, T.P., & Jordan, D.S. (1988). The instructional design environment. In J. Psotka, S.A. Massey & A. Mutter (Eds.), *Intelligent Tutoring System: lessons learned.* Hillsdale (NJ): Lawrence Erlbaum Associates.

SHIVA. (1991). *Advanced Courseware Development Environment.* CNRS-IRPEACS-Ecully, France.

DISCourse:
Tools for the Design of Learning Material

Harald Mispelkamp[1] & Luigi Sarti[2]

[1] Dornier Deutsche Aerospace, Germany;
[2] Istituto Tecnologie Didattiche, Italy.

Abstract

This contribution covers those areas of courseware design that can be supported with computerised tools, like learner modelling, instructional design and domain representation. In the DISCourse (Design and Interactive Specification of Courseware) framework the learner is modelled from both a static perspective and a dynamic one. The static model accounts for those learner characteristics which are largely independent from the specific domain being taught; the dynamic model monitors the student's progress with respect to the author's declared goals. The selection and application of suitable instructional strategies are based on GTE (Generic Tutoring Environment), an environment where *teaching expertise* is represented independently of the particular domain being taught. GTE's libraries provide *tasks, methods* and *objects* to navigate course structures, elaborate on individual contents, manage exercises and evaluate the student's progresses. In the paper more detail will be devoted to the area of domain and content representation. In the domain analysis an author produces a description of the entities of interest in the subject domain; this representation is independent of any specific instructional strategy, and is therefore highly reusable. The learning goal analysis is devoted to the description of the degree of mastery the learner should acquire for each given content element. The goals are expressed in terms of *knowledge, understanding* and *ability of application* of the given content element. In the content analysis an author elaborates on the domain representation, specialising it to the particular instructional purposes of the courseware under development. Topics of interest are selected, prerequisite links are added and the content elements are further typified to add structuring information which will be used in the strategy selection. The content analysis is tightly interrelated with the learning goal analysis, and these two are often performed concurrently.

1 INTRODUCTION

The DISCourse (Design and Interactive Specification of Courseware) project aims at the systematic support of all the phases of courseware development. DISCourse addresses both the design and the production of courseware, together with other authoring issues such as creating simulation-based learning environments, the reuse

T. de Jong and L. Sarti (eds.), Design and Production of Multimedia and Simulation-based Learning Material, 45-60
© 1994 *Kluwer Academic Publishers. Printed in the Netherlands.*

of learning material and aspects related to the learner's interface. The main objective of DISCourse is to develop and pilot test a modular, multimedia authoring environment that comprises tools to support authors in the various steps of the courseware development cycle.

The DISCourse approach to the design aspects follows the suggestions of the DELTA Exploratory Action project TOSKA (TOSKA Consortium, 1991) and differentiates the courseware design activities according to the various sources of knowledge involved:

- knowledge on how to model the learner;
- knowledge on what instructional strategies to use;
- knowledge on how to structure the domain.

Thanks to such a separation an author can specify domain knowledge without the requirement for a simultaneous specification of instructional knowledge or learner characteristics. In these three areas the DISCourse project identifies, validates and uses generic structures to build and integrate tools that support authors in the related design tasks. The genericity of the tools makes it possible to support the authors in a variety of courseware domains and instructional tasks.

This paper mainly focuses on the design of courseware material. Section 2 addresses those aspects of learner modelling an author is involved in at design time. Section 3 deals with the definition of instructional strategies. Section 4 covers the domain authoring, structured into three conceptually separate steps: the *domain analysis*, that is the acquisition and representation of a reusable knowledge model (Section 4.1); the *learning goal analysis*, i.e. the definition of the tasks a learner should be able to perform as a result of the instructional process (Section 4.2); the *content analysis*, consisting in a re-elaboration of the domain structure by applying the learning goals in a specific learning context. After a conclusive section, the paper reports a number of references for those readers interested in a more detailed exposition of the DISCourse approach.

2 LEARNER MODELLING

The DISCourse project takes a pragmatic position in the creation of design support tools: the purpose of the learner model is to ensure that learning process is proceeding in the best possible way for a given student *with the given system*. The evaluation of the quality of the learning process is determined in terms of the *author's intention* rather than in terms of a cognitive model of the domain (Moyse et al., 1993): the author declares abstract pedagogical goals for the various units of learning material, as they are used in a specific context.

The DISCourse learner model has a *static* and a *dynamic* aspect. The static aspect attempts to pre-define a set of learner classes which will be confronted with the courseware. The learner attributes involved in the static model are based on such aspects as prior knowledge, learning style, learner control, IQ, and motivation.

The dynamic aspect attempts to maintain a set of relationships connecting the instructional material, its *learning function*, the static connotation of the learner and a dynamic, summative measure of the level the learning function is satisfied with. E.g., it is possible for an author to predict that if a student is represented by a given set of attributes, the fruition of a particular learning material will result in a certain degree of activation of the prior knowledge related to a given topic, or in a rise in motivation.

The concept of learning function is introduced in Shuell, (1992). Shuell identifies a set of psychological processes, such as raising attention, expectations and motivation, activating prior knowledge and perform monitoring, that foster effective learning in the student. For a detailed discussion on how the concept of learning function integrates in the literature and on its usefulness in the context of domain authoring, the reader can see Moyse et al. (1993). Here, it is worthwhile mentioning that in DISCourse the learning function is an attribute of the learning material in a specific context: for each piece of learning material the author has to state the learning function it serves for the various learner classes; for each element in the content description (see further on), at run-time the application of each learning function to that topic is registered, to determine the degree to which the author's goals have been satisfied. Table 1 lists the learning functions identified by Shuell (Johnson & Sime, 1993); an author could add other functions to the list.

The currently available learner modelling tool prototype supports the author in the following tasks:

- selection of the relevant learner attributes and their values;
- selection of a representative subset of learners to validate the attributes and their values;
- analysis of the learner attribute data including a classifier program providing facilities for the author to view the learner populations in a number of different ways;
- selection of possible overlay values;
- tailoring of the maintenance engine that keeps track of the overlay values in the overlay model;
- assessment of the initial learner knowledge.

3 INSTRUCTIONAL STRATEGIES

In the design support area concerning instructional strategies DISCourse supports the authors in defining the instructional mechanisms to be used for teaching the topics in question. For this task DISCourse today offers the mechanisms that GTE (Generic Tutoring Environment) provides.

GTE (Van Marcke, 1992) is based on the representation of *teaching expertise* in terms of *instructional tasks*, *instructional methods* and *instructional objects*. Tasks provide a way of refining the specification of what needs to be achieved and methods specify variations of how a task may be satisfied: alternative methods which can satisfy the same task allow for adaptation to the learner. Instructional objects add specific domain dependent knowledge, in that they encapsulate information on how the domain knowledge will be used inside an instructional process and link the instructional tasks and methods with the multimedia material which will be used in the interaction with the learner.

Table 1 *The learning functions identified by Shuell*

Learning Function	Tutor Initiated	Learner Initiated
Expectations	Provide Overview (map, diagram);Statement of purpose.	Identify purpose for using program.
Motivation	Give opportunities for interaction; interesting material.	Personal interests; look for ways to make it personally relevant. Make it a game.
Prior knowledge activation	Remind learner of pre-requisite information.	Ask self what is already known about the topic.
Attention	Highlights, animation, audio supplements.	Identify key features. Record notes.
Encoding	Provide diagrams and/or multiple examples/contexts; Suggest mnemonics.	Generate mnemonics images and/or multiple examples/contexts.
Comparison	Encourage comparison with diagrams, charts, questions.	Look for similarities; Draw diagrams, charts.
Hypothesis Generation	Encourage student to think of and try various alternative courses of action.	Generate possible alternatives and corresponding solutions.
Repetition	Guided practice and/or reflection. Multiple perspectives/examples.	Systematic reviews.
Feedback	Provide instructionally relevant feedback and correctives.	Seek answers to self-posed questions.
Evaluation	Have next action by student based on student's evaluation of feedback received.	Ask "What do I currently know?" "What do I need to know?"
Monitoring	Check for understanding.	Monitor performance. Self testing.
Combination, Integration, Synthesis	Provide ways to combine and integrate information;-e.g. with graphics or multimedia.	Establish categories; construct tables; seek higher-order relationships.

Examples of instructional task are such tutoring activities as selecting a topic, introducing a topic, describing a concept, giving an exercise or supervising a student. Instructional methods to select a topic might range from asking directly the learner, to finding a topic which is still unknown to the student but related to his or her current knowledge. Typical examples of instructional objects are examples, counter-examples, exercises, explanations, analogies, hints, etc. An instructional object being categorised as a certain type of exercise states that the related material can play the role of an exercise inside an interaction with a learner. A series of abstract, generic instructional object types were identified, that are able to steer GTE's generic instructional library in the management of the instructional interaction. In this way the instructional object allows GTE to decide how to use the information inside the object. The classification of the instructional object types and the instructional libraries which operate on them are described in detail in Van Marcke et al. (1992).

The mechanism implemented in GTE relies heavily on the notions of selecting out of a set of libraries and tailoring these libraries for the topics to be taught. The libraries of instructional tasks and methods include:

- *navigate library*: contains the basic task and methods to navigate the overall course structure, up to the selection of the content to teach;
- *elaborate library*: contains the mechanisms to instruct about individual contents;
- *exercise library*: contains the tasks and methods to manage exercises;
- *test library*: is an extension of the exercise library, which allows to evaluate the students performance.

The currently available GTE environment supports the following authoring activities:

- development of a teaching plan for each topic;
- selection of the relevant instructional libraries;
- experiments with the selected libraries; this includes a simulation of instructional dialogues on a certain topic to determine in how far the selected libraries behave as expected;
- adaptation and combination of libraries.

The GTE system also includes a run-time engine which manages the interaction with the learner and is in charge of all those decisions left open at authoring time.

4 DOMAIN AUTHORING

The remainder of this paper presents the DISCourse proposal in the area of domain authoring and describes the activities supported by the tool prototype currently available.

Conceptually, the task of domain authoring is separated into three distinct activities: *domain analysis*, *learning goal analysis* and *content analysis*. The domain analysis is intended to provide a formal description of the entities which play a role in the domain of interest. In the learning goal analysis an author describes the tasks a learner should be able to perform after the fruition of the courseware being developed. The content analysis reviews the domain representation from the perspective of the learning goals.

4.1 Domain analysis

The domain analysis provides a reusable overview of an area of knowledge; such a description is independent of specific learning goals. The representation is structured as a graph where the *domain objects* are nodes and the *domain links* are edges. The domain objects are named and labelled as *top*, *class* or *instance*: an object is *top* if it represents a root class in the graph, i.e. no superclass is defined for such an object; *class* objects are on the contrary subclasses of some other object; *instance* objects represent individual elements, specific cases belonging to some class. Most of the semantics of a domain representation is generated by the links between the domain objects, organised into the six groups shown in Table 2.

Table 2 *The domain link hierarchy*

1. Hierarchical Structuring Link 1.1 is-a-class-of 1.2 is-a-subclass-of 1.3 is-an-instance-of	4. Spatial Link 4.1 is-located-at 4.2 is-located-under 4.3 is-located-behind 4.4 is-located-within 4.5 is-located-next-to
2. Aggregational Structuring Link 2.1 is-part-of 2.2 is-a-collection-of	5. Causal Link 5.1 is-effect-to 5.2 infers
3. Temporal Link 3.1 a-is-before-b 3.2 a-meets-b 3.3 a-overlaps-with-b 3.4 a-starts-with-b 3.5 a-happens-during-b 3.6 a-ends-at-the-same-time-as-b 3.7 a-equals-b (in time)	6. Activity Related Link 6.1 uses 6.2 is-performed-by 6.3 has-purpose-of

For a detailed description of the semantics of the domain links see Schmidt (1992). It is worth while mentioning here that although from a theoretical point of view the set of link types is applicable in a random manner, to make the author's task as convenient as possible it is recommended to use the hierarchical structuring links first, the aggregational links second and the other links afterwards. It seems in fact conceptually better to develop an outline map of the domain components, hierarchically organised, at an early stage of the analysis, so that each object that is to be included can be located at the correct level of abstraction.

We would like to stress the independence of the domain representation from any instructional aspect such as the required learning goals or the strategies the courseware will apply. As an example, no prerequisite relationship is yet considered in the domain analysis; such aspects will be dealt with in the following analysis steps. This approach is deemed to allow for an abstract, highly reusable representation of the domain subject which the author can specialise taking into account his or her specific instructional needs.

Figure 1 shows a fragment of the domain analysis the DISCourse consortium has carried out - as an application experiment - in the field of image processing. It is important to note that the picture refers to an early prototype of a domain graph viewer, and is not representative of the user interface of the final version of the editor, still under development at the present time.

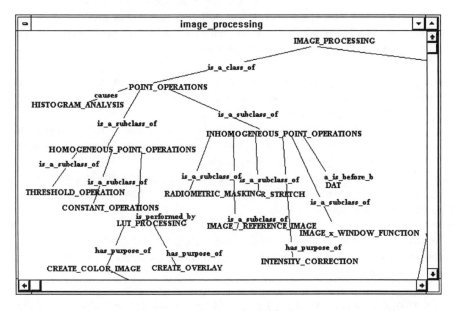

Figure 1 *An example of domain analysis in the field of image processing (fragment)*

4.2 Learning goal analysis

Within the learning goal analysis a variety of descriptive terms are supplied in order to support the author in the specific task of structuring the learning goals for the courseware design.

Generally the process of learning goal analysis is interdependent with the process of content analysis. In order to give a description of the actual contents that is to be taught, it is necessary to know the goals of the instruction (which usually will be tasks the learner is expected to perform) to make the necessary selections from the domain structure and vice versa. The goals can only be precisely described, if it is known which contents shall be taught. The deduction of an elaborate set of learning goals depends to a large extent upon the course objective and the individual perspective that the author takes as well as the needs of the target learner group. Starting from the course objective the perspective can be formed according to the following factors:

- single domain or combination of domains;
- target learner group attributes;
- goal tasks or specific job tasks, that are to be performed after the courseware instruction.

The goals should be classified. In terms of three categories, stating to which degree the learner should have knowledge of a domain (which might be procedural as well as descriptive). The goals shall be described in terms of performance in the following way (see right-hand column of Figure 2):

- Knowledge: the learner is expected to master the related topic at one of three different degrees, namely *'has an overview of'*, *'can reproduce complete knowledge of'*, *'can summarize knowledge of'*;
- Understanding: the learner is expected to show one of three different degrees of understanding of the related topic, namely *'complete comprehension'*, *'general understanding'*, *'beginning of understanding'*;
- Application: the learner is expected to be able to apply the related topic in one of three different cases, namely *'cases that were taught'*, *'new area of knowledge'*, *'more complex cases'*.

Individual goal tasks are marked and learning goals are described in free text form for each task. From the list of domain objects the author selects one or more for each goal (see Figure 2).

In case of a domination of theoretical knowledge (instead of practical tasks or skills) that is to be taught and especially if a combination of domains is required, it should be stated within the learning goal, which part of each domain will be selected and in which way they will be combined for the purpose of instruction.

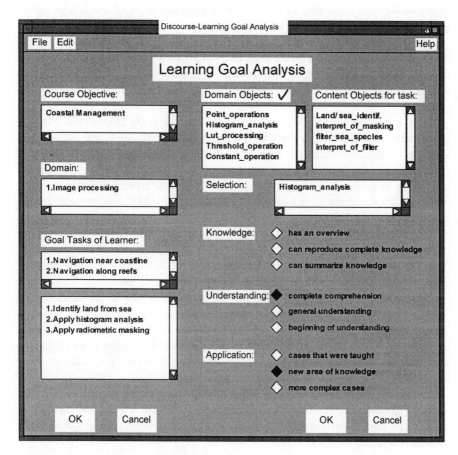

Figure 2 *Stating the learning goals*

In case of a combination of a more theoretical area of knowledge with a domain concentrating on the description of practical tasks or skills it will be possible to combine the two domains in the following way. Within the window on the left side starting from the course objective a list of goal tasks is being stated step by step. For the first goal task within the right side window a domain object will be selected from the list of available domain objects. Once the object is selected the classification according to the categories of *knowledge, understanding* and *application* can be performed. As a result an entry is made into the list of learning goals in form of goal tasks related to content objects, stating value triples of the type (*goal task, domain object, category of performance*).

In a large number of cases a mixture of theoretical knowledge and tasks, based again upon a number of skills, is to be expected for a variety of learning goals. In that case for each major task a cluster of knowledge can be stated that is relevant for the individual task.

The degree of granularity to which a specific object of the content analysis needs to be known, is determined by the level of description of the individual task, that the learner needs to perform after the instruction. Therefore the bottom level of the content analysis structure should only be designed after the learning goals have been stated.

From a methodological point of view there is no clear cut between the learning goal analysis and the content analysis. They both define what the learning contents is going to be, but from different perspectives. Within the first perspective, the learning goal analysis, the learning goals are applied to a domain (which is structured according to general principles) and serve as selection criteria in order to select objects from the domain and to provide guidance on which objects need further elaboration to which degree.

There is a logical implication to move from goal analysis to content analysis, but the author might choose to do it the other way around. Especially if the issue of re-usability is to be considered, it makes sense to provide the author within learning goal analysis not only with a window stating the domain objects in form of an alphabetical list to choose from, but to provide an option to inspect the list of content objects (in case one exists). In this case the author would state the learning goals according to the contents offered, e.g. stating the level of knowledge for a specific content object and describing the contents in a learner task oriented way. Within the goal task the contents is stated in a more general way, whereas the information what the learner will perform with this contents is stated explicitly.

Especially the evaluation phase requires the statement of precisely described learning goals. It is not enough to state which content the learner shall be able to master, the kind of performance and the degree of mastering a specific contents has to be determined as well.

4.3 Content analysis

The third component of the Domain Authoring Tool is the content analysis, structuring the domain according to the perspective of the learning goals of the courseware to be developed. The learning goals are used for the selection task in order to decide which elements of the domain are to be dealt with and to which degree they will be further elaborated. The content analysis typically elaborates on the domain representation and produces a graph which differs from the domain graph in the following:

- nodes (content objects) and links that may be relevant to the achievement of the learning goals are added; examples of these additional nodes are decompositions of one or more domain objects, and content objects that may be needed to support analogies;
- content objects are typified according to the hierarchy shown in Table 3;

- a further link type is available, in addition to the six link types of the domain analysis listed in Table 1: it is the *logical prerequisite*, which connects content objects in a logical sequence; this structure does not necessarily resemble the instructional sequence of the courseware, as the sequencing of instructional objects is influenced by factors such as learner model and instructional approach: it mainly serves the purpose of visualising the coherence of certain content clusters.

Within the Content Analysis even more than one domain representation can be combined, in order to serve the needs of the learning goals. Additionally to the selection and elaboration activity, the classification into knowledge type is performed; Table 3 lists the complete taxonomy of node types available in the content analysis. A more detailed dissertation on the semantics of such hierarchy is available in Schmidt (1992).

Table 3 *The content object hierarchy*

```
                          Generic Content Object

       skill
                    cognitive-skill
                    reactive-skill
                    interactive-skill
                    physical-skill

       knowledge
                    fact
                              system-fact
                              series-of-facts
                    procedure
                              linear-procedure
                              branched-procedure
                    concept
                              concrete-concept
                              system-concept
                              defined-concept
                    principle
                              process
                              principle-of-action
                              causal-principle
```

As already mentioned above there is no strict sequence that prescribes that the content analysis has to be performed after the learning goal analysis, but it is useful to follow this routine.

Within the content structuring there are two different methods of designing the content, one is graphically oriented whereas the other one is performed by giving a description and stating the attribute values alphanumerically.

The graphical version of content analysis is presented first. In order to perform the content analysis the results of the domain analysis are available in form of a graphical representation, showing the domain objects as well as the relationship classified according to the six types of predefined links. Figure 3 shows a (fragment) representation of the content graph derived from the domain representation of Figure 1, after the content analysis has been carried out. Note that only hierarchical structuring links are shown, other types of link being filtered out. The author builds the content graph starting from the domain representation, and modifying it by interacting graphically with the tool.

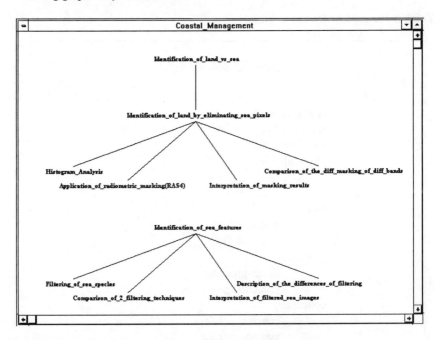

Figure 3 *A graphical representation of the courseware contents*

The marked domain objects are selected and transferred into the content analysis graph window. According to the description of the learning goals and the goal tasks the learner is supposed to restructure the selected content. The restructuring might concern a modification of link types and additionally a modification in terms of adding further objects. These modifications should be directed towards a further didactic elaboration of the contents description. During the content analysis the level of granularity has to be specified for a specific content of the courseware unit that is being designed.

This implies that the contents structure is designed including the bottom level, stating the content objects which will be part of the courseware, not on an abstract, but a concrete, instance level. Nevertheless it is purely an instructional decision process determining *what* will be taught, but this does not imply any decisions concerning the instructional methods of *how* those contents will be taught. The contents analysis tool does not offer any support concerning the methods and the selection of learning material.

The structure of the content analysis is not restricted in any way and it will be possible to connect the contents structure with any instructional method that the author chooses.

The alternative opportunity to design the contents structure is provided by the Content Object Description window (see Figure 4).

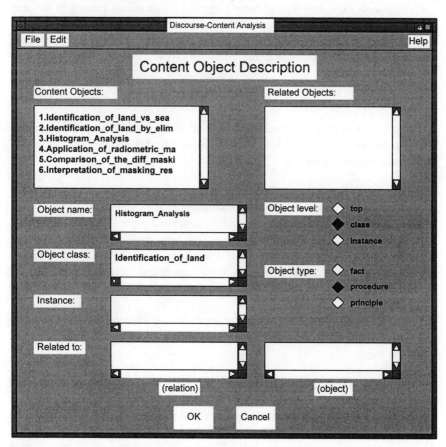

Figure 4 *Textual analysis of the courseware contents*

One reason why the author might choose to work directly within the Object Description window might be that he or she has already a well defined structure in mind and rather than tentatively working with a graphical structure, he or she might be able to describe the contents objects in a straightforward manner. The advantage of the graphical display is that the author gets a structural overview of all the objects, but if he or she does not need such a support, he or she can choose the description window instead. Within the description window is stated the object name, the related object class as well as instances and the types of relation (in terms of the predefined seven types of relationship) and the objects related to are being stated. For the object itself the level is being stated (default values are: *top*, *class* and *instance*) and the object type. Within the two top windows on the left hand the newly defined content objects are displayed and on the right-hand side the related objects that have been described are presented. If the author agrees with the statement he or she indicates so by the *OK* button at the bottom. After that the objects are integrated into the content graph and can be viewed within the graphic window.

Having analysed a domain and having defined a courseware content in the way described here an author has generated structural descriptions that allow for the other tools to navigate in an explicit domain and content representation and, moreover, have a high potential of being reusable.

5 CONCLUSIONS

We have described the conceptual framework on which the DISCourse environment bases its approach to the design of courseware. The remarkable features of the DISCourse workbench are:

- DISCourse supports the entire life-cycle of a courseware development project (although in this paper we have only analysed the design aspects);
- the courseware design activities are structured into learner modelling, instructional analysis, domain analysis, learning goal analysis and content analysis; such a separation allows for the provision of a set of specialised tools;
- attention is paid to reusability issues at the conceptual level: an example is the identification of a domain analysis step, independent of specific instructional decisions;
- reusability also affects the architectural level: the various tools are integrated into a single environment; inter-tool data exchange is granted by a common database sub-layer.

For the sake of completeness it is worthwhile here to devote some brief considerations on those aspects of the DISCourse workbench that this paper has not explicitly addressed so far. With the term *production* we identify all the activities related to the manufacture of the multimedia material to be presented to the learner. As a wide range of editors is available off the shelf to handle text, pictures, sound, video, etc., the DISCourse production effort is oriented toward the organisation (in both space and time) of such material into compound units and in the modelling of the learner interaction. The integration of multimedia material in a single compound unit is addressed with the adoption of MHEG, a recent ISO standard (MHEG, 93). The modelling of the interaction with the learner is described in Dykiel et al., (1993).

In the DISCourse workbench architecture all the specialised tools rely on the services of the CIS (Common Information Space), a database which stores all the half-products of the courseware development process. The CIS is designed to foster the reuse of already existing artifacts; in addition, it acts as a standardised integration means between application tools. When all the authoring activities are concluded all the components of the courseware are stored in the CIS, available to the run-time GTE engine. For a detailed description of the CIS structure and functionality see Chioccariello et al., (1993).

It is also interesting to briefly exhamine the links between the instructional objects, described in Section 3, and the pieces of multimedia learning material. Once an author has defined a set of instructional objects to be available to the GTE strategies, suitable multimedia material is to be associated to each instructional object in order to play the intended role inside the interaction with the learner. More than one unit of multimedia material can be associated to any given instructional object, to allow for further adaptation to the learner characteristics (e.g., to implement multilinguality). Those elements of the learner interaction which are relevant to the instructional process must be dealt with by GTE; for this reason a run-time communication protocol is defined between GTE and the multimedia units; whenever the interaction does not affect the strategy directly, it can be managed locally by the multimedia unit itself.

The DISCourse project is now in its third and final year: most of the tools exist as prototypes and are being tested using real-world examples; in particular, the courseware design tools are being used in the development of an application example in the area of Image Processing for Coastal Management.

REFERENCES

Chioccariello, A., Innocenti, C., Marcke, K. van, Persico, D., Sarti, L., & Viarengo, V. (1993). *New Conceptual Scheme Description for DBLM.* DISCourse Deliverable #27.

Dykiel, R., François, C., & Chalon, R. (1993). *Implementation Specifications for Multimedia Production Tools.* DISCourse Deliverable #24.

Johnson, R., & Sime, J. (1993). *Tutors use of feedback in Adaptation of GTE designs.* DISCourse Deliverable #9.

Marcke, K. van (1992). Instructional Expertise. In Frasson, Gauthier & McCalla (Eds.), *Proceedings of the Second Conference on Intelligent Tutoring Systems.* Montréal: Canada.

Marcke, K. van, Vedelaar, H., & Tubbax, B. (1992). *Preliminary description of instructional knowledge base.* DISCourse Deliverable #14.

Moyse, R., Johnson, R., & Sime, J. (1993). Learning Functions for Author Modelling. In P. Brna, S. Ohlsson & H. Pain (Eds.). *Proceedings of AIED 93 World Conference on Artificial Intelligence in Education*. Edinburgh.

MHEG (Multimedia and Hypermedia Expert Group) (1993). ISO/IEC CD 13522-1, *Information Technology - Coded Representation of Multimedia and Hypermedia Information Objects*. JTC1/SC29/WG12.

Schmidt, C. (1992). *Report on DISCourse Topic and Link Type Definition*. DISCourse Deliverable #18.

Schmidt, C. (1993). *Domain Authoring Tool Specification*. DISCourse Deliverable #20.

Shuell, T. (1992). Designing Instructional Computing Systems for Meaningful Learning In P. Winne & M. Jones (Eds.), *Foundations and Frontiers in Instructional Computing Systems*. New York, Springer Verlag.

TOSKA Consortium (1991). *TOSKA final report*. Public deliverable.

Acknowledgements: The DISCourse project is partially funded by the CEC under the DELTA D2008 contract. The ideas expressed in this paper are the result of the collaboration, interaction and discussion within the whole DISCourse consortium. In particular, Robin Johnson, Rod Moyse, Julie-Ann Sime and Karen Valley contributed to the development of the learner model; Kris van Marcke and Henriette Vedelaar to the instructional strategies and GTE; Christina Schmidt to the domain authoring aspects. With them and with all the other partners the authors are in debt.

Production of Interactive Multimedia Courseware with *Mathesis*

Norbert Benamou[1] & Augusto Celentano[2]

[1] SELISA, Paris, France;
[2] Politecnico di Milano, Italy, and R&S Informatica, Milano, Italy.

Abstract

Mathesis is a project aiming at defining and developing tools for authors and learners of computer based courses in a stand-alone environment, by including a broad range of tasks and functions that follow people involved in courseware during the whole life-cycle of course preparation and use. The analysis of the requirements of authors and students distinguished two kinds of services: the ones devoted to the management of the working sessions, and the ones devoted to the preparation and structuring of course material according to a wide choice of educational strategies. The courseware model of *Mathesis* structures a course as a set of lessons. Each lesson is built around one of three types of modules directed to distinct educational targets, exploiting at full extent the capabilities of interactive multimedia applications. The basic didactic modules are the units of learning material that follow a traditional educational strategy based on predefined paths and evaluation tests. Background information is supported by a hypermedia concept web, that is linked to the lesson context but can be freely traversed by the learner. Learning by doing is supported by practice exercises and simulations that allow learners to self-assess their progresses. A set of rules is applied to the learning objectives defined by the course authors, in order to build the logical succession of the modules within the lessons.

1 INTRODUCTION

Mathesis - Stand Alone Workbench for Learners and Teachers is a project aiming at defining and developing tools for authors, teachers and students of courseware products. Its name is the translation in Latin letters of the Greek word for *instruction* (μαϑησις). The scope of the project includes a broad range of tasks and functions that follow authors and learners during the whole life-cycle of courseware preparation and use.

Mathesis is a technology oriented DELTA project that originates as a consequence of two converging markets in Europe: the one of education and the one of multimedia publishing. It considers the evolution of these markets and aims at providing learners and teachers with an educational workbench which:

- Is strongly oriented towards flexibility in deciding the educational strategies to be implemented;

61

T. de Jong and L. Sarti (eds.), Design and Production of Multimedia and Simulation-based Learning Material, 61-82

- Provides an innovative functionality of interactive multimedia applications, especially for delivering multimedia courseware on CD-ROM;
- Operates on the most frequent stand-alone systems, MS-Windows and Macintosh.

In Section 2 we present a general overview of the project objectives which led to the definition of the *Mathesis* architecture, before emphasising, in Section 3, the approach which has been defined to model courseware and its production. Three main issues are considered in the production process:

- The courseware architecture and the subsequent diversity of roles and tasks in producing and structuring courseware (Section 4);
- The needs of services embedded in a stand-alone environment to support the authors in managing and configuring their work (Section 5);
- The possibility to develop portable software and platform independent courseware (Section 6).

The reader is referred to the Mathesis bibliography (Mathesis 1992a, 1992b, 1992c, 1993) for a complete description of the project.

2 *MATHESIS* OBJECTIVES

The primary objective of the *Mathesis* project concerns the provision of a stand-alone environment for both the authors and the learners of computer based courses, which will include a coherent set of tools for publishing and executing interactive multimedia courseware (Jonassen & Mandl 1990). The tools are grouped into three subsystems oriented to authoring, resource management and session management.

A *Courseware Authoring System* allows authors to organise courseware combining didactic modules (called *units of learning material*), simulation modules and a hypermedia network of information. Sequencing of the various modules can be controlled through the evaluation of the learner's progress and results. All courseware components rely on multimedia interactivity (animation), and the authoring system includes a multimedia composer.

A *Resource Manager* enables learners and authors to configure their work environment by expressing preferences regarding multimedia features, identifying and selecting courseware servers, and managing catalogues of available courses.

A *Session Manager* enables learners and authors to organise and keep track of their actions over time. A session gathers information sent by the *Mathesis* subsystems about the course preparation or execution, describing the user activity. The user can get a structured or timed view of his or her work, can annotate specific activities (Nielsen, 1986), put bookmarks at important stages of the sessions and come back to these marks, pause the session for some time, saving information such as the current stage of the course, and resume it later.

By speaking of authors, we address generically the producers of course material and structure, whose tasks involve at least three different roles: the *editor*, who defines the raw material, the *teacher*, who defines the educational context, and the *course designer*, who organises and integrates the material according to the educational context.

Mathesis aims at providing tools covering the three roles. Editing of the material is supported by an authoring tool, Apple Media Kit®, oriented towards multimedia interactive presentations. Defining the educational context and designing the course are supported by extensions of this authoring tool that are specifically targeted to educational applications. Since in *Mathesis* learners and authors work alone, structuring and integration tools are designed according to specific requirements of a self-learning environment. End users are provided with appropriate support tools that would help them to perform their educational activity in that stand-alone environment.

The second objective of *Mathesis* concerns the development of a multi-platform authoring environment for the production of multimedia courseware. Courses are designed as interactive multimedia applications controlled by education oriented strategies. A key issue for the project is the possibility to use distinct platforms for the production and the subsequent use of the courses, and to transfer a finished course across different hardware and software platforms. Two platforms are considered, Macintosh and MS-Windows, that cover almost all the currently relevant market of personal computing. Portability of the course material and compatible run-time executors are the technical foundations on which this issue is based.

The third objective is to prototype an educational server which will be accessed through local area networks and ISDN by the *Mathesis* stand-alone environment. Such a server is developed within the project to evaluate the environment and the reaction of customers to different strategies of courseware delivery, but is not intended to be a product by itself. Tools are defined to enable an author to store a new course on the server, and a learner to select a course and to launch it from the server.

3 THE *MATHESIS* MODEL OF EDUCATIONAL PROCESSES

The courseware model of *Mathesis* derives from an analysis of educational processes. It implies in turn some requirements on the architecture of the production and execution systems.

3.1 Course design

The design of a course is largely independent of being computer based or not. Its structure, its contents and its evaluation procedures are defined with respect to the educational goals, and only marginally depend on the tools employed (Besnainou et al. 1988; Ferguson-Hessler & de Jong 1990). At a rough analysis, a course is a set of lessons, and its design is bound to three major tasks:

1. The definition of the global educational goal, i.e., what learners will be able to perform and the knowledge they will acquire at the end of their training;
2. The definition of the educational strategies through which the goal will be approached and achieved. The strategies concern the organisation of the course, i.e., what is presented and in what order, the material resources available, the influence of learners profiles, i.e., cultural level and previous knowledge and skills, and the tasks to be performed by learners;
3. The production, collection and organisation of course contents into concrete elements, in order to best fit the educational strategy.

During course design the achievement of an educational goal is translated into a controlled navigation through a path, whose steps are lessons, tests, exercises, in general operations related to didactic activities. The design of these activities and of their mutual organisation follows from answering a number of questions (Weinstock & Bork 1986): What is the learning goal to achieve? How could the goal be split in sub-goals? What kind of intellectual activity should the author try to induce in the learner? What kind of interaction best supports the learner in his or her intellectual activity?

Several operations can be defined, that support lesson design and delivery. For each course an author has to define a set of activities that will be either performed by the courseware or driven by the learner. A sample list is the following one:

- *Information presentation*, that concerns the issuing of knowledge about facts by the courseware;
- *Variant selection*, that concerns the ability of the learner to distinguish among different information chunks;
- *Problem solving*, that requires the learner approach an unknown situation by adapting and applying a known method;
- *Concept browsing*, that concerns the ability of the learner to explore knowledge, to make generalisation, and to discover or create associations between concepts.

3.2 Educational strategy

Taking into account the above mentioned process in designing a course, an author may have difficulties for integrating a complex instructional dimension in a courseware instance. This is due to the fact that courseware, besides being a collection of lessons with their goals, steps and operations, is also a kind of interactive tutor, that must supply monitoring services normally issued by a human tutor.

In a computer based course, human interaction between the teacher and the learner does not exist, and the software has to find other ways for evaluating the learner progress, in order to adapt course execution to his or her pace. Evaluation is based on the user profile and is supported by tracing the user activity in course execution.

Educational strategies can be proposed according to several paradigms: program, information, simulation and strategy oriented.

Program oriented paradigm
A course is made of interactive applications whose execution is defined algorithmically, i.e., course sequencing and variant selection are systematically driven by a predefined schema.

The course design is based on collection of monomedia or multimedia data upon which four classes of functions act:

- *Presentation*: what the learner sees;
- *Interaction*: what the learner can input;
- *Test*: the way the learner input is analysed;
- *Action*: what action is performed after the user input is analysed.

Information oriented paradigm
The learner has access to a web of educational material (like an encyclopaedia) in which he or she can navigate according to some information exploration function, e.g., browsing or querying (SAFE, 1990a, 1990b).

The most appropriate area of hypertext and hypermedia techniques is in open learning, where the path through information and the time spent on the course is decided by the student.

The main issue to be defined is the kind of navigation tools and associated learning tools (e.g. self-assessment tools) that can be proposed to help the learner to fruitfully progress in web exploration.

Simulation oriented paradigm
The idea of learning by doing is well established in education. Practice and exercises are directed not only to evaluate the learner ability to perform a task or to apply the learned lesson, but can improve understanding of a problem by showing how it works in a real case, specially for simulations based on formal models of the world.

Strategy oriented paradigm
Some new systems emerged from the DELTA exploratory action (AAT, 1991; SHIVA, 1991), that propose a more flexible way to deal with the instructional dimension of courseware.

A set of pedagogical rules are applied to a network linking the didactic units to the concepts to be learned, allowing the system to plan the presentation order of the units to the learner. This information is integrated with the result of the test units, in order to update the course plan according to the user interaction.

4 THE *MATHESIS* ARCHITECTURE

The architecture of *Mathesis* derives from a model of courseware design that takes into account the objectives and the educational issues of the project. The model defines courseware as a (set of) interactive multimedia application(s) relying on shared media objects, whose execution is controlled by structures defined by educational strategies. The basic components of the model and their organisation reflect in activities in courseware design. Courseware is produced by authors and consulted by learners through the co-ordinated use of a set of tools.

4.1 *Mathesis* components

The basic components of *Mathesis* courseware are interactive multimedia applications (IMA), made of objects that encapsulate the presentation and the interaction functions. Multimedia properties of presentations are defined according to the capabilities of the running platforms. The interaction functions support several kinds of dialogue targeted to the needs of the course, e.g., questions and answers, commands or movement actions, time-based reactions, and so on.

The production of such objects requires tools specialised to the representation, input and output of content information and to the design of the information shape, and systems for cataloguing, retrieving and delivering such components.

Production tools are, for example, word processors for text, graphics programs and image processors for drawings and images, outliners and structure editors for the organisation of material. In general, several kinds of editors are requested to create and modify multimedia data.

The design of the course structure consists in the organisation of the basic presentation and interaction components in such a way that the learner can select and access them in some suitable order.

On this model of courseware structure the authors and the learners act through three sets of functions (Figure 1):

- The *Courseware Editor* provides authors with the functions required for producing the courses. The editor is directly responsible for the editing of the course structure, by assembling multimedia presentations, exercises, and units that access external tools. Basic media objects are produced and assembled with a variety of tools, some of which exist out of the *Mathesis* system (e.g., graphic and animation editing programs). Assembling and interaction control of IMA objects is made by a *Mathesis* specific version of the commercial product Apple Media Kit®;
- The *Courseware Browser* is a run-time environment enabling a learner to select and execute a course. The courseware browser allows transparent execution of any *Mathesis* course on both the selected platforms, Macintosh and MS-Windows;
- In producing and consulting courses, the author and the learner also need an environment supporting their activities and providing some general interest services: annotation, session management, access to remote educational servers,

and so on. Such an environment, called *Workbench*, will provide homogeneous services through a platform dependent look and feel.

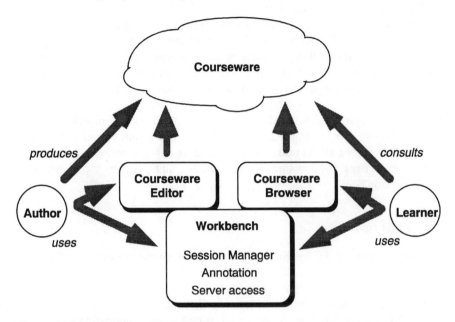

Figure 1 *The architecture of Mathesis*

4.2 Course organisation

The organisation of the course is defined by applying an educational strategy to the collection of lessons and lesson units. The lesson contents are set by the authors and refer to specific knowledge or procedure that has to be acquired or understood. A course lesson is usually defined in terms of concepts and *units of learning material* (ULM), that a user must visit and learn in order to progress in the course (ESM-BASE, 1991).

At the outermost level *Mathesis* does not prescribe any predefined path among the lessons. They are collected in a set, the user being able to select each of them from a menu. Learning objectives are defined and updated through tests performed during lesson attending.

Educational strategies can be mixed in different parts of a course, and a compound approach can suggest guided tours based on the relationships between the lessons, still leaving the user the possibility of a free choice. For example, within the lessons usually a program oriented strategy defines the instructional paths the learner must follow in accessing the lesson units, with intermediate evaluation steps that explicitly trace user progress.

In a subset of the lessons, a simulation oriented strategy can allow the learner to practise freely with a model of the specific lesson topics until he or she shows confident with the underlying theory.

When the learner has completed a lesson unit, a test, in the form of one or more exercises whose results can be formally analysed and evaluated, can assess if he or she has got a specific skill in presenting or using the concepts issued in the unit, and in performing the activities related to the taught domain. According to the test outcome the learner is driven to another unit, or sent back to repeat some unit already consulted.

A lesson is regarded as fulfilled when a specific global learning objective, defined by the course authors, is achieved. For example, the learner has visited all the lesson units and has passed all the tests. The local learning strategy, which is based on the learning objectives updated through the accessed units, defines the learner path within a lesson.

4.3 Lesson contents

A course is defined by instantiating, in a set of course lessons, the following elements (Figure 2):

- A set of units whose content is the learning material;
- A web of concepts the learner can consult as background information;
- A set of exercises and tests to assess user progress;a global learning strategy defined upon a set of objectives.

Units of learning material (ULM)
The ULM collect the multimedia information directly related to the course and organise them according to the program oriented paradigm. They represent the content of what the author wants to teach. According to the *Mathesis* objectives, a strong emphasis is given to handling of complex multimedia data in the ULMs.

Concepts
The hypertext paradigm can be used to provide background information, supporting the explanation of items found during course exploitation. This kind of information is stored in a *Concept Web*, a learner being able to enter it through a ULM and then to navigate in the web before going back to the main lesson stream.

Web nodes of information share with the other units the richness of presentation features, by means of links whose traversal executes multimedia scenes.

Exercises
In the course of a lesson unit, a learner will be able to launch exercises that have different goals: to assess the achievement of learning objectives, and to help the learner to evaluate his or her preparation.

In the first case the exercises are linked to the instructional strategy and can modify the order in which the ULMs are accessed. According to some test results the learner can be driven to repeat some units, or to integrate a 'normal' lesson route with supplemental units.

In the second case the exercise results do not influence the ordering of ULMs, acting simply as parallel branches that may be followed or not; in this sense they are simply a different kind of units, that may require a more active participation of the learner.

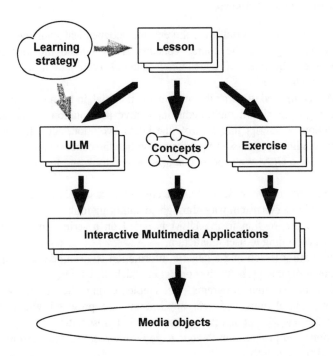

Figure 2 *The components of a course*

Media objects

The design paradigms proposed for *Mathesis* are based on interactive multimedia applications. Most media objects are not specific but common to all applications.

Available tools and standards in progress are more or less agreeing on the structure of an interactive multimedia application. Consequently, the differences are the controlling structures: algorithms in the program oriented design, webs in the information oriented design, models in the simulation oriented design, and rules in the strategy oriented design.

The various parts of a *Mathesis* courseware could thus share interactive multimedia objects, and should only specialise control structures and methods to drive their execution.

Learning strategy

Learning objectives represent the achievement of some educational result that the author wants to audit and evaluate throughout the progression of a learner in the courseware. They will be evaluated in the execution of ULMs and will control the learning strategy, which is the guiding mechanism which determines the choice or the proposal of the lesson units to the learner.

4.4   Units of learning material

The units of learning material are coherent and independent courseware elements that gather and organise the course contents. They embed the algorithms that implement the sequences of educational material presentation as well as the interaction with the user.

A ULM is composed of parts: the multimedia material, in form of nodes, each one of them being a consistent multimedia interactive presentation, encapsulating the user interaction; the script that controls the ULM evolution, according to the user actions; and the links to the external information like the concept web.

The design of a ULM is a process that uses several tools and functions:

- Multimedia interactive presentations are created by assembling and synchronising raw material in a consistent way, through an authoring tool;
- Algorithmic progression in the ULM is based on a script whose execution is performed according to user interaction;
- Links between a lesson and a generic information environment are exploited by navigation tools that preserve the context in which the user is;
- Execution of external programs for supplementing the lesson with richer executions, simulations and real applications are provided within the same scripting framework that drives the lesson content presentation;
- User actions and progression in course are monitored, and the learning objective is updated consequently.

As an example of lesson and ULM structures, let us introduce a lesson on mathematics aiming at introducing numbers and operations to children. The course is composed of a set of lessons that the learner can access without being forced to a predefined path, and of a set of learning objectives that the learner must achieve (Figure 3). A lesson on numbers could be organised as follows (Figure 4):

1. The first ULM, *Numbers Definitions*, defines several categories of numbers: natural numbers, integers, real numbers, and so on. Some tests are performed within this ULM to assess the learner's understanding. If it is over a predefined threshold, the next ULM is launched;
2. The second ULM, *Operations*, defines the various operations on numbers and explains how to perform them. This ULM will be more detailed in the following.

When the learner reaches a predefined level of understanding,, an exit test launches the third ULM;

3. The third ULM, *Quiz*, includes a questionnaire and a set of exercises on the lesson. Results of this quiz are expressed as values of learning objectives such as "Understanding of *Integers*, *Natural Numbers*, *Real Numbers*". A global performance test determines at the end of the quiz if the learner has to go back to one of the two first ULMs.

The second ULM introduced above concerns *Operations* on numbers and its goal is to explain the four basic operations: addition, subtraction, multiplication and division (Figure 5).

1. A first multimedia composition introduces the goals of the ULM. Within this composition, interaction with the learner is very limited;
2. A second multimedia composition concerns the addition operation. Within this composition (Figure 6), the learner interacts permanently with the software; according to the interaction, three different multimedia scenes are displayed, concerning the basic add mechanism, commutativity and associativity, with exercises being linked to each scene. While the multimedia composition runs, it sets values to some variables that can be used by the ULM (through message passing). In the example, two variables are used, Choice and Exercise1 (see Figure 5);
3. While the second composition runs, some tests are performed by the ULM on the values set by the multimedia composition:

   - If results of Exercise1 are good and the learner has chosen to study the subtraction, the multimedia composition *Subtract* is executed;
   - If results of Exercise1 are good and the learner has chosen to study the multiplication, the multimedia composition *Multiply* is executed;
   - If none of these two conditions apply, the learner can either quit the ULM or stay within the multimedia composition *Add*.

The way the example has been drawn shows that actions can be implemented by sending selected commands to a multimedia composition that unconditionally shows a scene, and tests can be defined by receiving a status about user actions from the multimedia scenes.

A lesson unit can thus organise the access to components of interactive multimedia compositions through a separate control mechanism that defines the structure of the unit itself, independently from the way the behaviour of the single scenes is defined.

Thanks to the separation between the algorithm and the presentation, graphic artists can design the scenes independently from their use. This leads to a high degree of re-usability both in the case of material purposely designed for the course, and in the case of material retrieved from existing sources.

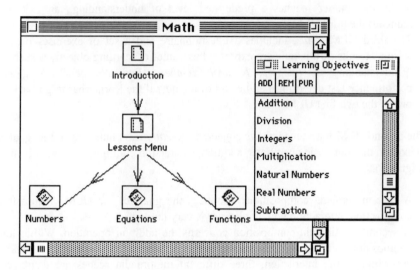

Figure 3 *Lessons and learning objectives*

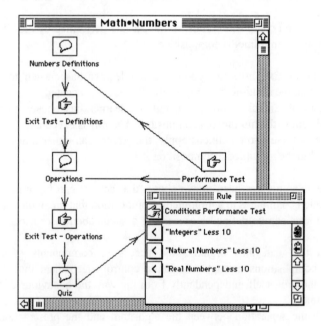

Figure 4 *A lesson structure*

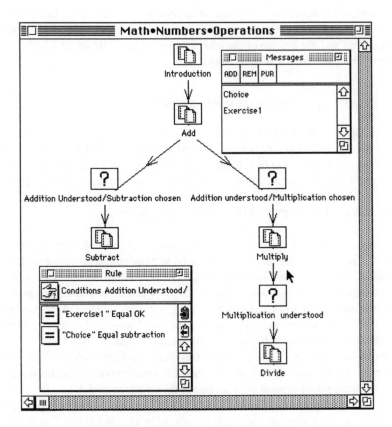

Figure 5 *A Unit of learning material*

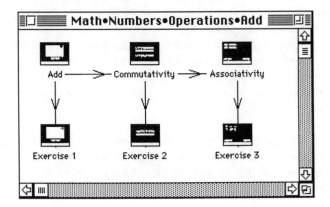

Figure 6 *A multimedia composition*

Also testing is enhanced by this organisation, because the look of a lesson unit can be tested independently from the controlling logical structure. The authors of the basic material and the authors of the course structure can established a well defined interface for the integration of their work.

5 *MATHESIS* MANAGEMENT AND CONFIGURATION

For a simple course, it will be possible for a single person to play all the roles implied by courseware production. However for a big and complex one these roles will almost certainly have to be split among the various actors of a production team.

To ensure an efficient management of the production process, *Mathesis* provides a set of general interest services, which support the production activities. These services, collected under the *Workbench* subsystem, cover:

- Management of one or several work sessions. Session management is a key activity, particularly for users that may need to pause and resume sessions over a period of time. Session management also involves informing the user about the non-completed tasks in a session, as well as the facilities and resources available. By creating various work sessions according to the roles played in the production process, it is possible to get supplementary points of view on the work performed;
- Annotating a session or a course. Annotation would allow authors to create thoughts or notes and associate them to objects in their work session, without inserting them formally in the courseware under production. Learners can organise note taking around the structure of the course accessed;
- Graphical display of a work session. A history of the session can be kept and used by the user. The history of a session is displayed in a graphical way that shows the relationships among the lessons and the units, the current activity, the possible continuations, and the path followed (Figure 7). A shorter representation, in the form of an ordered list of steps, traces the user route and the time spent. The production environment generates automatically information stored in the session according to the activities performed;
- Access to a server and/or management of a catalogue of educational resources. The basic idea of this service is to enable an author to update a catalogue or server of courseware that is available for learners. However this service can also be used by a production team as a common repository to store a courseware under production.

These services are especially useful to support the diversity of roles in the production process. They also concern learners and support the learning process. Due to their crucial role in *Mathesis*, they provide the basic functionality of the workbench and are implemented as independent tools.

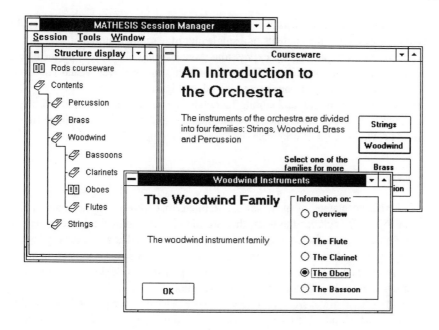

Figure 7 *Graphical display of a work session*

5.1 The authoring environment

In order to allow the authors to build their global learning strategy, the authoring environment organises the lessons in a network of relationships and dependencies. The definition of the learning objectives results in a set of rules that behave as constraints for navigation among the ULMs. A global map of the courseware organisation helps the author in selecting the various parts.

The structure of the courseware is presented with diagrams linking multimedia applications and lessons. The author is able to create, move and connect the lessons and the lesson components using a direct manipulation interface.

The lesson designer is used to edit the structure of the lesson. It implements three groups of functionalities related respectively to the learning objectives, the learning strategy and the learning rules.

Learning objectives are basically named variables whose values represent the degree of achievement of some knowledge or skill. The author creates a set of objectives by defining their names and types (e.g. on/off or score), that will be used in learning rules.

The learning strategy defines the structure of a lesson, and is presented as a diagram linking units of learning material and learning rules. As for the organisation of the lessons within a course, the author creates and links the ULMs, the tests and the rules; the interface mirrors the interface of the multimedia editor, that can be invoked for designing the contents of a single unit of learning material.

The learning rules are logical expressions over learning objectives and local data describing the ULM completion. They are built in a menu driven visual language, and associated to paths from one unit to the other (Figure 5).

In addition to the design and editing functions, the author can switch to a browser mode identical to that experienced by the student, and can take advantage of the services provided by the Workbench, like session auditing and annotation.

5.2 Exercises configuration

In *Mathesis* two classes of exercises are defined, that have different goals: a first class of exercises includes the tests, that are directed to assess the achievement of learning objectives, or the completion of intermediate steps that approach the learner to the objectives. A second class includes exercises whose purpose is to help the learner to evaluate, by practising, his or her preparation without a formalised assessment that could influence the course execution.

In the first case the exercises are linked to the learning strategy, and can modify the order in which the ULMs are accessed. According to the test results the learner can be driven to repeat some units, or to integrate the 'normal' lesson structure with supplemental units.

In the second case the exercise results do not influence the access to ULMs, acting simply as parallel branches that can be followed or not; from the courseware point of view they are simply a different kind of ULMs, distinguished by a more active participation of the learner.

Two reasons suggested the introduction of practice exercises in *Mathesis*: the first is to provide the user with some form of self-assessment that can be executed without penalties in case of failure. Exercises are an integration to conventional lesson units in the framework of 'learning by doing'.

The second reason is to allow the inclusion in a course of complex interactive material whose automatic evaluation can be difficult or ambiguous, or of material controlled by applications outside the *Mathesis* system. For example, a course on business planning could contain some exercise that uses a spreadsheet as a tool. While they are a special kind of ULMs, the increased complexity and the deeper user involvement distinguish them from the units based on presentation.

In *Mathesis* the term 'simulation exercise' denotes a kind of test or practice exercise that is related to some organised model of behaviour. This term includes 'true' simulations, e.g., artificial representations of some phenomenon or process of the real world, but also generic interactive practising environments that are related to operational aspects of the application field. Exercises can be executed according to flexible and configurable paths, and give the learner some degree of freedom in selecting the sequences and iterations of the exercise steps. They can be used as tests or as practice exercises according to delivering or not a final status that could be used for scoring purposes.

Simulation exercises are generated and executed according to the architecture illustrated in Figure 8. The author defines the semantics of a set of similar or related exercises with a *configurator*, building a conceptual class, which is an abstract description made of a set of data definitions and a control script.

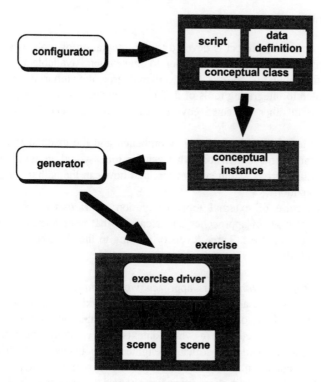

Figure 8 *Simulation exercises configuration and execution*

The conceptual class describes which are the exercise parameters, what variants are defined, how they are identified and selected according to the parameters, and how they are implemented in terms of basic multimedia scenes and interactive presentations.

From the conceptual class instances can be derived by assigning values to data, each instance describing a specific exercise. A *generator* interprets the instance by producing the actual exercise code, in form of a *driver* that is used to control its execution. The driver generates messages addressing the multimedia applications that compose the exercise, conveying commands and parameters from the conceptual description of the exercise, and returning information about the execution completion status.

By using this approach, the simulation exercises exhibit many similarities with the ULMs, the main difference being the greater flexibility in changing the control sequence of the exercise.

5.3 Integration of external tools

A specific part of the project is devoted to the integration of tools existing outside *Mathesis* into the Workbench, in order to make them available to authors and learners in the context of courses. To a certain degree, the authoring environment is itself dedicated to integrating tools of different type, since texts, graphics and audio are generated in other dedicated environments, and integrated in the courseware environment.

The possible relations between the Workbench and the external tools are more involved in the learner dimension: what generic tools would an author want to be called and utilised from within courseware, and how can the author set this up and control its execution?

The architecture of external tools integration in *Mathesis* derives from the investigation of a set of approaches and scenarios that have been explored during early stages of the project. Three levels of binding to the Workbench environment have been studied:

- *Workbench-specific tools.* This approach would imply a set of generic tools available at any time as an integral part of the Workbench, similar to the Desk Accessories available on Macintosh systems. The main question raised is about which tools are needed and in what contexts. For example, the functionalities required for a calculator in a structural engineering courseware are different than those in a course on statistical analysis (and a standard GUI calculator is inadequate for both). This observation first showed the ambiguity in the definition of 'generic' tools. They can be based on generic applications, but need to be configured for different context;
- *Usage from within courseware.* Here the term 'external tools' refers to off-the-shelf applications which are relevant to the learning domain. An author developing courseware on financial management might want the student to be able to do some exercises using a spreadsheet, with one of the market available products. This approach may lead the student to acquire or improve skill on a real product, leaving to each instance of the learning environment the choice about which product is to be used. Since the author does not know which product will really be used, it must address spreadsheet usage in a general way. In a rich spreadsheet program, then, only a small part of the functionalities are required for the exercise; will the other ones create confusion and distraction from the course itself? How can data be transferred between the spreadsheet and the courseware in a product independent way, and how much will a suitable customisation environment cost?;

- *Session configuration tools*. External tools can also be used to adapt the Workbench to specific situations. A courseware author may not know in advance if a videodisk player or a modem is available on a learner platform, but want to take advantage of them if they are. Or a learner or teacher may want to follow courseware at different levels of detail or at different learning paces according to previous familiarity with the material.

For each level a number of meaningful scenarios were set up and analysed. The more interesting ones, that led to the definition of the current integration architecture, come from the usage within the courseware. Free access to a program from within the *Mathesis* environment should not require any log or data exchange mechanism, other than those provided by the operating system (e.g. a clipboard).

Access to a tool that act as an integral part of the learning environment requires different solutions according to the role of the tool in the educational process, and to freedom the user is given in using it.

As a brief example, let us examine some possible learning scenarios which would involve the integration of a spreadsheet, each of which rouses a different set of integration problems:

- *Learning general financial management*. Courseware in the broad range of domains which actually use spreadsheets would benefit from the possibility of integrating a spreadsheet program into specific points of the courseware itself. This also involves invoking the spreadsheet already configured with some headings, formulae, and data, as well as text formats, colours, etc. In this context, it is important that the passage from the courseware to the spreadsheet be as 'seamless' as possible, and that the user not need to know how to use the program;
- *Learning how to use a spreadsheet*. Rather than a tutorial on a specific product, the course could be organised around the functions provided by a class of products. This is a common problem in professional training, and one could essentially imagine an off-the-shelf program being run from within the *Mathesis* workbench and commanded by a courseware script. The question then becomes what the range of possibilities are, whether the editing of such a script is coherent with the *Mathesis* authoring environment (e.g., what part of the course is actually made running the spreadsheet, what part is a simulation based on screen dumps). The above mentioned problem of data exchange is the main technical concern;
- *Learning new budgeting procedures in a company*. In a distributed environment in which a spreadsheet is used by a range of managers, secretaries, etc. for the preparation of budgets for different divisions, procedural changes may arise due to changes in accounting principles, law, etc. In this case, it would be useful for each user to run the program from within the *Mathesis* workbench, which could launch some courseware modules when the user is working on a determined section of the spreadsheet. The Session Manager could also keep track of the

effectiveness of these learning modules and, as a tool for learning needs capture, gather a set of data which can be used in planning future updates.

Due to the many facets of external programs usage, an integration architecture should be as open as possible, and provided with configuration and customisation functions in order to be adapted to a large range of needs.

This part of the project will find a concrete implementation in the production of a courseware about mathematics on CD-ROM, that is planned as exploitation of *Mathesis*. An initial reference architecture (Figure 9) has been designed around a demonstrator of a course on word processing standards, using Word for Windows as the learning tool.

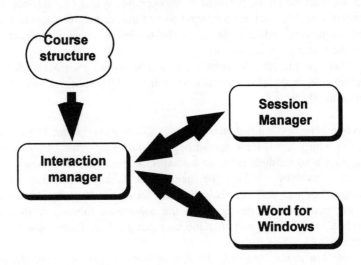

Figure 9 *Integration of external tools*

The course is structured around a flow of data and commands that specify the steps that must be executed by the word processor, or the events that must be considered by the learner.

The interaction manager, integrating the external tool with the *Mathesis* Session Manager, follows the course structure by driving the word processor to execute specific functions. It checks the messages received by the word processor, and transmits messages to the Session Manager when course steps are completed.

The word processing program is configured with a set of macros that replace the standard actions corresponding to menu items. Each macro performs the action of the menu item, then sends a message to the interface (through the DDE mechanism provided by MS-Windows), possibly with parameters describing command arguments (e.g. what text is involved).

The reference architecture is largely independent from the application, as long as it supports message and data exchanging at the OS level, and some form of internal macro or scripting facility.

6 PORTABILITY AND PLATFORM INDEPENDENCE

Portability is one of the main design constraints in *Mathesis*, and work is still in progress in the project. The two target platforms, Macintosh and MS-Windows, are equipped with several compatible software products, and experience about how to develop portable GUI based programs is widely available in the computer designers community. Nevertheless, the development of multimedia interactive applications gives portability issues another dimension, that of portability of multimedia data. As long as the hardware features are different, applications based on rich graphic, animation and sound, properly synchronised, require supports that go beyond a simple translation of the data formats.

In *Mathesis* the portability issues are implied by a simple question: How could we develop a courseware on one platform, and run it on another platform? The problems have been split in two parts: the ones coming from the courseware material (the multimedia presentations), and the ones coming from the operating environment (the Workbench).

An industrially and economically acceptable method that answers to the question, is based on a cross-platform language and run-time support for describing and programming interactive multimedia applications. Official standards like HyTime or MHEG are still in a pre-industrial stage, and cannot be realistically taken into account for wide distribution of huge multimedia material. On the selected platforms the only available compatible support is QuickTime™. A run-only version of the multimedia composer Apple Media Tool exists on MS-Windows, that interprets the Macintosh data formats. This ensures that courseware material developed on a Macintosh can be run on a MS-Windows machine.

The portability of the courseware design tools and of the workbench requires porting of the user interface and of the algorithms that process user actions. In order to ease the translation, the design has been split in three layers that communicate through a purely functional interface:

- The Man Machine Interface layer implements the GUI dependent functions and tasks. Its separation from the other layers ensures that user interface, while looking similar in both platforms, can take advantage of facilities of each operating system. All the tools included in the workbench environment will use a common look and feel;
- The Interaction layer defines the algorithmic part of the workbench modules that should completely independent from the specific platform. It is also in charge of co-ordinating the tasks between the MMI and the next layer, the Data layer;
- The Data layer provides a set of basic primitives that define basic operations on the data. It is separated from the Interaction layer in order to ensure cross-

platform independence from the data management systems used for archiving and retrieval of course related information.

REFERENCES

AAT (1991). *Advanced Authoring Tools, Final Report*, DELTA Project D1010.

Besnainou, R., Muller, C., & Thouin, C. (1988), *Concevoir et Utiliser un Didacticiel*. Les éditions d'Organisation.

ESM-BASE (1991). *The ESM-BASE project, Final report on Educational Systems based on Multimedia Databases of Learning Material*. DELTA Project D1012.

Ferguson-Hessler, M.G.M., & Jong, T. de (1990). Studying physics texts: Differences in study processes between good and poor performers. *Cognition and Instruction, 7(1),* 41-45.

Jonassen, D.H., & Mandl, H. (Eds.) (1990). *Designing HyperMedia for Learning*. Nato ASI Series F. Vol. 67. Springer-Verlag.

Mathesis (1992a). *Specification of the Mathesis Courseware Architecture*. DELTA Project D2009.

Mathesis (1992b). *Specification of the Mathesis Multimedia Block Server*. DELTA Project D2009.

Mathesis (1992c). *Specification of the Mathesis Workbench*. DELTA Project D2009.

Mathesis (1993). *Specification of the Mathesis Courseware Editor and Browser*. DELTA Project D2009.

Nielsen, J. (1986). Online Documentation and Reader Annotation. In *Proc of 1st Int. Conf. Work with Display Units* 526-528. Stockholm, Sweden, May 12-15 1986..

SAFE (1990a). *The SAFE project: Final report on Hypermedia Databases*. DELTA Project D1014.

SAFE (1990b). *The SAFE project: Final report on User Interfaces for Hypermedia*. DELTA Project D1014.

SHIVA (1991). *SHIVA: Manuel de Référence Provisoire*. Version 0. CNRS-IRPEACS.

Weinstock, H., & Bork, A. (Eds.) (1986). *Designing Computer-Based Learning Materials*. Nato ASI Series F. Vol. 23. Berlin: Springer-Verlag.

Acknowledgements: *Mathesis* is developed in the frame of the DELTA programme of the European Community as project D2009. The companies involved are: Selisa, Arborescence and Quai Nord from France, Epsilon Software from Greece, R&S Informatica from Italy, and Oxford Computer Consultants and Longman Cartermill from United Kingdom. The authors gratefully acknowledge their contributions to this work.

Open System for Collaborative Authoring and Re-use

Antonio Ulloa

Tecnopolis CSATA Novus Ortus, Italy

Abstract

The paper gives an overview of the OSCAR system which supports collaborative and distributed authoring of multimedia training materials. OSCAR refers to an application scenario featured by the distribution, both over local and wide areas, of the authoring resources such as actors involved, authoring tools, information base and equipment. Increasing needs of uniformity, quality, productivity and reliability of the course development process along with new opportunities for large scale training projects are making collaborative and distributed authoring one of the most promising sectors of the educational technology market. OSCAR, based on an open system architecture, provides multimedia communication facilities supporting distribution of the authoring process, a common information space allowing cooperation between different tools and actors, and high level services (*co-authoring services*) for multimedia authoring, collaboration, co-ordination, co-decision and re-use. In this paper the organizational and architectural models of OSCAR are described with a special emphasis on the authoring and co-ordination services offered by the system.

1 INTRODUCTION

OSCAR is an open authoring system supporting joint design and production of multimedia training materials. The system supports collaboration and communication between multiple actors involved in joint course development as well as the access to and re-use of existing training materials.

Increasing needs of uniformity, quality and productivity of the courseware development process along with new opportunities for large scale training projects are making collaborative and distributed authoring one of the most promising sectors of the educational technology market. Joint course development is currently taking place at European level in a number of frameworks and training programmes (OSCAR Consortium-deliverable 02, 1992).

In general, the design and production of quality multimedia courses is typically a complex, expensive, and long group working process, carried out by a multidisciplinary team including experts in several fields such as media production, programming, graphic, instructional design, project management, and contents domain of the course. Each team member plays a specific role and brings specific

83

T. de Jong and L. Sarti (eds.), Design and Production of Multimedia and Simulation-based Learning Material, 83-97
© 1994 *Kluwer Academic Publishers. Printed in the Netherlands.*

contributions, thus arises the need to co-ordinate different roles and contributions within a coherent view of the whole course development process.

Courseware authoring systems, available today on the market, neither recognise this diversity of roles, nor allow the people playing them to work together effectively.

Secondly, the existing authoring tools are primarily aimed at the software implementation phase of the development process: they don't help the course team in the early stages of the development process as well as in the decision making process.

Thirdly, the authoring tools available today on the market do not support the concept of 'courseware life cycle', including maintenance, re-use, modification and update to correct or make more current the content of a course, or the adaptation of a course from one spoken language to another, or from one industry to another, or from one kind of media to another.

OSCAR addresses the above problems, co-authoring services facilitating collaboration, co-ordination, co-decision and re-use in courseware development projects.

2 OSCAR ARCHITECTURAL MODEL

OSCAR refers to an application scenario featured by the distribution, both over local and wide areas, of the authoring resources such as actors involved, authoring tools, information base and equipment. In other terms, the application scenario is based on the collaboration of multiple actors and on the distribution of the courseware development process over several workplaces. To this end, in the OSCAR model the following processing environments can be identified:

- the authoring workstation;
- the workgroup environment;
- the joint courseware project environment.

The authoring workstation is the execution environment of an authoring application and represents the physical workplace of an individual author. The workgroup environment is an aggregate of authors working on strictly related activities, consisting mainly of usage of common information and sharing of physical devices, applications and communication facilities. The workgroup environment plays a central role in OSCAR as most of the co-authoring services are designed to serve the needs of a workgroup involved in a courseware project. The workgroup environment is the fundamental element of a *joint courseware project environment*. It consists of a collection of workgroups co-operating in a given project over several sites, even remotely located. The workgroups perform parallel development of courseware modules or execute different activities of the courseware development process. In both cases, they need to exchange information and integrate their results.

The OSCAR architecture has been specifically devised to fit the requirements of the application scenarios described above. The services provided by the OSCAR architecture have been grouped in layers to better represent their organisation and relationship as shown in Figure 1.

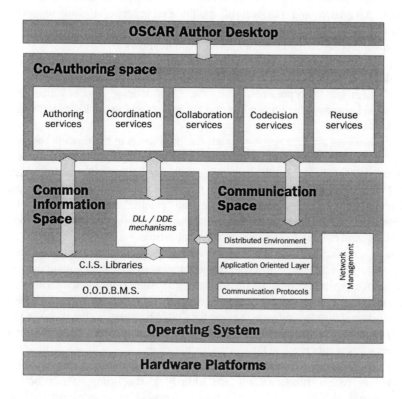

Figure 1 *The OSCAR architecture*

The *OSCAR hardware/software platform* is based on a client/server model, which refers to industry standard systems. Such a platform allows the coexistence of the MS-DOS and UNIX worlds in order to combine the versatility of personal computers with the networking and transaction capabilities of workstations.

An Object Oriented Database Management System (OODBMS) runs on a server under UNIX while the client applications run under MS-WINDOWS on PCs connected to the host system by means of an Ethernet LAN (Local Area Network).

The *Communication Space (CS)* supports distribution and networking services for multimedia information exchange and for the access to local and/or remote data bases of existing multimedia training materials. The *Communication Space* is essentially based on the interconnection of LANs by means of Integrated Services Digital Network (ISDN) and satellite.

The *Common Information Space (CIS)* implements information management services with regard to all the information objects generated during the courseware development process. The *CIS*, based on an object oriented model, allows input, storage, navigation and retrieval of multimedia information and supports co-operative work. It ensures integration, distribution, sharing and re-usability over different authoring activities and authoring team members.

OSCAR provides four classes of co-authoring services: authoring, collaboration, co-ordination, co-decision and re-use (OSCAR Consortium - deliverable 04, 1993). All of them are incorporated within the *Co-Authoring Space* which ensures integration between different services and uniform access to the lower infrastructure OSCAR services.

The *Authoring services* support design and production of multimedia courseware. In particular, OSCAR provides tools to specify the instructional elements of a courseware, tools helping authors in laying out effective instructional strategies and tools to implement the actual instructional materials. In order to exploit existing tools and make the OSCAR system more flexible, external authoring tools, whether available on the market or coming out of other research projects, can be incorporated in OSCAR and tailored to specific training applications.

The *Co-ordination services* support the organisation and management of courseware projects (i.e., courseware project management, quality assurance, work flow control, project documentation management). The Co-ordination services allow a courseware authoring team to decide on the authoring methodology which best fits their needs and then to configure the way the OSCAR system works according to the chosen approach. Once the approach is defined and selected, the Co-ordination services support adherence to the chosen methodology.

The *Collaboration services* support group communication and sharing of information. Such functionalities are aimed at supporting synchronous and asynchronous collaboration between people working in a given activity of the courseware development process. In particular, this group of services allow two or more authors to co-edit a document of courseware specifications or to co-operate on the same courseware material, and to get their different contributions integrated at the end.

The *Co-decision services* support remote group decision making among authors that are not together either in the same place or at the same time in a courseware development project, by providing means to facilitate and organise both formal and informal asynchronous discussions in a work group via mechanisms that support their definition and flow control.

The *Re-use services* support the reusability of existing training materials and/or half-fabricates through mechanisms of retrievability and adaptability of courseware components and/or half-fabricates of the courseware development process. The Re-use services refer to two main classes of tools: CIS (Common Information Space)

Browser and Conversion Tool Kit. The first is meant to facilitate retrievability, while the second and the third tackle problems related to adaptability.

The *OSCAR Author Desktop (OAD)* provides user interface functions, allowing applications to interact with people in a consistent and intuitive way. OAD offers tailored views of OSCAR which can be considered as a sort of virtual workspaces for the different authors involved in a courseware development project. Each workspace provides guidelines, tools, functionalities and information relevant to specific role(s) within the courseware development process. According to the profiles of the user (which role he/she plays) and to the courseware development methodology adopted, the OAD configures itself providing a methodological guide to the user and allowing a task oriented activation of the system facilities. Phases, activities and tasks of the courseware development methodology are used as meaningful handlers to activate the related supporting tools: each authoring task is mapped in a proper tool activation to allow the author to carry out the task itself.

3 AUTHORING SERVICES

The main goal of the OSCAR Authoring Services (AS) is to provide the authors with a homogeneous handle to the tools and to the data they work within a courseware development project.

The tools that are going to be available inside the AS for the design and production of courseware are preferably tools that are already available on the marketplace or from other research projects. As the tools require integration between each other and within the OSCAR environment, a uniform mechanism is defined to integrate tools in the AS. This avoids ad-hoc solutions for individual tools. Moreover it is set up in this way a kind of module, a framework to which the tools can be attached. In this way an eventual new tool has to be integrated just with that module and not with all of the other OSCAR tools and services.

3.1 **Authoring model**

The OSCAR Authoring Services refer to the authoring model described within the DELTA Discourse Project because Discourse authoring tools are incorporated within the OSCAR system. The description of the authoring model is general and broad: it starts at the very first activities, the 'birth of the idea', and ends with the very last activity, where the courseware is being used.

The authoring process is described in terms of the following 15 authoring tasks (DISCOURSE Consortium - deliverable 02, 1992):

- *Conception*: this involves understanding the start-up situation in which a courseware project might be undertaken. It is an activity consisting of identification, analysis and recognition;

- *Instructional Specification*: the aim of this task is to specify a minimal set of global specifications to be defined a priori from an instructional perspective rather than a programming perspective. This set is minimal in the sense that it contains the basic specifications that have always to be defined;
- *Program Specification*: this aim of this task is to determine the platform that will be used, and the kind of modules that will be incorporated (learner model, domain model, etc.). It designs the courseware as a program;
- *Content Definition*: starting from the topics already defined in the Instructional Specification task, this task must further develop all the topics and sub-topics in a hierarchy. It is necessary to define for each topic the instructional objects (e.g. exercises, examples, descriptions...) that will be used for instruction, and how these objects are interrelated;
- *Learning Objectives/Prerequisites Definition*: the aim of this task is to describe in detail the learning objectives in terms of contents (what the learner should master) and performance (what the learner should be capable of doing having mastered the contents);
- *Instructional Strategy Definition:* this task aims to define the instructional mechanisms to be used for teaching each of the topics and sub-topics previously defined;
- *Learner Model Definition*: this task develops the learner model whose aim is to indicate to what extent the learner masters each of the defined topics;
- *User Interface Definition*: this task defines how the instructional system will interact with the student and vice versa. It must define the general interface styles and develop the framework in which all the required interactions will fit;
- *Material Development*: this task aims at developing the Learning Material (Graphics, Text, Video, etc.). Material is not necessarily developed from scratch but it could be often retrieved and modified from some previously developed product;
- *Documentation*: this task performs two main activities: providing the documentation required for maintenance and further developments, and for the use of the courseware;
- *Testing*: this task performs instructional effectiveness testing rather than technical testing. This task is typically carried out by delivering the course to a sample group of learners;
- *Configuration*: this task prepares the courseware to run on its target Hardware/Software platform;
- *Distribution*: this aim of this task is to make the courseware available to the target destination. This is not always a relevant task for the Authoring process;
- *Management*: the management issues in an Authoring process are not significantly different from management issues in any other software development process;
- *Use:* the use task does not appear to be an Authoring task but it is one of the aspects in an Authoring process.

Those tasks should cover the large majority of real authoring processes but, of course, not all the tasks have to appear in all of those. It is quite possible that many authoring processes only use a subset of this set of authoring tasks. The list of tasks can be further split-up in 6 groups to make evident how those tasks are organised in time.

The following figure (Figure 2) indicates how tasks are laid out in time. The diagram is intended to indicate the general time relationships between tasks; in practice, the interaction is very much freer and less precisely ordered. However, some general indications of time relationships may well be useful for authoring process support.

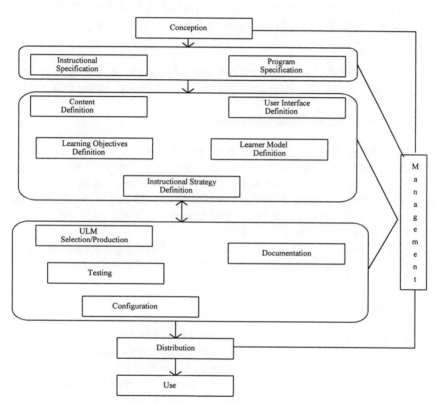

Figure 2 *Approximate time dependencies between authoring tasks*

3.2 Functionalities of the Authoring Services

The OSCAR Authoring Services includes 'user functionalities' and 'architectural functionalities'. A set of user functionalities provide the authors with a well chosen and reconfigurable set of tools. A set of architectural functionalities provide the

OSCAR Authoring Services with a framework into which the tools can be incorporated.

The user functionalities correspond to the functionalities of the tools that are available to the authors. The selection of the tools to be made available to the users can be made according to two strategies:

- Select tools on the basis of the type of courseware that must be produced (traditional CBT, simulations, hypermedia, etc.);
- Select tools with respect to the activities the authors have to undertake. An explicit model of the authoring process (as the one proposed in Section 3.1) is needed in order to predict the nature of the activities an author will be asked to undertake, and then link the activities to the possible tools that can be used to carry them out.

Since it seems likely that future courseware is not going to belong to a single category but will be a mix of technologies, the second strategy seems to be the best fitting to our case.

The major architectural functionalities are:

- The AS defines how to adapt the tools of the toolset in such a way that they could retrieve and store information from the Common Information Space. This is achieved by using the OSCAR Author Desktop as a communication channel;
- The AS defines (starting from the 'desktop' concept) a sort of 'workspace' that allows the authors to access, at a given moment, only the tools and data with which she/he is working at that moment;
- The AS is reconfigurable in such a way that the 'Desktop workspace' of a given author is always up-to-date with his\her position within the authoring process.

3.3 Integration of external tools

So far, some external tools have been already incorporated within the OSCAR Authoring Services. They are Multimedia Toolbook, Generic Tutoring Environment (GTE), and Word for Windows. The inclusion and integration of those tools within OSCAR were made with regard to interoperability between the same tools, re-usability of courseware half-fabricates and co-operative working.

Multimedia Toolbook can be considered a sort of de-facto standard in the sector of the hypermedia and multimedia production tool. Thus, it has been incorporated within OSCAR in order to provide typical hypermedia production facilities integrated with the other OSCAR services.

GTE (Van Marcke, 1990) allows authors to define the elements of the courseware at an instructional level and, at run time, selects dynamically teaching strategies and their related teaching material to respond as well as possible to the demands of each individual teaching situation. GTE has been adapted to OSCAR in a way that, at run time, it is able to select teaching material developed with Multimedia Toolbook.

Word for Windows has been customised to better support the courseware specification and in general to better document joint courseware development projects.

In addition, Multimedia Toolbook and Word for Windows have been customised to permit synchronous and asynchronous co-operative work on the same teaching material or on the same document.

All those tools have been integrated with the Common Information Space (CIS) so that they can store, share and retrieve relevant information within the semantic network of CIS objects.

4 CO-ORDINATION SERVICES

Co-ordination Services are realised through a set of tools supporting the co-ordination of authoring activities and actors working together in a courseware project (OSCAR Consortium - deliverable 04, 1992).

The intention is to provide means to make the courseware development more effective and efficient, improving quality and productivity of the development process, without imposing a single rigid co-ordination approach to all courseware projects.

Why Co-ordination is useful to courseware projects? Because the courseware development process is a complex process made up of many different concurrent activities, each requiring different skills (often covered by multiple actors), and each dealing with information objects most of which are common to two or more activities. From this perspective to co-ordinate the process (i.e., to co-ordinate its activities and actors) means to manage the interdependencies between activities in order to ensure that people be able to co-operate at the right moment having at their disposal all the needed information.

The Co-ordination theories suggest that one useful way to undertake this step is to analyse *common objects* between activities since those objects constrain how each activity is performed with respect to the other dependent activities.

Different ways of use of the common objects by the activities will result in different kinds of interdependencies.

4.1 Collaborative Authoring Model

In order to analyse interdependencies in joint courseware development, a model of collaborative authoring has been defined using the AMIGO Activity Model (Pankoke-Babatz et al., 1989). The OSCAR co-authoring model can be considered as a means for specifying the regulations required for the co-ordination of several individual authoring tasks, thus reducing the co-ordination effort required by the participants(OSCAR Consortium - deliverable 01, 1992).

The Collaborative Authoring Model has been structured into different components; roles, functions, message object types and rules. With this subdivision, it is possible to predefine *who*, (i.e. which actor may exchange) *when*, (i.e. at which point in time) *what*, (i.e. which message) with *whom*, (i.e. with which actor). Following is a description of the four components. Figure 3 shows the components used to represent the collaborative authoring model.

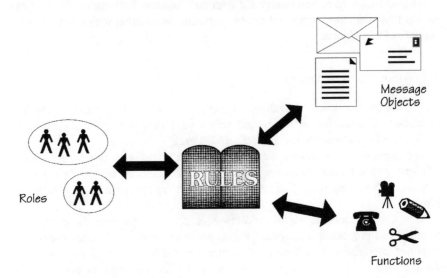

Figure 3 *Collaborative Authoring Model*

Role: The role component defines the names of the roles involved and the assignment of communicators to Role instances. The main attributes that characterise the role class are:

- Role class name;
- Functions which role instances may execute;
- Functions which role instances may request;
- Message Object Types which role instances may consume or produce.

Function: The function component declares the individual operations to be performed.

The function represents the operations which will be performed within a group activity. It is predefined specifying the set of operations to be performed by the functions. The main attributes that characterise each function component are:

- Name of each function;
- Input parameters;
- Output parameters.

Message Object: Each Message Object Type represents the class of all messages of identical structure.

The Message Object component defines the name and internal structure of all messages which occur. It contains either information produced by one actor, which is consumed by the receiving actor, or information about activity regulations.

Message Objects are related to roles and functions; they may also contain a description of how the communication activity should proceed after the receiving role has completed its actions. The main attributes that characterise the function components are:

- Address and role of recipients;
- Address and role of originator;
- Request which indicates the intention of the message;
- History of the message;
- State of the message;
- Relations among messages.

Rule: The rule component defines the actual communication procedure for executing an activity.

The regulations given in the rule component coordinate the flow of Message Objects between the participating actors' role. So it can be said that the main purpose of the rule components is to give a declaration of the co-ordination of the activity objects.

Co-ordination is achieved by having the rule component of the activity define what actions should take place if a message arrives at the activity or if a deadline is reached. Such actions determine which function is to be executed, which message should be sent to which role and so on.

The actors taking part in the activity might use the rule component as the basic information describing what they should do and how they should act in the activity itself.

One of the major requirements of the Co-ordination Services is the flexibility. It should be avoided to impose a single rigid project management approach to all courseware projects.

4.2 Functionalities of the co-ordination services

Co-ordination services can be viewed as a set of tools which support:

- project management and quality assurance;
- group communication management;
- system configuration.

4.2.1 *Project management*

The subset of functionalities related to courseware project management do not stress the conventional project management issues such as resources allocation, time scheduling, work breakdown structure that are already addressed by existing project management tools.

More courseware oriented functionalities are offered with regard to the definition and/or the selection of co-authoring models able to fit specific requirements of actual courseware projects carried out on distributed and collaborative bases.

The objectives of the courseware project management toolset are: to facilitate communication between different actors and different activities within the project and to monitor the authoring process.

The project management tools do not impose a single, rigid project management discipline. Instead, they allow a courseware authoring team to decide on the most appropriate authoring methodology and to tailor the project management tools to better support the approach chosen. The same model should be visible and make explicit to all the members of the team.

This category of tools support the creation, sharing and controlled updating of structured documents. The documents describe aspects of the authoring process, as defined by the authoring team, and include aspects such as: overall authoring methodology and plan, courseware requirements specification, overall design, design of the domain representation, reasons for selecting or creating particular instructional methods, learner modelling approach, design decisions for the user interface, testing and evaluation.

It is generally agreed that careful documentation of software design, implementation and testing is a major factor contributing to the successful management of large or complex software projects. In addition, it is argued that a well specified documentation process is seen as a major contribution to quality assurance.

For these reasons, one of the main functions of the courseware authoring project toolset is to support the creation, sharing and controlled updating of structured documents.

At the most basic level, the project documentation states the decisions taken during courseware development, for example which presentation strategies are used and which instructional principles. However, it is envisaged that the documents resulting from an authoring project will themselves be available as a resource for future authoring projects. Thus, it is important that the documents state not only what decisions were taken during the authoring process, but also to state what the rationale was behind the decision.

4.2.2 *Quality assurance standards in courseware production*

Co-ordination Services support quality assurance in courseware projects implementing international standards (e.g. ISO 9000).

Quality control (QC) is performed by all team members on a continuous basis. Quality assurance (QA) is generally performed by specified individuals at the conclusion of the various courseware project phases and, ultimately, constitutes a formal review of the completed deliverables.

Thus quality should be pursued by all the actors working in a courseware project and should be built into all the stages of the courseware development process.

This is another reason for which individuals have to view their role as part of a team and have to move toward a common goal. When an issue or problem arises, individual team members identify the issue, recommend alternative solutions, and select the best solution that will allow achieving the goal.

Each phase of the development process includes quality assurance tasks. People involved in such tasks use QA Review Forms that serve to formally document reviews.

Within the courseware project management toolset it is important that authors have available a set of standards for courseware development which they can refer to and use during the authoring process. Those standards which take the form of procedures to be carried out during development, such as completion of relevant forms, can be enforced as part of the documentation process. Other standards which take the form of guidelines and recommendations can be available for reference, but cannot realistically be enforced; it is up to individual authors to meet the stated requirements.

4.2.3 Group communication management

The group communication can be managed following two different approaches:

- mediator oriented approach;
- role oriented approach.

In the first one, the exchange between the group members is mediated and co-ordinated by a central coordinating entity that applies the activities specifications in order to automate functions of the co-ordination process. An activity comprises all the regulations required to coordinate the flow of communication among the group members, and it has all knowledge about roles, message objects, functions and rules. So it can be considered as a complete unit and for this reason it can act as a mediator.

The advantage of this approach lies in the fact that it is simpler to manage the synchronisation and co-ordination conditions and to recognise exceptions, errors and deadlocks.

The major disadvantage lies in the lack of individual support for human actors playing roles in the activity. The actors must derive all their knowledge about what they are supposed to do from the messages they receive from the activity, but they are completely free in their decisions. The disadvantage is that the activity can progress only when they do what they are requested to do.

In the second approach the exchange between the group members is managed by the roles themselves. So the activity can be seen as a set of roles, where, for each role, regulations are given defining what this role is supposed to do in which situation, and with which other role it exchanges which messages.

The power of this role oriented approach is that role specific splitting of work is reflected in the regulations of each role.

The major disadvantage is that detection of error situations, deadlocks and controlling or tracing could be rather difficult because the knowledge about the activity and its state is completely distributed among the various roles.

OSCAR is essentially based on a mediator oriented approach, but it also refers to the second type of approach. The reason for this lies in the fact that in the modelling phase a methodology based on scripts was followed. So the activity has been seen as a unique entity described by a rule based procedure. The roles must follow these rules.

For this reason the management of the activity co-ordination is easier if it is introduced as a specific entity, that is very similar to a role, and then if the mediator oriented approach is used.

As in the authoring system, very often the co-operation of role instances is not completely regulated and the support for role players is required. It is therefore necessary to also follow the role oriented approach. In this way it is possible to have the advantages of both the approaches.

To support Group Communication the Co-ordination Services provide tools for all the different stages of an activity:

- specification supports for Roles, Message Objects, Functions and Rules;
- administration of activities templates and instances;
- instantiation supports;
- run-time supports.

4.2.4 *System configuration*

This subset of functionalities help the project manager and/or the system administrator to configure, in a friendly way, the OSCAR system in accordance to a given co-authoring model.

To this end, mechanisms are provided to define workspaces and their interrelations. The workspaces are defined on the basis of activities being performed within them, roles/actors having access, tools or methods associated, information objects included, relations to other workspaces.

5 CONCLUSION

OSCAR is an authoring system being developed within the CEC DELTA programme. The system implements models of collaborative and distributed development of courseware which, focusing on communication paths within the work group involved in the development process, permit the specification of regulations and procedures for the co-ordination of the individual authoring tasks. OSCAR is being developed as an open system referring to de-jure or de-facto standards and able to incorporate external tools. It includes:

- multimedia communication facilities supporting the distribution of the authoring process and the access to remote resources;
- data base of training materials and half-fabricates of the courseware development process, acting as a common repository where information shared by various applications are consistently managed, concurrently made available to and updated by different actors;
- high level services supporting collaboration, co-ordination, co-decision and re-use in courseware projects.

A first prototype of the OSCAR system has been completed and the following step will involve its experimentation, under realistic conditions, by aerospace companies in a pilot test of joint courseware development. The pilot test will also result in practical guidelines for joint courseware development at European level.

REFERENCES

Marcke, K. van (1990). A Generic Tutoring Environment. *In Proceedings of the 9th European Conference on Artificial Intelligence (ECAI).* London: Pitman Publishing.

OSCAR Consortium - deliverable 01 (1992*). Refined model for collaborative authoring and reuse.*

OSCAR Consortium - deliverable 02 (1992). *Training needs and authoring requirements of aerospace industries.*

OSCAR Consortium - deliverable 04 (1993). *Final overall architecture specifications.*

Pankoke-Babatz, U., Danielson, T., Patel, A., Pays, P.A., Prinz, W., & Speth, R. (1989). The Amigo Activity model. *Computer Based Group Communication.* Ellis Horword.

COSYS - An Approach to Production of Flexible Learning Material

Peter Busch[1], Mette Ringsted[1], Hanne Shapiro[1] & Finn Grønbæk[2]

[1] Centre for Competence Development & Media Integration,
Danish Technological Institute, Denmark;
[2] Dept. of Computer Technology, Danish Technological Institute, Denmark.

Abstract

This paper discusses production of flexible learning material and co-authoring issues in a DELTA pilot project COSYS, where five end user testbeds are set up in Europe to explore new approaches to production of flexible (and multimedia) learning material. The paper describes the COSYS project, the Generic COSYS Concept and the implementation of this concept in the five application pilots.

1 THE COSYS PROJECT

COSYS (Distributed Course Production and Delivery System) is a strategic project for industry and organisations providing or using courseware: Publishers, producers, educational providers, company departments and customers/users.

The main objectives of the project is to pilot a distributed course production and delivery system comprising the whole production and delivery cycle in five different real life user environments in Europe. Based on a model developed in COSYS: The Generic COSYS Concept, the application pilots will enhance and integrate advanced standardised computer software and communication technologies to target their specific training environments.

The COSYS user environments represent different production scenarios and involve major actors from both the publishing world, professional course producers, industry and professional organisations who have all joined the project with a direct commercial interest in enhancing current production environments. Already at this point in time COSYS has had a measurable impact on the policies and strategic plans of the companies participating in the project.

When writing this article - January 1994, COSYS has just started its third phase, the test and evaluation phase. Prior to this there has been 1) an analysis, specification and modelling phase, and 2) a prototyping and development phase. The third project phase will run for most of 1994, and COSYS will end in the first months of 1995 delivering a COSYS handbook describing the Generic COSYS Concept and Reference Model, the different testbed implementations of the concept, and an evaluation document evaluating the project from both a formative and a summative point of view.

99

T. de Jong and L. Sarti (eds.), Design and Production of Multimedia and Simulation-based Learning Material, 99-110

With the variety of test scenarios in terms of types of actors involved, technological level, size of organisations, and organisational structure COSYS will also be of relevance to a wider European course production environment for publishers, in-house training departments, and different forms of training/course production networks. The COSYS concept will also be applicable to other domains where large quantities of information must be processed across different organisations or departments. An exploitation marketing plan for COSYS is currently under preparation featuring both low end and high end solutions based on initial market assessment and user reactions, consortium internally and externally.

2 THE AIM OF THE COSYS PROJECT

The aim of the COSYS project is to pilot a distributed course production and delivery system which facilitates:

- Exchange and handling of information concerning training demands and supply;
- Tailoring, translation and version control of existing material;
- Co-authoring with:
  - ◆ On-line access to raw material from the material database;
  - ◆ On-line help facilities and help desk functions;;
  - ◆ Communication facilities such as e-mail, computer conferencing and groupware.
- Different output formats depending upon technological platform among users, concerning text, examples could be ASCII, RTF, MS-Word, etc.;
- Different distribution channels depending upon technological platform among users, e.g. paper, disks, CD-ROM, On-line;
- Management of administration, security, billing and copyrights;
- Generation of training materials for a given target group by accessing, browsing, picking and mixing material from a database.

To meet the needs of different user groups and their technological settings and constraints, the COSYS project will explore and implement selected solutions to a general on demand concept:

- Bandwidth on demand, i.e. adequate communication solutions in the pilot environments (dial-up lines, X.25, ISDN);
- Printing/publishing on demand, i.e. customised output formats, structure, layout, quality and number of copies and delivery media;
- Training on demand, i.e. the integration of information and training systems facilitating the production of course material to certain target groups within very limited time.

The on demand concept is a central part of COSYS. It is implemented in the COSYS Concept to enable the users to configurate and implement a tailored version of COSYS that will meet exactly their needs on their premises. The on demand concept is embedded in COSYS in all areas of the concept from the configuration and implementation of a COSYS system to the end users' use of COSYS.

3 THE COSYS SYSTEM

The COSYS system is built as a tailorable generic concept covering the whole functionality of the course material production process. The concept is modulized and can be implemented in various configurations depending on the specific user needs, i.e. if the user writes all course materials using MicroSoft Word and only uses MicroSoft Word, there is no need for implementing a configuration of the COSYS model that supports direct formatting and printing of different word processor formats. Another example is that the application pilots have different needs and approaches concerning copyrights and royalties. They vary from company internal security needs for managing copyrights of distributed material to the extent of a publishing house wishing only to present highly compressed picture material on the users' screen to ensure that no violation of copyrights due to Print-Screen Commands will be made during pick and mix from the COSYS system.

3.1 The generic COSYS concept

The Generic COSYS concept covers on-line, distributed or LAN-based databases containing course material. The databases are accessible via telecommunication lines, via disk based subsets of the databases or via LAN connections. The concept supports a set of functions covering:

- Collaborative Authoring of course material;
- Archiving of course material;
- Ordering of course material;
- Delivery and Distribution of course material;
- Management and Administration.

The concept supports flexible delivery on demand of user tailored course materials both printed on paper and as interactive, hypermedia documents and multimedia CBTs. Through remote access and telecommunication services, the concept supports development, production and delivery of course materials throughout Europe. And common production tools such as commercially available word processors, desktop publishing and hypermedia software can be supported as both input and output interfaces to the course database.

3.2 The application domain

The generic COSYS concept is implemented in five different real life production environments - the Application Pilots (AP). Each application pilot will demonstrate and evaluate a scenario based on existing training activities, and will include time saving procedures for production and distribution of services and new approaches to course production. The five application pilots are:

- AP1. EGIN (COMETT 2 UETP), a cooperative cross-European network of SMEs and branch organisations as a distributed production and delivery unit in the graphical branch. AP1 will test course production in a distributed scenario; the use of telecommunication in course production; the use of pick and mix system in course production; and the use of a distributed print service;
- AP2. COSTEL, (COMETT 2 Pilot Project), a network of large scale traditional public and private providers of open learning courses based on self study material, video and audio - co-authoring expert material - locally/nationally tailored and implemented with an electronical Print-on-Demand service. AP2 will test course production in a distributed scenario; the use of telecommunication in course production; the use of pick and mix system in course production; the use of an advanced distributed print service. AP2 will also test the production on demand for training provision to SMEs in remote areas, and the transfer of a tailored AP2 COSYS solution to an industrial environment;
- AP3. Océ, (European private company), a Multinational European producer of copiers, plotters and laser printing systems testing and evaluating the practical use of the COSYS model and prototype in the process of producing, reviewing, translating and maintaining user training manuals. AP3 will test the use of the COSYS model in the process of producing, reviewing, translating and maintaining user training manuals. Computer aided translation (CAT-module) will be added to the AP test; further an investigation of translation barriers and storage options for service manuals will be performed;
- AP4. Philips, (European private company), in house industrial training represented by a multinational company testing and evaluating the practical use of the COSYS model and prototype in multimedia CD-I production and maintenance of integrated information systems to support on-demand training and product information services in a distributed organisation. AP4 will test the COSYS model with regards to CD-I production. The definition of projects based on storyboard from a MultiMedia Specification Tool; asset specification extracted from the MultiMedia Specification Tool; data acquisition on line and off line from subcontractors and/or commissioner; storage of production data in Asset Management database; final assets incorporated in Product database; assets integrated in CD-I software and disk pressing and distribution;
- AP5. Industriens Forlag, (Danish publishing company), a publishing company represented by a commercial national publisher testing production and delivery of training materials to course providers and trainers. AP5 will test the production of

a product catalogue for customers (electronic and paper based); the on-line pick and mix of titles in a catalogue with external users (modem); the use of navigation software and administrative prototypes for internal users in the publishing company; and external author communication via computer supported systems (Lotus Notes and BBS).

The generic COSYS concept has been developed during the last two years based on a survey with regard to State of the Art in the areas of existing standards and techniques and tools to design, build and implement instructional multimedia databases; and specific user requirements from each application pilot. During the last two years the generic model has been developed in an iterative process as a central part of the prototype development of the system, and the COSYS concept is now being implemented in tailored prototype versions for the pilot tests. The COSYS concept will during the next year be refined and enhanced based on the experiences gathered from the application pilot tests.

3.3 The target audience

The multimedia course production and delivery system is seen as an integrated part of the user environment, where the interaction between publishers, authors, producers, customers (providers and teachers) and the use and re-use of course-(modules) determines the structure and the interfaces in COSYS.

The five application pilot environments all represent a technology level past first generation of computing and flexible learning production and provision. And the five application pilot environments together represent a very diversified field within the area. As such, the test sites are real-life working environments representing the following types of actors:

- Publishers including publishing organisations with staff dealing with copyrights and price structures, electronically based services, management and co-authoring of materials, stylesheets for DTP and metaphors for hypermedia;
- Technical and administrative support for production, archiving and delivery of flexible learning materials and help desk services;
- Producers of printed materials (printing on demand), video, audio, CBT, CD-ROM and CD-I;
- Distributors of flexible learning materials. Distribution of printed materials, video- and audio cassettes, CD-ROM, CD-I, floppy disks with CBT materials and electronical distribution of learning materials through the pick and mix system;
- Authors including designers, writers and editors of flexible learning materials;
- Providers of flexible learning materials, libraries of flexible learning modules for pick and mix of learning materials.;
- Trainers who can tailor training materials through the pick and mix system targeting the students.

3.4 Services - flexibility in the COSYS system

The test of the COSYS system in the different application pilot environments cover a wide range of aspects of distributed course production and delivery environments ranging from company internal services to a publishing house offering publishing on demand.

To cover the different basic requirements of the application test pilots, the COSYS system is modulized and flexible, giving the application test pilots the possibility of picking and mixing from a wide range of services to make a customised version of a course development, production, and delivery system.

To obtain this high scale flexibility for the COSYS system, the functionality of the system is divided into a set of services, making it possible for users to choose a customised version of the COSYS system to fit exactly their needs:

- Some of the services in the system are internal, whereas others can be accessed externally by the end user;
- Some of the services are provided as integral parts of the system, whereas others may be added later by the end users;
- Some of the services are provided by software tools or communication services, whereas others are provided as human actions and communication.

3.5 Workbenches - the modulized COSYS system

The services are integrated and organised into four conceptual workbenches:

- *Management and publishing workbench*
  The management and publishing workbench provides services for administration, management and control of the development, production and distribution of course materials.
- *Collaborative development workbench*
  The collaborative development workbench provides services for the distributed collaborative creation of courses and training materials on paper and as multimedia.
- *Production and distribution workbench*
  The production and distribution workbench provides services for ordering, retrieval, master creation, duplication and distribution of course materials.
- *Systems maintenance and user support workbench*
  The system maintenance and user support workbench provides services for maintaining the technical systems and services, and provide users in the environment with adequate support.

4 THE CO-AUTHORING ENVIRONMENT IN COSYS

4.1 Co-authoring in COSYS

Focusing on the material production process, the Co-authoring definition in COSYS covers a number of activities. The overall environment can be characterised as distributed on-line production of flexible (multimedia) course material. In the different application pilot environments the three issues: distributed, on-line and multimedia are optional, but basically the general demands for the test beds are that they should be able to support these features.

Setting the stage for co-authoring in this environment raises the demands for specifications of functions included in the co-authoring process and functions undertaken elsewhere.

4.2 Functional description

The definition of the co-authoring environment encompasses the following functions:

- *Project initiation*
  The trigger is usually the requirement from a client for a new publication or course, or the identification of a potential market. The project initiation support facilities should encompass a short guide to the format of the specific material to be produced: Course aim, objectives, training plan, training aids and materials, training resources, course duration, target trainee profile, trainer/instructor profile, copyrights and acknowledgements to mention some;
- *Instructional design*
  This is the process where the master plan for the training materials is made. The instructional designer gives guidelines to and discusses developments with content creators.
  This aspect of co-authoring either takes place in a collaborative fashion, with the instructional designer working with the content creator or on a separate basis - where tasks are allocated by editors or project leaders. Both these models need to be supported by the COSYS system facilities;
- *Production Planning*
  The aspect of production planning covers the identification and allocation of the components of a course/publication to different content creators. As such, it is only a subset of management and administration of a production which is included in the definition of co-authoring here. From the COSYS point of view the tools to support co-authoring should be those developed to support the general management and administration, rather than tools specific to co-authoring;
- *Content creation*
  Content creation is the core activity of co-authoring, the process where materials are actually developed, the authors are writing and the media producers create

graphics, audio etc. This process follows the guidelines set out by project management, instructional designers and editor.

In the COSYS project the primary requirements for content creation are first to support text and hypertext authoring and then support the authoring of other media. Furthermore, the collaboration can be described as being more like serial collaboration than actual CSCW.

The test environments want to be able to support their authors on common word processors by providing them with stylesheets and help facilities rather than requiring them to use applications with which they are unfamiliar, however optimal they may be from other perspectives (database, open information interchange). At the same time, in the test environments there is interest in seeing the potentiality of more sophisticated tools for co-authoring, so these should be supported in the workbench;

- *Project management*
The project is managed according to the project plan, made by the project manager as a result of discussions with the involved partners. Project management allocates the needed staff to the project;

- *Editing*
Editing of materials is divided into pre- and post editing. Pre editing is setting up guidelines (outlining and annotation) to the authors. Post editing is reviewing the developed materials, i.e. quality control concerning the content and the guidelines;

- *Content composition*
This activity encompasses the extraction of content from a database and presenting it to the author in a suitable form, and extracting content from the authoring tool and putting it in the right place in the database.

It is not necessarily the purpose of content composition in co-authoring to carry out composition for final publication, although in the case of content with a simple presentation this may be done simultaneously. The use of stylesheets (which integrate composition and content creation) is again a requirement, with an alternative being an SGML sensitive editor;

- *Layout mastering*
The layout mastering is the provision of formats for content in a form that will be suitable for customers of the COSYS system. There are two aspects to this:
  - ◆ Final layout for the complete document;
  - ◆ Access via the pick and mix system.
A need has been identified for stylesheets/formats which can give an indication of the presentation of the full document and support the generation of order forms etc.;

- *Browsing, picking and mixing*
This covers giving the customers the ability to browse, but only down to a defined level of detail: Picking and mixing takes place by ordering components from the content provider.

Authors on the other hand, need to browse and to have the facility to modify materials. Their need can be met by loading content into stylesheets.

Material will be transferred to local sites in some testbeds whereas in others it will be held in central databases for on-line querying.

These elements serve as the basic co-authoring workbench building blocks in the COSYS pick and mix system, and requirements to the co-authoring building blocks can be consolidated to:

1. Help files to support authors in their use of tools and their interpretation of specifications;
2. Authoring stylesheets or context sensitive editors for content creation and content editing;
3. Presentation stylesheets for potential customers downloading elements of course material;
4. Applications which can extract content from stylesheets for automatic placement in databases;
5. Applications which can extract content from databases for automatic placement in a content viewer, made available to potential customers;
6. An application that customers can use to browse content in remote or local databases.

5 STATUS OF IMPLEMENTATION.

The implementation of the generic COSYS concept in the different application pilots vary based on different technological settings, different requirements, different organisational settings and different business areas and purposes of the implementation of the concept.

Application pilots 1 and 2, both distributed network organisations, implement the Generic COSYS Concept with emphasis on:

- The distributed access to materials, i.e. a disk based access to the material databases;
- The possibility of customising and tailoring the material database to meet local needs, thus keeping the relations to and consistency with material shared within the network;
- The use of low-end telecommunication facilities for user and content creator access (2.400 - 14.400 modems) or access via remote disk based editing of databases;
- The use of High-end telecommunication facilities for production, i.e. transfer of print files from database to distributed print services;
- The use of an agreed set of structured formats for different datatypes within the organisation, i.e. SGML based MS-Word stylesheets, etc;
- The support of common end user platforms, PC-Windows and Macintosh.

The basic units to be picked and mixed from the databases are books, chapters, articles, course modules, video in approximately 15 minute sequences, CBT-modules on self contained subjects, etc.

The end user will typically compose a course material from modules gathered into chapters, chapters taken directly from the database, background articles, video-lessons, CBT modules and series of overhead folios.

The Generic COSYS Concept is implemented in AP1 and AP2 as a Visual Basic Pick & Mix prototype, Lotus Notes for distributed co-authoring, various connected databases (MS-Access, Lotus Notes and Sybase) and communication facilities ranging from telefax and mail distribution, over low-end telecommunication to the use of ISDN and distribution of final layouted/formatted platform independent electronic documents.

Application pilot 3 implements the Generic COSYS Concept in a corporate environment with emphasis on:

- Direct access to the database from the working environment, i.e. FrameMaker;
- Context sensitive/intelligent presentation of subset of material from database, i.e. the database only presents valid subsets of material for the task performed;
- Computer aided translation of original material;
- Validity of data in database, i.e. input quality control;
- Cost savings in the production process of multi lingual materials;
- The acceptance of the changed working situation for technical and pedagogical writers.

The basic units to be picked and mixed from the database are sections, paragraphs, phrases, words and graphics.

The end user will typically compose material from sentences and paragraphs taken from the database and mixed with new material composed on the fly. The result will be material with links directly to the database for approximately 60% of the content.

The Generic COSYS Concept is implemented in AP3 as an integrated functional extension to FrameMaker giving direct access to a Sybase database. Communication is implemented using local area networks, Lotus Notes and file transfer via high speed modems (> 19.200).

Application pilot 4 implements the Generic COSYS Concept in a corporate environment with emphasis on:

- The management of the production process of CD-I titles;
- The re-use of material in certain CD-I titles, i.e. classification of pictures for retrieval and reuse;
- A multi-platform and operation system production and environment, (Windows, Macintosh, Novell, OS 9);
- Platform independence and transferability of materials;
- Easy updating of materials;
- Direct production/generation of CD-I titles from database.

The basic unit in the COSYS system will range from video and audio sequences, single screens, pictures and screen objects to full specifications of a whole CD-I title.

The end user will operate in two different situations 1) the production of new titles from scratch, where focus will be on the specification and content generation processes, and 2) the updating and reproduction of existing titles.

The Generic COSYS Concept is implemented in AP4 as a network and data integration of multiple platforms, where tools for different purposes, i.e. asset databases, animation, specification, design and production tools best suited for the production tasks are integrated with external and non-digitised material to form the whole production cycle.

Application pilot 5 implements the Generic COSYS Concept with emphasis on:

- A cost effective business;
- New effective and more informative distribution scenarios, i.e. the electronic catalogue;
- More consistent and effective company internal production and administrative tasks;
- More effective editorial processes.

The basic unit of the COSYS system will be chapters, i.e. selfcontained course material modules that can be picked and mixed to a targeted book.

The end user will typically search for relevant chapters in the electronic catalogue, mix the chapters to a customised book, and order the book printed in small series, i.e. 7 - 12 copies.

The Generic COSYS Concept is implemented in AP5 as a database holding the chapters in Ventura Publisher format and a series of software programmes enabling the generation of customised electronical catalogues in Windows Help format. The editorial and project managing processes of distance production of new material is guided using stylesheets and Lotus Notes.

The above mentioned implementations have been prototyped and enhanced during the last one and a half year, and are now implemented for test production in the different application pilots. During the spring, summer and autumn of 1994 the implementations will be evaluated and further enhanced for production, and at the end of the year, a handbook with the Generic COSYS Concept and reference models will be published.

REFERENCES

DELTA 2011, COSYS Technical Annex: Design and implementation of a computer based course production and delivery system COSYS

DELTA 2011, COSYS Deliverables:
D/WP01-1:   Report on market needs
D/WP01-2:   Report on technical possibilities and constraints
D/WP02.1-1: Description of a generic scenario based on the application pilots

D/WP02.2-1: Specification of user requirements and services
D/WP03:   Description of the architechtural model for distributed course
             production delivery
D/WP04.1-1: Implementation of a generic multimedia database - phase 1
D/WP05-1:   Implementation of management and administrative tools
D/WP06-1:   Co-authoring workbench - phase 1
D/WP07-1:   Implementation of pick & mix system - phase 1
D/WP08-1:   Communication network and services - phase 1, distributors and users
D/WP10-1:   COSYS Evaluation Handbook. An external perspective.
D/WP04.1-2   Implementation of a generic multimedia database - phase II
D/WP04.2-1   Prototype of interface to the multimedia database
D/WP05-2   Specification of management & administration, Procedures & Tools
D/WP06-2   Co-authoring Workbench - phase II
D/WP07-2   Implementation of Pick & Mix System - phase II
D/WP08-2   Communication network and services - phase II

Published papers:

Grønbæk, F. (1993). *Multimedia documentation and free text retrieval.* The Nordic
    BRS Search Usergroup Conference, 15 May 93, Copenhagen DK/Oslo N.
Ringsted, M. (1992). *Transnational Project Management.* COMETT II Pilot
    Conference in Glasgow, Nov.92.
Ringsted, M., & Shapiro, H., DTI. (1993*). New Production Concepts in Flexible
    Learning - The COSYS/COSTEL Case.* Toronto University, April 93.
Ringsted, M., (1993). *Multimedia and regional development.* COMETT Conference,
    Ireland , September 1993.
Ringsted, M., Busch, P., Grønbæk, F., & Shapiro, H., (1993*). A European
    Perspective in use of Technology in Flexible Learning.* The Nordic Conference
    under Nordic Forum for Computer Aided Higher Education, Aalborg, Denmark,
    August 93.
Ringsted, M., Busch, P., Grønbæk, F., & Shapiro, H., (1993*). Design and
    Production of Flexible Learning Material.* Tele Teaching Conference,
    Trondheim, Norway, August 93.
Ringsted, M., Busch, P., Grønbæk, F., & Shapiro, H., (1993*). Production of flexible
    and modulized course material in COSYS.* The NATO Advanced Research
    Workshop: Collaborative dialogue technologies in distance education, April 24-
    27 1993, Segovia, Spain.
Shapiro, H. (1993). *Training infrastructures and services in remote areas.* Inverness
    Scotland, June 1993.
Shapiro, H., (1992). *Copyright and Electronic Publishing in COSTEL/COSYS AP2.*
    COMETT II Pilot Conference in Glasgow, Nov 92.
Shapiro, H., (1993*). Design of distance and flexible learning in vocational training.*
    Feasibility study for the Greek Ministry of Education, Department for Vocational
    Training, September, 1993.

DISCOURSE:
The Design and Production of Simulation-based Learning Environments

Kenneth Tait

Computer Based Learning Unit,
The University of Leeds, UK

Abstract

A component of the Discourse project addresses the tools required for the design and production of multimedia simulation environments for learning. The educational and training use of simulations has two drawbacks: most simulations are designed and produced as single applications; and learners have difficulty in exploiting the learning opportunities presented by simulations. The work addresses these two aspects by developing a systematic methodology for the design and production of a simulation based on an abstract representation of the model which drives the simulation, and by embedding the resulting simulation in an environment which supports pedagogically beneficial learning activities and gives support to the learner by proposing useful tasks, encouraging prediction, and providing explanations which elaborate the simulated events These aims are ambitious, but progress to date is encouraging. Equations for a model can be derived directly from a bond graph representation, and this can be developed into a simulation by the systematic addition of an animated diagram and display mechanisms for graphs and values using generic tools. An entity-relation graph (such as a bond graph) suitably annotated by an author and combined with a graph interpreter and a task space can provide the knowledge-base for explanation and question answering using techniques already developed.

1 INTRODUCTION

In building and using a simulation-based learning environment there are four aspects to be considered. Creating the model which drives the system, making an executable model into a controllable simulation, adapting or redesigning the interface to promote learning, and providing learner support. This is illustrated diagrammatically in Figure 1 where the learner support has been shown as a further layer surrounded the learner interface. This is the typical situation where the learner support is provided through teachers or trainers. Where the learner support is provided as part of a computer-based learning environment then it is likely that the learner support will be intimately linked with the learner interface, though it remains important to recognise the two separate functions: one of allowing the learner to operate the simulation and the other of helping the learner to learn from using the simulation.

111

T. de Jong and L. Sarti (eds.), Design and Production of Multimedia and Simulation-based Learning Material, 111-131

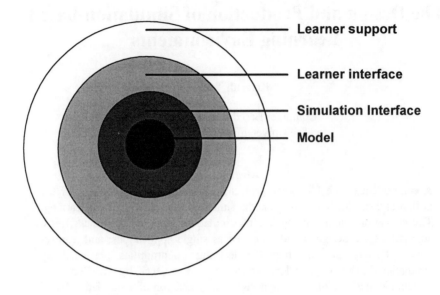

Figure 1 *Simulation-based learning environment*

The model at the centre of a simulation-based learning environment is often nothing more than a set of mathematical equations. Such a quantitative model is made executable by adding a solver which when given an initial state can calculate the next state after a small interval of time. By iteration a succession of states is generated which describe the behaviour of the model over time. Qualitative models operate somewhat differently, but in essence they serve the same role.

An executable model provides all the raw data but may be awkward to use and manipulate as a simulation. A simulation has, in addition to the model, a convenient means of setting parameters of the model, specifying the initial state and of displaying the behaviour in a more readily understood form through, for example, graphs and animation. The facility to change the parameters while the model is running can provide dynamic control.

A simulation which is to support learning needs a richer interface. The assigning of values to parameters, the specification of initial conditions and the control during execution need to be achieved in ways which directly correspond to the concepts or procedures that are to be learned. Thus, although a change in the behaviour of a model of part of the human body may be achieved by altering a parameter value, medical students may need an interface which allows them to achieve this same change by apparently controlling the amount of a drug administered. Similarly, a simulation of a chemical plant should, for training purposes, be managed through an interface where the controls and data correspond to the control panel which exists in the real system.

It is worth considering, in outline, the way in which learners learn from their use of simulations. Most simulation environments allow users (from our point of view, learners) to set up initial conditions and to start and stop the model so that events (in the form of data, graphs, animation and so forth) can be observed. Either these events will be consistent with the learner's understanding of the concepts and procedures involved in the system modelled or they will not. In this latter case learners must either adjust their understanding or interpret the evidence differently. In either case there is opportunity for learning. Thus there are three phases to a learning episode which uses a simulation: (1) preparation/ planning when the simulation is set up to behave according to the learner's expectations or hypotheses; (2) observation/performance, and (3) reflection/debriefing on what has happened. The preparation/observation/reflection structure gives a terminology suited to simulation in which there is no dynamic control in the middle phase. In those simulations in which the second phase involves dynamic control (through which the learner contrives to achieve some goal related to the behaviour of the simulation) then the planning/ performance/debriefing terminology may be more appropriate. It is likely, in this case, that the learner support in the third phase is substantial and consist of systematic debriefing. However, in all case, this tripartite structure to learning episodes can be seen. (A discussion of this will be found in Byard et al., 1991.) The important role of reflection and debriefing suggests that there is the need to be able to replay a simulated episode and to examine further data not seen in the original run or view data differently during such a replay.

Simulations can be difficult to learn from (Forbus, 1991; Self & Twidale, 1991) and learners do not always learn from simulations without further help and support. As has already been pointed out, learner support is usually provided through human tutors or trainers who engage in preparation and planning with the learner and also, and more importantly, in debriefing and reflection. If simulation-based learning environments are to play a role in distance and open learning then this support must be provided by the environment itself. This is not a new idea, De Jong et al. (1991) describe work done in the SIMULATE project in which an 'educational layer' was added to a simulation model nevertheless the nature of this educational layer and how it is able to support learners has still to be resolved.

2 THE DESIGN AND PRODUCTION OF SIMULATION-BASED LEARNING ENVIRONMENTS

In creating a simulation-based learning environment there are two roles: that of modeller and that of author. The modeller ensures that the simulation is sufficiently accurate, the author adds pedagogical knowledge to the system so that it is an effective learning environment. In identifying these two roles there is no assumption made about the number of people involved.

Specifying the model as a set of mathematical equations is not straightforward, nor is verifying that the model is valid. The Discourse project aims to provide a modelling tool kit through which the mathematical model can be built at a conceptual level and then translated to a set of equations. At the moment three stages are envisaged: a schematic representation, an abstract representation, and the automatic generation of the mathematical equations.

The schematic representation is essentially the linking of objects which represent elements of functionality. These can be arranged on the screen and connected systematically in various ways. This provides an editing environment for the model builder. Each block in the schematic belongs to a single energy domain and blocks in different energy domains are linked by transducers. The representation also includes information blocks and information flows through which information about the state of one part of the model affects the behaviour of another. This is illustrated in Figure 2 which shows the interface for the model editor of the DISCOSIM system described by Tavernier and Lefèvre (1993).

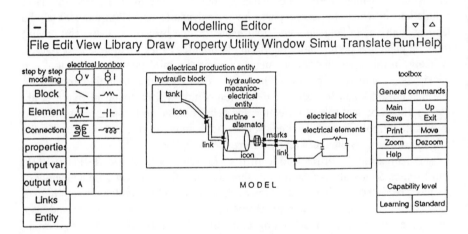

Figure 2 *The model editor (after Tavernier and Lefèvre, 1993)*

From the schematic representation an abstract representation of the functionality is created. This is a bond-graph. Bond-graphs represent the functionality of physical systems as energy flows and can be generically applied across different energy systems such as electrical, mechanical, thermal and hydraulic. When the bond-graph formalism is extended to take account of information blocks and information flows we have an extended bond-graph. An important feature of bond-graphs which can be utilised in learner support is that causalities are represented or can be determined (Karnopp & Rosenberg, 1975; Rosenberg & Karnopp 1983).

Given any bond-graph (or part of it) it is possible to generate a set of equations (the Procedural State Space Subroutine, or P3S) which represents its functionality. Examples of the three representations (the schematic-electrical in this example, the bond graph, and the P3S equations) for the same system are given in Figure 3.

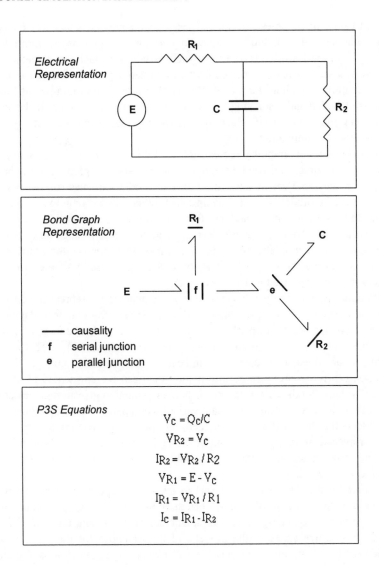

Figure 3 *Three representations of a model*

2.1 The simulation

As was noted earlier, simulation is a model with an interface. This interface allows the user to experiment with the model and view the behaviour of the model. One of the advantages of a simulation (over the real system) is that the behaviour can be represented through different modalities. Typically a simulation will provide numerical data, graphs and an animation. Numerical data is usually in the form of tables of values of variables over time. These variable may be actual variables in the model (that is variables in the P3S equations) or values, which may be more directly meaningful to the learner, derived from such variables through some mathematical formula. Derived values may be represented qualitatively rather than quantitatively by, for example, dividing the range of a variable into a small number of intervals which are labelled and displaying the label when the value is in a particular internal rather than the value itself. Such qualitative representations can the basis for components of an animation.

The most common graphical representation of the state of the model is a plot of a variable against time. This can be elaborated in several ways: plotting more than one variable on the same set of axes; plotting two model variables (or two variables derived from the model variables) against each other with no time axis; using other representations than points; and so forth. However, the essential feature of a graphical representation is that it shows in a single diagram the changes that have taken place over a simulation episode. The learner may observe the representation building up during the episode, but at the end of the episode all the information remains and can be viewed in a single diagram.

Animation is, essentially, an elaboration of the quantitative representation seen in graphs and the qualitative representation which is derived from numerical data. Thus in an animation, an object or part of an object will move or change its size indicating by its position or dimensions the values of one or more variables. The colour or shading of an object may change to indicate some qualitative change. Thus, an animation can represent no more information than can be represented in graphs or tables of values, but the key difference is that an animation gives a representation of a number (may be all) of the significant variables at a particular time, in other words it represents the state of the model moment by moment and as time progresses each state is replaced by its successor and at the end the learner can only see the final state: the earlier states are no longer observable except by replaying the episode with the same initial conditions.

In order for the learner (or any user) to take advantage of the simulation there must be a method of control. Control has three aspects: setting up or changing the initial conditions, assigning values to parameters of the model, and specifying the way the successive states of the model and its behaviour for the duration of an episode (or its replay) are represented and displayed. Again, in some simulations it may be possible to interact with the system while it is running thus providing dynamic control.

2.2 The learner interface

Although every simulation has some kind of interface, the features and functionality of that interface may not readily support all the tasks that a user may wish to carry out. In particular this is true when the user is a learner, although it could be argued that every user is in some sense a learner.

Learning goals are difficult to describe precisely but it seems clear that the learning goals associated with simulation based learning can be divided into those concerned with controlling the system (procedural goals) and those concerned with understanding the system or the principles and concepts which underpin the system. It may also be necessary to distinguish between learning about the model and learning about the real system through the model (conceptual goals). Where the goals are procedural it is likely to be critical that the skills acquired with the simulation transfer to skills required when controlling the real system and the functionality of the model can remain hidden without any detriment to learning. In the case of conceptual goals the learning is always, in the final analysis, about the real world as distinct from the understanding the simulation model. Whether making the workings of the model visible to the learner aids this process or not is a difficult question and may depend on the fidelity of the model and the particular goals of the learner.

Any discussion as to the extent to which our knowledge of the real world rests only on models must be put on one side here, though it is worth noting that the mental models of understanding need not have any relationship (either analogically or metaphorically) with the mathematical model of the simulation or any of its representations in the simulation-based learning environment.

It is often more convenient from an educational point of view to speak of learning tasks rather than learning goals. Although learning goals cannot be ignored it is for the teacher using experience and pedagogical expertise to devise learning tasks which they believe will help learners to achieve the desired learning goals. One element of learner support is, therefore, the provision of a repertoire of appropriate learning tasks and it is these learning tasks which are the springboard for the first part, which we have termed planning, of a simulation-based learning episode.

It has already been noted that learning goals can either be procedural or conceptual and it is possible to classify the learning tasks designed to achieve those goals in a similar way. Our tripartite view of working with simulations leads us to consider learning tasks as having a similar structure. However, these three phases differ depending on whether the task is associated with procedural goals or learning goals. Table 1 gives a brief description of what might be involved at each stage for each class of tasks.

In a procedural task the learner interacts with the simulation during the simulation episode, adjusting and changing in order to maintain or achieve some desired state, or to cause a series of events to take place whereas in a conceptual learning task the element of interaction is less important and may not even exist, rather the learner conducts experiments.

Although intervention (by a human tutor) does sometimes occur during the learner's interaction with or observation of the simulation, this is not always liked by learners and can probably only be justified if the learner's action or inaction may result in the simulation episode being of little value. However, it is during the third phase when expectations are not matched with what actually happened that learning which leads to conceptual change takes place. It is this propensity to bring about conceptual change which is relevant to procedural learning as well as conceptual learning that gives simulations their educational potential (Hartley et al., 1991).

Table 1 *Learning activities during a simulation episode*

Procedural	Conceptual
Planning: determining in advance a sequence of actions or how to attain a desired state	Prediction: setting up initial conditions so that the predicted behaviour occurs
Performance: fulfilling the plan without losing control of the simulation or allowing and undesirable state to occur	Observation: comparing the expected behaviour with the actual behaviour
De-briefing: looking back at and discussing both what was done and what should have been done, and comparing the planned actions with the actual ones	Reflection: trying to explain the differences between the expected behaviour and the actual.

3 LEARNING SUPPORT FOR SIMULATIONS

Although simulations are extensively used in learning the evidence is mixed as to their general effectiveness (Self & Twidale, 1991; Klahr & Dunbar, 1988; Shute & Glaser, 1990). It is therefore important to verify that the style of simulation learning environment envisaged does support learning and attempt to identify difficulties in its use. To this end a simplified prototype was constructed and used with a small sample of students. The subject matter was calcium homeostasis in humans and the model was built using Stella. StellaStack was used to provide a suitable interface using HyperCard and the complete environment was implemented on an Apple Macintosh computer (Figures 4, 5 and 6).

As well as control of the simulation and the display of graphs, the interface allowed the learner to sketch graphs before the model was run so that when the graph was displayed a comparison could be made. Access to brief built-in explanations of the main aspects of calcium homeostasis we provided. An investigation was conducted using this system: this will be described briefly.

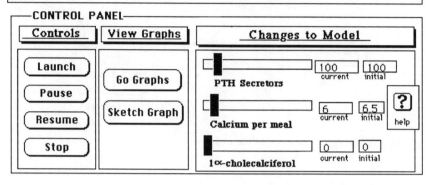

Figure 4 *The control panel of the experimental simulation*

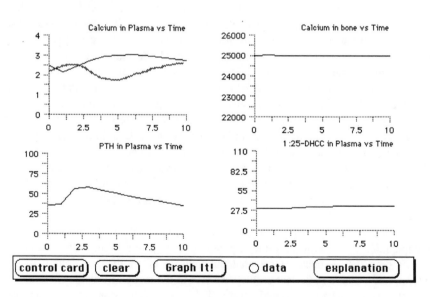

Figure 5 *Comparing a predicted graph with one produced by the simulation - the broader line in the first graph is the one drawn by the subject*

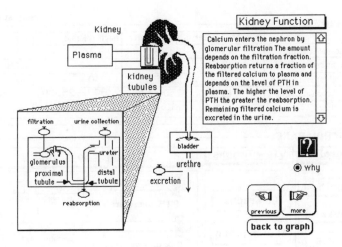

Figure 6 *Explaining the function of the kidney*

3.1 An experiment

The subjects for the study were students in their third year of study at Medical
School who were randomly put together in pairs to encourage the articulation of
their thinking while working with the simulation. A video recording (including
sound) was made of each experimental session and an experimenter was present to
ensure the experimental procedure was followed and to provide extra support for the
learners when its absence would have jeopardised the experimental procedure.
Experimental materials were designed so that each pair of subjects could work
through two tasks in sequence under the supervision of an experimenter. Each task
ran for about 30 minutes with total contact time not exceeding 120 minutes.

In order to measure learning gain each experimental subject was given a pre-test
and a post-test on the topic of calcium homeostasis and related knowledge. As part
of the experimental tasks, subjects sketched graphs which predicted the performance
of the model. These were seen as a source for evidence of belief change and a
context for students' explanations of graphs. After the post-test subjects completed a
further questionnaire designed to elicit subjects' perceptions of the usefulness of the
simulation-based tasks.

Two classes of tasks were devised: *manipulation* tasks and *diagnostic* tasks. In
manipulation tasks subjects were required to change the values of parameters,
predict how they expected these manipulations to affect the functioning of the
system, and observe the effect on the variables in the model. In diagnosis tasks the
subjects must infer the cause of observed data and state what interventions are
needed to bring the system back to normal.

Four tasks were used: two different manipulations and the diagnosis of two
different diseased states. In the diagnostic tasks the subject did not know the nature

of the disease whereas in the healthy case the abnormal functioning of the model (which was to be identified with a diseased state) resulted from setting the levels of PTH secretion, calcium per meal and $1\propto$-cholecalciferol before launching the model.

One experimental hypothesis was that the manipulation tasks, which allowed subjects to observe data not normally available in ways which are feasible within medicine, would improve conceptual understanding of the domain A second experimental hypothesis expected that tasks which related the simulated data to functional goals (medical decision-making skills) would support greater learning than those which did not.

Six treatment conditions were defined and assigned to one of eight subject pairs with two conditions being used twice to balance the design (Table 2).

Table 2 *The experimental design*

Subject Pair	First Task	Second Task
1	Manipulation 1	Manipulation 2
2	Diagnosis 1	Diagnosis 2
3	Manipulation 1	Diagnosis 1
4	Diagnosis 1	Manipulation 1
5	Manipulation 2	Diagnosis 2
6	Diagnosis 2	Manipulation 2
7	Manipulation 1	Manipulation 2
8	Diagnosis 1	Diagnosis 2

After the pre-test was given each pair were given a warm-up task which required the subjects to predict what would happen when a normal patient has a calcium-rich meal. After this each pair of subjects completed two tasks from a possible four, in accordance with their assignment to experimental condition. During the perceptions questionnaire (part of the post-test) there was opportunity for an informal debrief in which there was a chance for questions and subjects were allowed to comment on the experimental procedure.

The experiment and outcomes of the investigation are fully reported in Pilkington and Tait (1993) but it is helpful to draw out the main conclusions here. Subjects were favourable to the environment, thought the graphs useful and judged that more detailed explanation would be helpful. Although all subjects benefited from using the simulation, some expectations about the utility of different tasks were not supported by the results. In particular one diagnostic task was more efficacious than the other and the effect of mixing manipulation with diagnostic tasks was not as great as was anticipated. This argues for careful choice of learning tasks and underlines the fact that simulations in themselves are not necessarily effective learning tools unless used to perform appropriate tasks. Three misconceptions were identified which the use of the simulation did not overcome. This emphasises the need for further learning support, for example in the form of explanation similar to that which might be given over the shoulder by a human tutor or by different learning tasks.

As a consequence it is clear that if the simulation learning environment itself is to provide support for the learner it must have knowledge of both the learning goals and of learning tasks. It also must have knowledge about the modelled system which is more than that contained in the executable model to provide the basis for explanation.

3.2 The learning support system

To use a simulation-based learning environment effectively learners must be able to relate the different kinds of information presented to them in graphs and through the animation. The Discourse approach supports this in three ways: by providing tasks which focus the exploration of the learner, by generating explanations of the model and its behaviour, and by providing linked background knowledge. It is worthwhile noting at this point that courseware produced by the wider Discourse project will be able to contribute by making available the preparatory teaching which leads up to the tasks and the background knowledge through courseware. A new prototype learner support system is under development, however at the present stage the learner support system is independent and presents both task information to the learner and uses a hypermedia system to make background knowledge accessible to the learner.

3.2.1 *Tasks*

To allow explanation to be placed in context the learner support system will possess a space of tasks that are designed to achieve learning goals. A useful classification of tasks is given in Table 3.

Table 3 *Classification of tasks*

	Normal System	**Faulted System**
Manipulation	Investigation of behaviour of the system under various conditions	Control of the system so that the behaviour is normal (treatment)
Diagnosis	Verification that unusual behaviour is normal	Identification of the fault in the system

Tasks are specified to meet particular learning goals. The specification for a group of related tasks consists of configuring the model, specifying the task objects and then selecting those task objects appropriate for each task. Configuring the model consists of associating cases with faults (if the tasks include diagnosis), specifying the mechanisms through which the learner will be allowed to manipulate the model or correct the fault, and determining the sets of graphs which are relevant to the tasks. For each individual task the controls (sliders in the current prototype) and the ranges of their associated variables are fixed, including domain specific information such as the normal clinical range for the variable. The author determines the variables to be graphed, the ranges for the axes, and labels each graph as essential or optional. Essential graphs are those for which the learner will have to make a prediction as part of the task. The author also supplies an introduction to the task and a debrief. Figure 7 shows the model configuration interface and Figure 8 shows the task specification interface. (These are taken from the current prototype learner support system which has the functionality of the prototype used in the experimental investigation together with functionality to support explanation generation.) A fuller discussion of the specification and role of tasks will be found in Pilkington (in preparation).

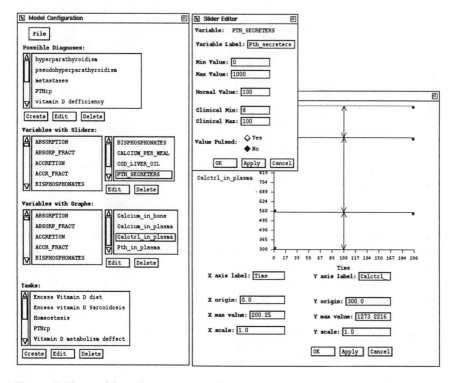

Figure 7 *The model configuration interface*

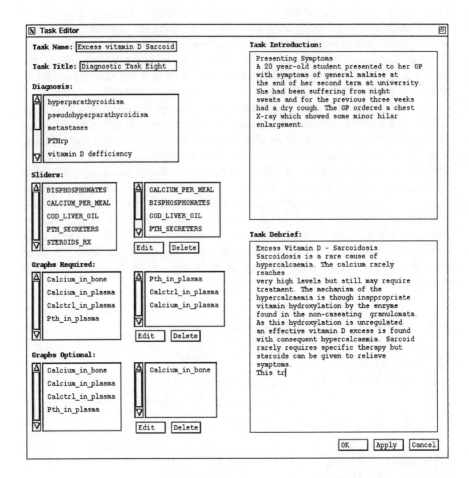

Figure 8 *The task specification interface*

Tasks can be linked together to form a space of tasks. The relationship between the tasks is used to determine the next task to be offered to the learner though the learner is free to choose any available task. Two dimensions on which tasks are organised (more may be added later) in the space are complexity of the model and learner familiarity with the cases. For the domain of calcium homeostasis mentioned earlier then three levels of complexity can be seen: normal system, fault in primary regulation, and fault in secondary regulation and the learner support system would require satisfactory performance at one level before suggesting that the learner proceed to the next.

3.2.2 *Hypotheses and predictions*

To make experiments with simulations effective the learner must have some expectations about the behaviour of the model. Explanation can be considered as the provision of information sufficient for the learner to be able to understand the differences between what was expected and what happened. Thus the learner support system must have some way of eliciting expectations from the learner.

If a learner has any understanding about the behaviour of a system then this is represented as one or more hypotheses which might be in the form of a set of rules or as a possibly incomplete mental model (Norman 1983). Rather than try to elicit hypotheses from a learner it is more practical to require the learner to predict.

The key form of prediction used in Discourse is to require the learner to sketch the graph of a particular variable against time for an episode as described earlier in discussing the experimental work already carried out (Pilkington & Tait, 1993). Other forms of prediction, which may be incorporated in later versions, include requiring the learner to specify a set of propositions about the expected behaviour, each of which can be tested for its truth at the end of the simulation episode, possibly in the form of a 'hypothesis scratchpad' as discussed by Van Joolingen and De Jong (1991), and De Jong et al. (this volume).

As was mentioned earlier learner performance is used to determine the next task to be offered. In the medical context the tasks require that the learner determine the fault (if any) and specify the treatment (that is change the control of the model) to obtain a desired behaviour. It is this performance which is used to determine the next task. Whereas the sketched curve is used in explanation generation.

3.2.3 *Explanations*

It is neither possible nor desirable to anticipate all situations that might occur in a learner's exploration of a simulation. Therefore any explanation which relates directly to the experience of the learner must be generated. Such generated explanations will be in the form of text and their purpose will be to relate the different items of information presented to the learner in various modes. The sources used in explanation generation are the model (as distinct from the equations) represented as entities and relations (Stella provides an example of this), and the graphs (including the graph sketched by the learner).

In generating explanations answer schemes and rhetorical predicates (McKeown, 1985; Tattersall, 1991) are used to organise the available knowledge prior to its expression as text. Annotation not only links the abstract model to the domain (physiology in the context used in the present prototype) but also provides a method of allowing the author to elaborate the model to enhance explanation. For example, annotation will allow explanation to be expressed in qualitative rather than quantitative terms: this is characteristic of human discussion and reasoning. Thus annotation will attach to an entity in the model (and hence variable associated with that entity) qualitative attributes such as 'high', 'normal' and 'low'.

By interpreting graphs as sets of connected features answer schemes and rhetorical predicates can also be used to generate explanations of the functionality of the model and of its behaviour as represented by the changing values of variables. It will also be possible to generate explanations which compare and contrast the trajectories of different but (causally) linked variables. All explanations will be in response to implicit or explicit questions In the prototype the rhetorical predicates and answer schemes will be specified in the LOOM (1991,1992) knowledge representation system with Penman (1988a, b, c) as the means of generating sentences. It is interesting to note that the same two systems are being used in the proposed development of intelligent electronic books (Amador et al., 1992).

3.2.4 *An illustration of explanation generation*

Figure 9 shows two graphs: an indication is given in the next section of how (after identifying the features of the graphs) and interpretation of what is happening during the experimental episode will be generated. In this illustration the information presented in the text is really no different from that present in the graphs which means that for explanation which is helpful to the learner The interpretation must be elaborated with domain knowledge concerned with the significance of the graph features. It is intended to achieve this by requiring the author to annotate typical graphs so that the graph features can be linked to domain events and as a result the interpretation will be in terms of the domain rather than abstract graph features. Furthermore the explanation needs to be linked to the context (task, goals), divided into pieces and given in stages. This is discussed in Hartley et al. (1990) and by Pilkington (1992).

3.2.5 *Interpreting a graph*

Comparing and contrasting the features extracted from the graphs by the Graph Interpreter will lead to:

1 At first
>   Graph Attribute Quantity *(level of* **calcium**) *(concentration of* **PTH**)
>   Similarity
>   Time Compare (At the same time
>   Graph Attribute Feature *(is* **calcium, stable**) *(is* **PTH, stable**)
>   Graph Attribute Range *(range* **calcium, normal**) *(range* **PTH, normal**))

2 Next
>   Graph Attribute Quantity *(level of* **calcium**) *(concentration of* **PTH**)
>   Difference
>   Graph Attribute Feature *(is* **calcium peak**) *(is* **PTH trough**)
>   Graph Attribute Range *(is* **calcium very high**) *(is* **PTH very low**)
>   Time Contrast (occurs before, **calcium peak, PTH trough**)

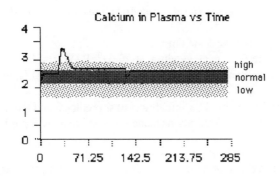

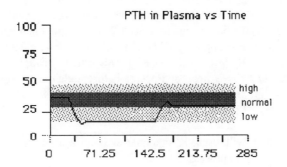

Figure 9 *Two graphs from a calcium homeostasis simulation*

3 Then,
>   Graph Attribute Quantity (*level of* **calcium**) (*concentration of* **PTH**)
>   Similarity
>   Graph Attribute Feature (*is* **calcium, stable**) (*is* **PTH, stable**)
>   Difference
>   Time Compare (At the same time
>   Graph Attribute Range (*range* **calcium, high**) (*range* **PTH, low**))

2 Next
>   Graph Attribute Quantity (*level of* **calcium**) (*concentration of* **PTH**)
>   Difference
>   Graph Attribute Feature (*is* **calcium trough**) (*is* **PTH peak**)
>   Similarity
>   Graph Attribute Range (*range* **calcium, normal**) (*range* **PTH, normal**)
>   Difference
>   Time Contrast (occurs before, **calcium trough, PTH peak**)

4 Finally,

> Graph Attribute Quantity (*level of* **calcium**) (*concentration of* **PTH**)
> Similarity
> Time Compare (At the same time
> Graph Attribute Feature (*is* **calcium, stable**) (*is* **PTH, stable**)
> Graph Attribute Range (*range* **calcium, normal**) (*range* **PTH, normal**))

This can be organised by the compare-contrast predicate and (when redundancies have been eliminated and substitutions made for repetitions) will produce:

> Deleting redundancies and substituting for repetition:
> *At first* both *level of* **calcium** *and concentration of* **PTH** *is* , **stable** and normal *Next* The graphs differ in that *level of* **calcium** *is,* **peak** whilst *concentration of* **PTH** *is,* **trough** and **calcium very high** whereas *is* **PTH very low** Also occurs before, **calcium peak PTH trough** Then both *level of* **calcium** *and concentration of* **PTH,** *is* **stable** but *range,* **calcium high** whilst *range,* **PTH low** *Next level of* **calcium** *is* **trough** whereas *concentration of* **PTH** *is* **peak** and occurs before, **calcium trough PTH peak** but both graphs *range,* **normal** *Finally* both *level of* **calcium** and *concentration of* **PTH stable** and both *range* **normal**.

The Penman system will, using its grammar and lexical rules and its knowledge of the predicates, be able to process this into:

> At first both the level of calcium and the concentration of PTH are stable and normal. Next, the graphs differ in that the level of calcium is at a peak whilst the concentration of PTH is at a trough and calcium is very high whereas PTH is very low. Also, the calcium peak occurs before the calcium trough. Then, both the level of calcium and the concentration of PTH are stable but calcium is high whilst PTH is low. Next, the level of calcium is at a trough whereas the concentration of PTH is at a peak and the calcium trough occurs before the PTH peak but both graphs are in the normal range. Finally, both the level of calcium and the concentration of PTH are stable and both are within the normal range.

3.2.6 *Questions and question-answering*

In principle every explanation is an answer to an implicit question. The two categories of questions which the explanations will answer are "What is...?" that is elaboration questions and "What happened?" which is a cause-consequence question and should result in an explanation that not only describes what happened but indicates the causal chain which led to the observed behaviour. Elaboration questions will be answered using the annotated model. To answer cause-consequence questions it will be necessary to use causal links in the model and knowledge about the behaviour of the model obtained by interpretation of the graphs. Current work has developed answer schemes and rhetorical predicates to extract from the annotated model the knowledge to answer elaboration questions. However, the present learner support system does not use bond-graphs, instead it uses the simpler system dynamics representation (as used by Stella) and a scheme has been devised to add causal links automatically to the representation. Work is now in progress on determining the answer schemes and rhetorical predicates necessary for causal explanations.

4. ISSUES

There are a number of issues still to be resolved in addition to those already mentioned.

The modelling component of Discourse uses (extended) bond-graphs as a stage on the way to producing an executable model. It is claimed that all systems can be represented as bond-graphs but whether this representation is appropriate for building simulations embedded in a learning support environment has yet to be demonstrated. Another attraction of bond-graphs is that the notation allows causal links to be marked or derived. However it is not clear how to annotate a bond-graph so that all the knowledge required for learner support is coherently represented.

Ideally the basis for this representation should be produced during the modelling process so that once the model has been built and tested the representation can be annotated by an author to provide the knowledge base for the learner support.

Explanation generation (or question answering) still requires some work. Previous work in the ESPRIT Project Eurohelp (Hartley et al., 1991) convinced us that answer schemes and rhetorical predicates can be devised for the kinds of explanation-giving and question-answering situations encountered in simulation-based learning. This has proved to be so. The weakness of the Eurohelp work was the inadequacy of the text generation although this was improved by Tattersall (1991) it was felt that a more generic approach was required which led us to adopt the LOOM knowledge representation system and the PENMAN system for text generation. These systems continue to be developed and the control of the PENMAN system has required the acquisition of substantial expertise. It is hoped that by the end of the Discourse project the capability to generate explanations with links to the hypermedia system containing the background knowledge will have been satisfactorily demonstrated.

REFERENCES

Amador, F.G., Berman, D., Borning, A., DeRose, T., Finklestein, A., Neville, D., Norge, Notkin, D., Salesin, D., Salisbury, M., Sherman, J., Sun, Y., Weld, D.S., & Winkenbach, G. (1992). *Electronic 'How things work' articles: A preliminary report*. Technical Report 92-04-08. Department of Computer Science, University of Washington.

Byard, M., Berkum, J. van, & Tait, K. (1991). Tools to Support the Design and Application of Instructional Strategies for Simulations. In: K. Tait (Ed.), *Towards the Specification of Integrated Support Tools for Authors Constructing Intelligent Simulation-based Learning Environments*. DELTA Project SAFE (D1014), Report SIM/22,48-62. Brussels: CEC.

Forbus, K. (1991). Towards Tutor Compilers: Self-explanatory simulations as an enabling technology. In: L. Birbaum (Ed.), *Proceedings of the International Conference on Learning Sciences*. Charlottesville, VA: Association for the Advancement of Computing in Education.

Hartley, J.R., Byard, M.J., & Mallen, C. (1991). Qualitative modelling and conceptual change in science students. In: L. Birbaum (Ed.), *Proceedings of the International Conference on Learning Sciences*. Charlottesville, VA: Association for the Advancement of Computing in Education.

Hartley, J.R., Pilkington, R., Tait, K., & Tattersall, C. (1990). Question interpretation and answering. In: J Breuker, EUROHELP: *Developing Intelligent Help Systems*. Final Report ESPRIT 280, Brussels: CEC.

Jong, T. de, Tait, K., & Joolingen, W. van (1991). Authoring for intelligent simulation based instruction: a model based approach. In: Cerri, S.A. & Whiting, J. (Eds.). *Learning Technology in the European Communities*, 619-637. Dordrecht: Kluwer Academic Publishers.

Joolingen, W.R. van, & Jong, T. de (1991). Supporting hypothesis generation by learners exploring an interactive computer simulation. *Instructional Science, 20*, 389-404.

Karnopp, D.C., & Rosenberg, R.C. (1975). *System Dynamics: a Unified Approach.* New York: Wiley.

Klahr, D., & Dunbar, K. (1988). Dual space search during scientific reasoning. *Cognitive Science, 12*, 1-48.

LOOM (1991). *Users Guide*. Unpublished USC/ISI Documentation.

LOOM (1992). *Reference Manual*. Unpublished USC/ISI Documentation.

McKeown, K.F. (1985). *Text Generation*. Series on Natural Language Processing. Cambridge: Cambridge University Press.

Norman, D.A. (1983). Some observations on mental models. In D. Genter & A.L. Stevens (Eds.), *Mental Models*. Hillsdale NJ: Lawrence Erlbaum Associates.

Penman (1988a). *The Penman Primer*. Unpublished UCS/ISI Documentation.

Penman (1988b). *The Penman User Guide*. Unpublished UCS/ISI Documentation.

Penman (1988c). *The Penman Reference Manual*. Unpublished UCS/ISI Documentation.

Pilkington, R. (1992). *Intelligent Help: Communicating with Knowledge-based Systems*. UK: Paul Chapman.

Pilkington, R. (in preparation). *A task space for simulation-based learning*. Deliverable 38 DELTA Project Discourse. CBL Unit, University of Leeds

Pilkington, R., & Tait, K. (1993). *Learning with Simulations*. Deliverable 40, CEC DELTA Project DISCOURSE (D2008), CBL Unit, University of Leeds.

Rosenberg, R.C., & Karnopp, D. (1983). *Introduction to Physical System Dynamics.* Mcgraw-Hill.

Self, J., & Twidale, M. (1991). Learner Modelling Tools in Simulations. In: K. Tait, *Towards the Specification of Integrated Support Tools for Authors Constructing Intelligent Simulation-based Learning Environments.* DELTA Project SAFE (D1014), Report SIM/22,48-62. CEC, Brussels.

Shute, V.J., & Glaser, R. (1990). A large-scale evaluation of an intelligent discovery world: Smithtown. *Interactive Learning Environments, 1,* 51-77.

Tattersall, C. (1991). Exploiting text generation techniques in the provision of help. *Seventh IEEE Conference on Applications of AI. Miami.*

Tavernier, A., & Lefèvre, J. (1993). *DISCOSIM Graphical Modelling Formalism.* Deliverable 45, DELTA Project DISCOURSE (D2008), UMDS, University of London.

Acknowledgements: The work reported here is the work of two teams: at the Computer Based Learning Unit in Leeds: Rachel Pilkington, David Hintze, Rod Williams, Roger Hartley and Andrew Cole; at UMDS in London: André Tavernier, Stevo Durbaba and Jacques Lefèvre.

SMISLE: System for Multimedia Integrated Simulation Learning Environments

Ton de Jong[1], Wouter van Joolingen[1], David Scott[2], Robert de Hoog[3], Laurent Lapied[4], & Robert Valent[5]

[1] Faculty of Educational Science and Technology, University of Twente, The Netherlands; [2] Marconi Simulation, United Kingdom; [3] Department of Social Science Informatics, University of Amsterdam, The Netherlands; [4] Framentec-Cognitech, France; [5] Engineering Systems International, France.

Abstract

The SMISLE project (System for Multimedia Integrated Simulation Learning Environments) has two main objectives. First, it aims to define exploratory learning environments based on simulations that incorporate instructional support for learners in such a way that effective and efficient learning will result. Second, it aims to provide authors of these simulation learning environments with an authoring toolkit that not only presents technical, but also conceptual support. Providing *support to the learner* can be done in many different ways. The project started with an inventory of potential instructional support measures and selected four types of measures that now have been implemented: progressive model implementation, assignments, explanations, and hypothesis scratchpads. The simulation environments that incorporate these support measures are designed around five different models each carrying a specific function. The *runnable model* is an efficient representation of the domain that will make the simulation run; *the cognitive model* is the representation of the domain that is tailored to learning and instruction; the *instructional model* incorporates the instructional support; the *learner model* keeps track of knowledge and characteristics of the learner; and the *interface model* decides upon the appearance of the simulation environment to the student. Together these models form the resulting application for the learner, which is called a MISLE (Multimedia Integrated Simulation Learning Environment). The main task of an author is to create the different models in the MISLE, with the exception of the runnable model which is automatically generated from the cognitive model. Creating the different models essentially means that an author has to select, specialise and instantiate generic *building blocks* (that can be regarded as generic templates) that are offered in *libraries of building blocks*. For each of the models there is a separate library of building blocks and a set of *dedicated editors* for specialising and instantiating the building blocks. Additionally, authors are guided through the authoring process by a *methodology* and they have access to *instructional advice* which provides them with ideas on which instructional support measures to apply.

T. de Jong and L. Sarti (eds.), Design and Production of Multimedia and Simulation-based Learning Material, 133-165
© 1994 *Kluwer Academic Publishers. Printed in the Netherlands.*

1 INTRODUCTION

In contemporary theories of learning and instruction, learners are no longer seen as persons who copy knowledge that is presented to them by a teacher, but as active agents in the learning process. This view has led to new approaches to the design of instructional environments. One of these new approaches is *scientific discovery learning* or *exploratory learning*, in which the learner is not given direct instruction about the domain to be mastered, but is invited to discover the important concepts and relations in the domain him or herself.

The main assumption behind the idea of exploratory learning is that knowledge discovered by the learner will be based more firmly in the learner's knowledge base and have stronger links with the learner's prior knowledge than knowledge that is just told. Knowledge that is discovered is seen as more intuitive, qualitative knowledge. Also the skills needed for the exploration itself are seen as important skills, since they may help a person in dealing with unfamiliar situations in a more effective way.

These notions have received particular attention through the introduction of *computer simulations* as an instructional device. Computer simulations can play an important role as a training device for reasons of safety, economy and for social reasons (de Jong, 1991). More important, however, is that simulations are well suited to exploratory or discovery learning since they contain a model that has to be discovered by the learner.

Computer simulations are quite popular in instruction (de Jong, van Andel, Leiblum, & Mirande, 1992), but in spite of their popularity there is no conclusive evidence of their effectiveness and efficiency, with some studies showing effects (Shute & Glaser, 1990; Grimes & Wiley, 1990; Faryniarz & Lockwood, 1992), whereas others fail to find advantages of simulations (Carlsen & Andre, 1992; Rivers & Vockell, 1987; de Jong, de Hoog, & de Vries, 1993). The reason for the possible ineffectiveness of computer simulations is that learners, while interacting with a simulation, encounter difficulties which they cannot overcome on their own. These problems concern, for example, the adequate execution of exploratory processes such as formulating hypotheses (van Joolingen & de Jong, 1991; Njoo & de Jong, 1993a,b), the switching between hypotheses and experiments (Klahr & Dunbar, 1988) and the burden of regulatory processes such as planning, keeping track of what has been done and checking (Shute & Glaser, 1990). A possible solution for these problems is to provide learners with support in addition to a pure simulation.

A second problem with the use of computer simulations in instruction concerns another actor: the author. The above mentioned inventory (de Jong, van Andel, Leiblum, & Mirande, 1992) showed that simulations are almost always created using general programming languages. Languages for non-programmers, such as authoring languages, are generally employed for creating drills and tutorials. This indicates a potential market for *authoring tools for simulations*. Taking into account our assertion that simulations should be surrounded with instructional support for the learner, these authoring tools for simulations should also assist the author in creating the additional learner support. Since simulations and instructional support for learners will be new areas for many potential authors, adequate authoring tools should not only provide technical support, as all contemporary authoring languages do, but also need to *provide the author with conceptual design support.*

The two issues discussed above – providing learners with simulations that have integrated instructional support and providing (non-programmer) authors with authoring tools that include both technical and conceptual design support[1] – are the key elements of the SMISLE project. The following sections outline the approach and achievements of the SMISLE (System for Multimedia Integrated Simulation Learning Environments) project. Section 2 gives an overall impression of the types of simulation learning environments that can be created using the authoring environment that is under construction: the SMISLE toolkit[2]. Section 3 presents the general 'architecture' of the applications for learners (the so-called MISLEs, which stands for Multimedia Integrated Simulation Learning Environments). The authoring process with the SMISLE toolkit consists of selecting, specialising and instantiating building blocks from libraries of building blocks. Section 4 describes the building blocks that are available in the SMISLE libraries and Section 5 subsequently presents the functionality that is present in the SMISLE toolkit for browsing, inspecting, selecting, specialising, and instantiating generic building blocks. Section 5 also describes two features of the SMISLE toolkit that assist authors in their work: an authoring methodology and pedagogical advice.

2   (MULTIMEDIA) INTEGRATED SIMULATION LEARNING ENVIRONMENTS

A (Multimedia) Integrated Simulation Learning Environment (from now on we will use the short term *MISLE*) presents the learner with a simulation and instructional support. Currently four types of instructional support have been selected. These are *model progression* which means that a learner may work through a succession of more complex and more precise domain models, *assignments* that help the learner to set targets while working with the simulation, *explanations* offering the learner direct access to domain information, and *hypothesis scratchpads* that help the learner in formulating hypotheses. Figure 1 displays the interface of a typical MISLE. It shows a number of windows of which the upper left window contains the simulation

---

[1] The author we have in mind for working with the SMISLE authoring toolkit is a domain expert not necessarily having programming experience.

[2] The functionality and interfaces as presented in the present paper are based on SMISLE version 1.11 which was released in February 1994. The SMISLE project will continue until the end of March 1995 and will use results of ongoing evaluation studies to adapt functionalities and interfaces. SMISLE 1.11 is built in Smalltalk 80 and VisualWorks™ (ParcPlace Systems) and is portable over Windows, Macintosh and Unix platforms.

itself (with input variables that can be changed by the learner and a display of output variables); the bottom left window gives the learner access to overall control functions; the remaining windows are each associated with one of the four types of instructional support. In the interface we have included an example of a simple simulation on controlling the heating of a house; input variables are the leaking to the outside world, the heating of the house itself, opening or closing a window, and the outside temperature, the output variable is the inside temperature. Learners working with a MISLE will normally switch regularly between operating the simulation window and use of instructional support, either on their own or on system initiative. Each of the instructional support measures is treated in detail in Section 4.2.

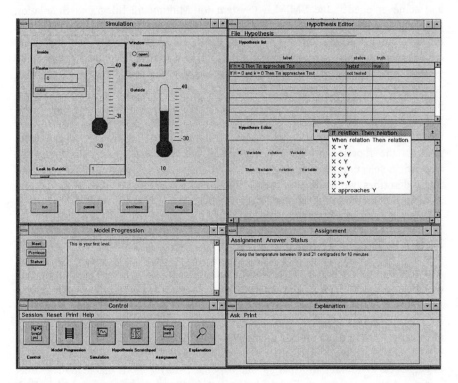

Figure 1 *An example of a MISLE interface*

3   THE ARCHITECTURE OF MISLEs

This section describes the architecture that underlies simulation learning environments (MISLEs) that can be created with the SMISLE authoring environment. We have divided a MISLE into a number of functionally different units that are called MISLE models. We distinguish the following models:

- *Runnable model*
  In a MISLE the runnable model will make the simulation run. The runnable model is itself an abstract description of a particular domain. The runnable model has as its objective to enable an optimal fast and efficient simulation. It will, therefore, often have a numerical character, but it may also be a qualitative causal model.
- *Instructional model*
  The instructional model contains the instructional function of the MISLE. It carries all the instructional measures available to the learner, such as (for example) the possibility of presenting explanations.
- *Learner model*
  The learner model is able to store (or infer) information regarding a learner. This information can then be used for activating instructional measures.
- *Interface model*
  The interface model contains all kinds of graphical objects, windows etc. enabling the learner to interact with the MISLE.

This four-partition follows a division into components which is commonly used in describing Intelligent Tutoring Systems (see for example Wenger, 1987). The domain related model of these four components (the runnable model), however, will, quite often, not be a good basis for instruction. First, we will not, for example, want learners to master complex sets of differential equations. Also, since the runnable model needs to be efficient, (abstract) variables, that are necessary for the learner to master, might be absent in the runnable model (see van Joolingen & de Jong, 1992). Second, as the 'domain representation' will be used by the other models (instructional, learner, and interface model) the runnable model probably would not contain sufficient information for the other models to function. For example, if the instructional model prescribes the generation of a causal explanation, the cognitive model will have to be structured in such a way to allow this kind of explanation.

To solve the first problem, we introduce the concepts of *conceptual model* and *operational model* (de Jong, Tait, & van Joolingen, 1992). These two models are the instructional domain representations, one for conceptual domains (domains in which no inherent procedure is present, for example electrical circuits), the other, required in addition, for operational domains (domains that have an inherent procedure, for example flying a plane). These two models represent what we want the learner to know or master at the end of the training session. Conceptual models may contain different models of the same system; for instance one model may give detailed information on the behaviour of a system whilst another may describe its causal structure.

To solve the second problem mentioned we introduce *extensions* of the conceptual model and operational model that provide the (extra) necessary information for the instructional, learner and interface models to operate. These extensions are added to the conceptual and operational models on the basis of requirements from the instructional, learner and interface model.

Together we have called the conceptual model, operational model and their extensions the *cognitive model*. This cognitive model plays a central role in SMISLE applications. Figure 2 displays a diagram of the different models.

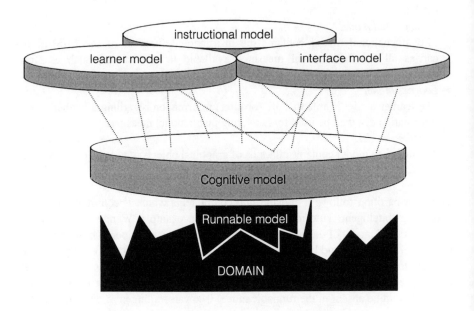

Figure 2 *Different models as identified in the SMISLE project*

4 THE SMISLE LIBRARIES

For a specific MISLE, authors will create the different MISLE models on the basis of building blocks from *libraries of building blocks* offered in the SMISLE authoring toolkit. For each of the MISLE models identified in the previous section, a library of building blocks will be available to the author. Only the runnable model is not created directly by the author but is generated from the cognitive model. Figure 3 gives a simple illustration of the relation between the libraries (part of the SMISLE authoring toolkit) and the resulting application (the MISLE).

Clearly a project like SMISLE will not be able to deliver an authoring toolkit that can be used for creating MISLEs of any kind, including all types of domains and all types of instructional measure etc. The present section outlines the choices (and thus restrictions) that have been made in the project for the different models in the MISLE, which, naturally, comes down to the choice of building blocks to be made available in the libraries of the MISLE.

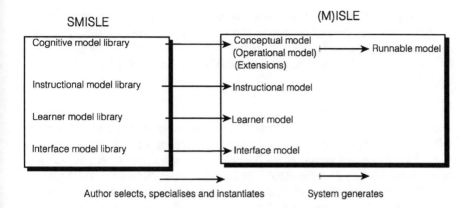

Figure 3 *Schematic relation between model libraries and models*

4.1 The cognitive model library

The cognitive model which is present in an application (MISLE) fulfils a dual role. First, it provides a description of the domain which is tailored to fit its use in instruction. This has two aspects: the representation of the knowledge that the learner should acquire in the course of exploring the simulation, and the provision of support to the other components of the MISLE (in particular the instructional model) so that they can function properly. For instance, the latter could include methods for determining the complexity of a domain model which is important in instructional theory. Second, the runnable model employed by the MISLE is generated automatically from this more qualitative description of the domain, rather than being directly encoded in a special purpose simulation language or a general programming language.

In concept at least, a *cognitive model* is composed of a *conceptual model*, an *operational model*, and some *extensions*. The extensions are present purely to support the other components of the MISLE. The conceptual and operational models are the counterparts of the conceptual and operational domains which were described in Section 3. Three libraries are provided to support the construction of the cognitive model. The *functional block library* and the *petri net library* are used to build the conceptual model, whilst the *operational model library* is used to build the operational model.

4.1.1 *The conceptual model library*

We have decided that the types of systemic model that the formalism must capable of representing are *lumped parameter* and the *process interaction view of discrete event simulation*, possibly coupled together. There are separate libraries for these two sorts of model namely the *functional block library* and the *petrinet library* respectively.

The functional block library
The formalism usually used to describe lumped parameter models is that of ordinary differential equations. Systems of differential equations may be represented by networks of *functional units* such as adders, multipliers, integrators, etc. So, one way in which models may be constructed is by connecting together such units. In general, these functional units are multi-directional - for example, an adder can compute the value on one of its terminals given the values on the other two - but this is not be the case for all of them (such as explicit sources and sinks). A network representation has the advantages of reducing the scope for syntactic errors in the description, and eliminating the need both for the explicit introduction of temporary variables and for the equations to be ordered.

Any given type of functional block has a fixed number of *terminals*. A terminal may be an *input* or *output* terminal, or it may be *bi-directional*. Terminals are connected by links. A link may connect two bi-directional terminals (in which case the link is represented by a simple line), or an output terminal to an input terminal (in which case the link is represented by an arrow).

A functional block may be composed of other functional blocks, called *sub-blocks*, in which case it is a *compound (or complex, or non-primitive) functional block*. The terminals on a compound block correspond to the free terminals of its sub-blocks. A *free terminal* is a terminal which is not linked to any other terminal.

A subset of the library of functional blocks allows systems to be modelled using the formalism of *bond graphs* (Karnopp, Margolis, & Rosenberg, 1990). When it is appropriate to model a system in terms of energy flowing between its constituents this provides a concise graphical notation. In this representation systems are described as collections of elements which may store energy, transform energy, dissipate energy, etc. These elements are called *ports*. A 1-port has just one energy flow in or out of it, a 2-port has two energy flows, etc. The basic n-port elements are shown in Table 1. *Bonds*, denoted by half arrows, indicate the sign convention for the directions of the energy flows. A pair of variables is associated with each bond: an effort variable, e, and a flow variable, f. The product of these variables has the dimensions of power. Sometimes one wishes to neglect the energy flow associated with an interaction. This may be the case when observing or controlling a system. In this case the interaction is indicated by a full arrow which is called an *active bond*. The basic 2-port elements provided in the library are the modulated transformer and modulated gyrator which have active bonds.

Table 1 *The symbols, names, and relations of the basic n-port elements*

Symbols	Names	Relations
$\dfrac{e}{f}$ ⟶ R	linear resistor	$e = Rf$
$\dfrac{e}{f}$ ⟶ C	linear capacitor	$f = dq/dt, q = Ce$
$\dfrac{e}{f}$ ⟶ I	linear inertia	$e = dp/dt, p = If$
Se ⟶	effort source	$e(t)$ given, $f(t)$ arbitrary
Sf ⟶	flow source	$f(t)$ given, $e(t)$ arbitrary
$\begin{array}{c} m \\ e1 \;\downarrow\; e2 \\ \xrightarrow{\;\;} \text{MTF} \xrightarrow{\;\;} \\ f1 \qquad f2 \end{array}$	modulated transformer	$e1 = m.e2$ $m.f1 = f2$
$\begin{array}{c} r \\ e1 \;\downarrow\; e2 \\ \xrightarrow{\;\;} \text{MGY} \xrightarrow{\;\;} \\ f1 \qquad f2 \end{array}$	modulated gyrator	$e1 = r.f2$ $r.f1 = e2$
$\begin{array}{c} e2 \mid f2 \\ e1 \;\downarrow\; e3 \\ \xrightarrow{\;\;} 0 \xleftarrow{\;\;} \\ f1 \qquad f3 \end{array}$	0-junction	$e1 = e2 = e3$ $f1 + f2 + f3 = 0$
$\begin{array}{c} e2 \mid f2 \\ e1 \;\downarrow\; e3 \\ \xrightarrow{\;\;} 1 \xleftarrow{\;\;} \\ f1 \qquad f3 \end{array}$	1-junction	$f1 = f2 = f3$ $e1 + e2 + e3 = 0$

One n-port may be joined to another n-port by selecting one bond from each (they must not have been used already to create a connection) and identifying them. Corresponding relationships are established between the effort and flow variables of the two bonds. More complicated connections may be established via the 3-port junctions. Figure 4 shows representations of a simple harmonic oscillator and a damped harmonic oscillator using the bond graph notation.

The bond graph notation is not supported directly by the modelling tool. Instead bond graphs appear as complex building blocks in the library of functional blocks (i.e. they are constructed from simpler functional blocks) as is illustrated by Figure 5

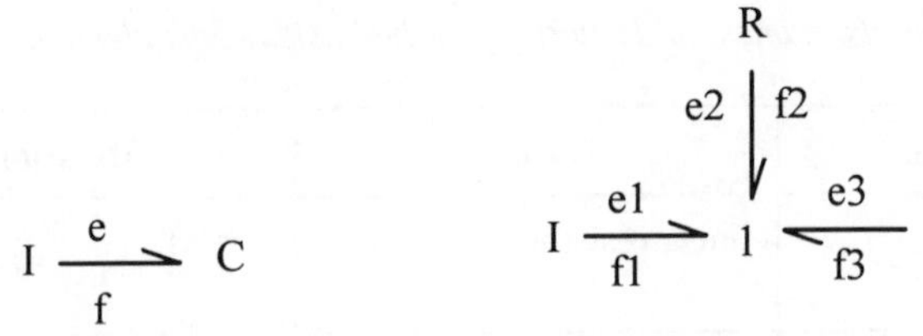

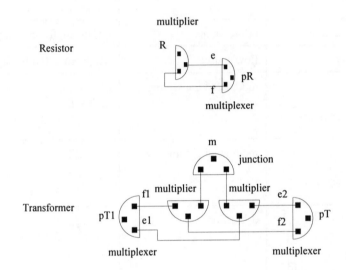

$$I \xrightarrow[f]{e} C$$

$$I \xrightarrow[f1]{e1} 1 \xleftarrow[f3]{e3}$$

Figure 4 *A simple oscillator (left) and a damped oscillator (right) in bond graph notation*

Figure 5 *The implementation of various n-ports in terms of functional blocks*

in which the networks corresponding to the resistor and transformer are shown. Figure 6 shows the functional block representations of the bond graphs of Figure 4. Note that the graphical notation of bond graphs is not fully supported. In particular the modelling tool will not automatically take care of the conventions for power flow. For this reason new 2-ports called '0-inverter and '1-inverter' have been introduced so that the direction of a power flow may be reversed. A similar approach has been taken in DYMOLA (Cellier, 1991).

The petri net library
The formalism used to implement discrete event models is that of *extended petri nets*. This formalism is also used to represent operational expertise and is described in more detail in the next section. The petri net formalism may be used to describe the behaviour of adders, multipliers, etc., so a fully integrated description of

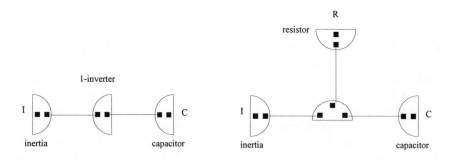

Figure 6 *A simple oscillator (left) and a damped oscillator (right) in functional block notation*

behaviour may be obtained which mixes lumped parameter and discrete event models. Functional units such as adders are represented in the library of extended petri nets as complex transitions. Figure 7 gives an example. The fact that basic functional blocks may be represented in this way is important for the working of the system, but is largely irrelevant as far a the author is concerned. Extended petri nets may be used to represent causal structures which include inhibition.

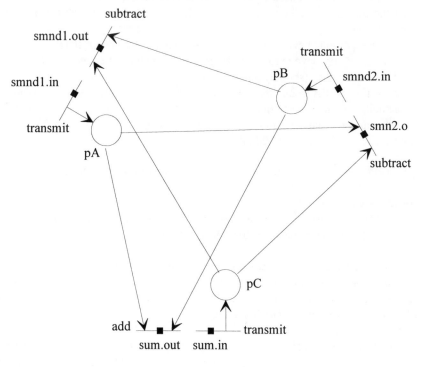

Figure 7 *The petri net for 'adder'*

4.1.2   The operational model library

The formalism used to model operational expertise is that of *extended petri nets*. Standard petri nets will not be described here other than to say that they are composed of places (represented by circles) and transitions (represented by bars) connected by directed arcs (represented by arrows), but a description may be found in (Petersen, 1981). However, the additional features that we use are described in this section. An operational model must have an associated conceptual model, for it describes how some system is manipulated. We shall use petri nets to represent tasks with their places being used to represent directly observable aspects of the state of the system and their transitions being used to represent actions performed by the operator on directly accessible parts of the system.

Standard petri nets may be used to model parallelism and synchronisation – which is obviously required in the representation of operational expertise. Also, they can express the logical constraints on the ordering of actions, and show the results of those actions. However, given that we wish to represent operational expertise, they cannot express certain ideas which are important for us, such as:

1. that an action cannot (or should not) occur if some condition holds;
2. that the operator may interact with a continuous system;
3. that the operator may have to interact with a dynamic system, which involves several issues:
   * the operator may have to wait for the system to reach a certain state;
   * one action may have to (or should) occur a certain time after another action, i.e. the operator must (should) wait;
   * an action whilst being treated as elementary in most respects nevertheless actually consumes some time.
4. that the operator may have to perform a computation;
5. that a task may be decomposed into sub–tasks.

Consequently some additional features are required, the principal ones being:

1. *Inhibitor arcs*
   An *inhibitor* arc may run from a place to a transition. The presence of a token in the place prevents the transition from being enabled.
2. *Concrete actions*
   Transitions have already been associated, conceptually, with actions of the operator. We now allow the association of a *concrete action* with a transition. Such an action either sets the value of some input variable of the system or gets the value of some output variable of the system.
3. *Coloured tokens*
   Concrete actions associated with transitions may be parametrised, and they may return results which may be used as arguments to other actions. These values are carried around the net by *coloured tokens*.

4. *Conditional transitions*

   A *delayed transition* has a time interval associated with it. If a delayed transition is selected for firing then it does not actually fire until the specified period of simulated time has elapsed.

5 *Transitions dependent on events in the associated conceptual model*

   The enabling conditions for *state dependent* transitions depend on logical expressions which involve the values of one or two output variables of the associated conceptual model. Such a transition is not enabled unless the logical expression evaluates to true and it satisfies the usual enabling condition.

6. *Arithmetic transitions*

   An *arithmetic transition* has an associated arithmetic operator and produces an output token whose value is determined by applying the operator to the values of its input tokens. The number of operands required by an operator is fixed and their order is usually significant. In order to take this into account new features, called *terminals*, are introduced on all transitions. A terminal is either an *input terminal* or an *output terminal*. Arcs no longer connect places to transitions (or vice versa), instead they connect places to terminals (or vice versa). A terminal may be connected to at most one place, but a place may be connected to any number of terminals. An input terminal may have an arc coming into it, but not one leaving it, whilst an output terminal may have an arc leaving it, but not one coming into it.

7. *Compound transitions*

   A *compound transition* has a petri net associated with it which will be referred to as its *sub-net*. The terminals on a compound transition are determined by its sub-net. Each terminal corresponds to a *free terminal* on a transition of the sub-net. A free terminal is a terminal which is not linked to anything by an arc. When a non-primitive transition fires it does not immediately put out tokens at its output terminals. Instead execution of the sub-net is started.

4.2   The instructional model library

Providing learners with instructional support in exploratory environments can be done in many ways. The project started with an inventory which resulted in a list of 23 different types of instructional measures (de Jong, van Joolingen, Pieters, van der Hulst, & de Hoog, 1992), and this list certainly is not exhaustive. From this list of instructional support measures four types of support were selected to be included in the instructional model library for SMISLE. To select these measures we used a number of criteria which included that measures should be applicable to conceptual and operational domains and also that they should form a more or less coherent combination. This coherence was achieved by adopting two basic approaches to instruction. One is the *mental model approach* as it is reflected in the work by White and Frederiksen (1989; 1990). The most essential characteristic of this approach is that a domain is learned by exposure to a sequence of models that gradually progress to some target model. The second approach is the *cognitive apprenticeship approach* as it is described by Collins, Brown, and Newman (1989). The mental model approach was developed in the context of teaching conceptual domains, the cognitive apprenticeship approach is applicable to operational domains. Both approaches have in common that students' faults are prevented. The latter characteristic of both approaches means that there will be no heavy burden on a 'learner model'. The specific instructional support measures that resulted are: model progression, assignments, explanations, and hypothesis scratchpads. Each of these support measures is discussed in detail in one of the following subsections.

4.2.1 *Model progression*

The basic idea of offering model progression in a simulation environment is to gradually unfold the properties of the domain to the learner, by offering a sequence of models. Model progression is used to avoid a confrontation of learners with a model that is too complex with respect to their prior knowledge. Model progression has been applied in systems such as QUEST (White & Fredriksen, 1989; 1990), NEWTON (Teodoro, 1992), and DIBI (Plötzner & Spada, 1992). In the SMISLE instructional model library we provide possibilities for:

- *Simple to complex ordering.*
  Simple to complex progression means that models with only a few variables develop towards models with a large number of variables. For example, a simulation environment about mechanics can start with frictionless motion in one dimension and move to motion with friction in three dimensions.
- *Changing the 'order' of the model.*
  We make a distinction between zero and higher order models, differing along the dimension of precision, i.e. going from qualitative descriptions to quantitative ones.
- *Changing perspective on the model.*
  This includes offering different ways to describe the same domain, for example using different variables. An important difference between this dimension and the ones listed above is that there is no ordering implied by the different perspectives; this means that the author has to supply this ordering.
- *From partial task to complete task.*
  Learners start with performing parts of the complete task and gradually they get control of the complete task. This type of model progression refers to operational domains, whereas the first three refer to conceptual domains.

4.2.2 *Assignments*

Confronted with an educational simulation the learner's general (often not stated) goal is to 'discover' the model behind the simulation. Such an 'assignment' may be too vague for a learner to work with, leading to undirected exploratory behaviour.

Therefore, we may introduce assignments in order to give learners some grip and to direct them through the model. Assignments can be given before the simulation starts, before a set of simulation runs, or at any moment in the simulation. We have distinguished six types of assignment:

- *Investigation*
  Investigation assignments prompt the learner to find the relation between specific variables.
- *Optimisation*
  In an optimisation assignment the learner is asked to change values for input variables in such a way that the output variable(s) acquire certain values that can be described as maximal, minimal, or optimal.
- *Fault diagnosis*
  In fault diagnosis the learner is confronted with a model that does not behave as it should; the assignment is to find the faulty relation.
- *Specification (prediction)*
  In specification assignments the learner is asked to predict (calculate) the unknown value for some output variable.
- *Explication*
  In explication assignments the learner is asked to give an explication for a specific phenomenon in terms of causal relations. This means that the MISLE shows the learner input values together with output values from the simulation and the learner has to give an account of what is displayed.
- *(Normal) operation*
  An important class of operational tasks concerns the normal operation of devices. This involves the starting, maintaining and shut down of processes. In these types of assignments output variables are specified, and the learner has to provide input for some of the input variables, whereas other input variables are under control of the system. For example: keeping a plane in the air has specified output variables (distance from the ground > 0); the learner has to provide values for input variables (the position of the wing flaps for example); and some input variables (wind direction) are under control of the system.

Normal operation is an assignment associated with operational domains, optimisation assignments can refer to both conceptual and operational domains, and the remaining assignments refer to conceptual domains[3]. Three of these assignments (investigation, explicitation, and fault diagnosis) focus *directly* at relations in the model, the other three do so *implicitly* by asking for specific values of input or output variables. Table 2 gives a structured overview of assignments present in the SMISLE instructional model library.

---

[3] Fault diagnosis assignments only refer to operational domains when the operational task *is* fault diagnosis, in that case, however, fault diagnosis is normal operation.

Table 2 *Structured overview of the different types of assignments*

Specification		Normal operation		Optimisation	
$Varl_1$:	specified	$Varl_1$:	to be varied	$Varl_1$:	??
$Varl_2$:	specified	$Varl_2$:	to be varied	$Varl_2$:	??
$Varl_3$:	specified	$Varl_3$:	varied	$Varl_3$:	??
$Varl_4$:	specified	$Varl_4$:	varied	$Varl_4$:	??
$VarO_1$:	??	$VarO_1$:	specified	$VarO_1$:	specified
$VarO_2$:	??	$VarO_2$:	specified	$VarO_2$:	specified
Investigation		**Explicitation**		**Fault diagnosis**	
$Varl_1$:	to be varied	$Varl_1$:	varied	$Varl_1$:	to be varied
$Varl_2$:	to be varied	$Varl_2$:	varied	$Varl_2$:	to be varied
$Varl_3$:	to be varied	$Varl_3$:	varied	$Varl_3$:	to be varied
$Varl_4$:	to be varied	$Varl_4$:	varied	$Varl_4$:	to be varied
$VarO_1$:	displayed	$VarO_1$:	displayed	$VarO_1$:	displayed
$VarO_2$:	displayed	$VarO_2$:	displayed	$VarO_2$:	displayed
$R(Varl_1,VarO_1)$: ??		$R(Varl_1,VarO_1)$: ??		$R(Varl_1,VarO_1)$: specified	
				$R(Varl_2,VarO_1)$: specified	
				$R_f(Varl_x, VarO_y)$: ??	

'specified' and 'varied' are author actions
'displayed' is system action
'to be varied' is learner action
'??' indicates 'values' (which can be single values or ranges of values) to be given by learner

4.2.3 *Explanations*

Explanations are instructional measures by which learners are offered information on concepts that play a role in the simulation model, or they are offered relations between variables directly. Explanations are used to present learners with (lacking) prior knowledge that they need for a fruitful exploration (e.g. definitions of variables) or to give learners relations between variables directly when they fail to discover them. Explanation as an instructional support measure with simulations has been used for example by Shute (1991) and Leutner (1993). In a MISLE the following types of explanation can be offered:

- *Class dependent*
  A 'class-dependent' view gives the place of a concept in a class hierarchy.

- *Structural*
  A structural explanation lists the super-part or sub-parts of a concept.
- *Functional*
  In functional explanations the role of an object in a process is presented.
- *Modulatory*
  A modulatory explanation lists how 'one object or process affects (or is affected by) another process or object'. In SMISLE 1.11 only one modulatory relation which is the 'causes' relation is provided.
- *Attributional*
  An attributional explanation lists the attributes of a concept.
- *Covariance*
  Two concepts may show covariance without having a modulatory relation. Different types of covariance relations exist such as 'monotonic increasing', 'feedback', and 'asymptotical'. A covariance explanation informs the learner on the relevant covariance relation between two variables.
- *Analogy*
  An analogy presents the learner with a similar variable or relation as the one under study, but now in a different (type of) system, or it refers to some real world application
- *Additional information*
  In additional information the author may put any information he or she likes.
- *Condition-action pairs*
  This explanation tells the learner which conditions have to be fulfilled for a certain (learner suggested) action to be performed, or which action is preferable under certain conditions. This explanation refers to operational domains only.

The author may select specific types of explanation that he or she wants to use in the MISLE that is created. There is, of course a restriction that the domain should allow for certain explanations (for example, if no causal relations exist, no modulatory explanations can be given). For each explanation the learner indicates the object he or she wants an explanation on and selects the types of explanation wanted from a list of available explanations.

4.2.4 *Hypothesis scratchpads*

Research has shown that creating hypotheses is one of the most difficult aspects of discovery learning (Klahr & Dunbar, 1988; Njoo & de Jong, 1993a; 1993b; Chinn & Brewer, 1993; Dunbar, 1993). Hypothesis scratchpads are learner instruments designed to support the learner in stating hypotheses about the simulation. The idea of hypothesis scratchpads is based on the 'hypothesis menu' in systems such as Smithtown (Shute & Glaser, 1990), Voltaville (Glaser, Raghavan, & Schauble, 1988) and Refract (Reimann, 1991). The role of hypothesis scratchpads has been empirically investigated by van Joolingen and de Jong (1991; 1993) and van Joolingen (1993). Hypothesis scratchpads contain the elements necessary for composing hypotheses. For conceptual domains these elements are: variables, relations and conditions. Hypothesis scratchpads for operational domains comprise similar elements. Instead of variables, however, these operational scratchpads contain 'actions', which themselves consist of variables and value changes (e.g. increase Var₁). Conditions in the conceptual scratchpad refer to constraints on the validity of the hypothesis, in the operational scratchpad they may be enabling or triggering conditions.

Learners can use the hypothesis scratchpad to compose a hypothesis from the elements that are provided: save the hypothesis which will put it on the hypothesis list; load a hypothesis from the list and allow further editing; mark the truth value of a hypothesis [true/false/unknown]; and, finally, mark a hypothesis as being tested [yes/no]. Figure 8 gives an example of a hypothesis scratchpad in this case for the conceptual domain of the heater that was displayed in Figure 1.

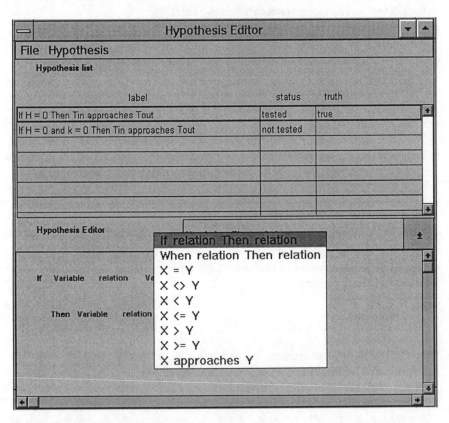

Figure 8 *Example of a hypothesis scratchpad.*

4.2.5 *An example of an instructional measure building block*

The preceding sections gave an overview of all generic building blocks in the
SMISLE libraries that are at the author's disposal for creating instructional support
measures. In this section we provide a more detailed example of one of the
instructional measures present as a building block in the SMISLE libraries: a *normal
operation assignment*. The purpose of this type of assignment is that the learner
practice a task in the simulation environment. For example, in the case of a flight
simulator, a normal operation assignment would mean operating the simulation of
the aircraft under specified circumstances. Typically, a number of normal operation
assignments together will allow practice in a number of varying conditions.

In a MISLE a normal operation assignment (when selected by the learner or
activated by the MISLE) sets up the simulation in the state from which the
assignment should start. The learner is told the goal of the assignment (e.g. take off,
fly to position X and land safely) and starts operating the simulation. During the
activity of the normal operation assignment, the MISLE checks if the task is carried
out correctly. This is done by checking *constraints* which were set by the author.
These constraints specify the boundaries within which the learner may operate, e.g.,
in the case of the plane: the height is greater than zero. Once a constraint is broken,
(height < 0, the plane crashes) the learner's attempt is terminated and an appropriate
message is displayed. Alternatively, the learner can reach the goal (safely on the
ground in place X), in which case the assignment is terminated successfully.

The functionality for setting up the simulation, checking the constraints and
informing learners of their success or failure are present in the library building block
representing a normal operation assignment. In order to include a normal operation
assignment in a MISLE, all the author has to do is create a copy of the building
block and specify the initial state for the assignment, the constraints and the target of
the assignment. E.g. for the assignment for flying the aeroplane to X, the author
specifies the position of the plane at the start of the assignment, the fact that the
height should be always greater than zero and the coordinates of the target position.

Apart from the details of a normal operation assignment, the author also has to
specify when the assignment may become active. This is done by attaching *enabling
conditions* to the assignments, which specify the state of the MISLE at which the
assignment can become active. MISLEs that are created with SMISLE 1.11 put most
initiative (for selecting assignments, asking explanations etc.) in the hands of the
learner. The only system initiative is the progression to a subsequent model level and
the activation of assignments and explanations. Although these actions are initiated
by the learner, the system may define minimum requirements that should be met (in
terms of achieved assignments) before a specific instructional measure may be
activated.

In Section 5.3 the tool (the instructional model editor) will be discussed which the author uses in the process of specifying instructional measures and the tool for specifying enabling conditions.

4.3 The learner model library

Since, as was explained in Section 4.2.5, in the current state of SMISLE most initiative is on the learner's side, SMISLE 1.11 only needs limited learner modelling capabilities. In the (near) future we foresee more sophisticated system initiative which partly will be based on a learner model. For creating this learner model a MISLE keeps a record of relevant events. These events fall in two main categories: interaction with the simulation and interaction with the instructional support. The history is recorded as a sequence of these events, but the data are also collected in more global records, like records of the number of variables varied, the total number of interactions etc. SMISLE enables the author to determine which of these events should be included in the learner model. Events that are recorded can be used for creating enabling conditions (see Section 5.3).

4.4 The interface model library

The learner interface communicates both the results of the simulation and the information regarding the instructional support to the learner. For this purpose there are six windows on a typical MISLE screen: one simulation window, four windows, each associated with one type of instructional support (model progression, assignments, explanations and hypothesis scratchpads) and a generic control window (see Figure 1). The four instructional measure windows display the current active instructional measure of the associated type and, if applicable, control the interaction of the learner with instructional support. So, the hypothesis scratchpad window allows the learner to state hypotheses, whereas the assignment window allows the learner to select assignment as well as provide answers to them. These windows are predefined and are not changed by the author and hence have no associated library in SMISLE. The same holds for the control window.

The interior of the simulation window is defined by the author, who can access a library of interface building blocks. The building blocks in this library are visible elements of a display which can be coupled to variables in the cognitive model. The SMISLE interface library includes graphs, tables, gauges, dials, thermometers, buttons, numerical displays, etc. Also, the author can import (static) graphics from other applications to be displayed in the interface window and create sequences of bitmaps to generate animations. In Section 5.5, the tools used to create the simulation interface and to access the library of interface building blocks are described.

5 BUILDING A MISLE

In Section 4 we have presented an overview of the generic building blocks an author has available. The present section describes the SMISLE toolkit that an author may use for browsing, inspecting, selecting and instantiating the building blocks, in this way creating the different models that together constitute a MISLE. First, we will describe how an author may browse, inspect and select building blocks from the libraries (Section 5.1) and then we will detail the dedicated editors for instantiating building blocks in the Sections 5.2 to 5.5. Finally, authors are supported in the SMISLE toolkit by an authoring methodology (Section 5.6) and pedagogical advice (Section 5.7)

5.1 Browsing, inspecting, and selecting building blocks

Building blocks that have been selected by the author can be specialised (by changing the value of specific slots) or instantiated (which means that domain variables are included in the building blocks). Authors have access to the libraries of building blocks for selecting a building block in three different ways. First, they can choose the option 'Create Cognitive ('Instructional', 'Learner', or 'Interface') Model', in which case they are presented with lists of relevant building blocks from which they may choose. Browsing building blocks is done by scrolling through the list. Second, authors may choose the option 'Libraries' in which case they are presented with a tree representation of all libraries with basic building blocks as the leaves of the tree. After selecting a basic building block (e.g. investigation assignment) the associated editor is shown so that the author may inspect the contents of the building block. Third, authors may perform a certain task by choosing the option 'Authoring', in which case they are shown a task decomposition in the form of a tree, of which basic tasks (e.g. create investigation assignment) form the leave ends.

5.2 Creating the cognitive model

The task of creating the cognitive model consists of taking building blocks from one of the three cognitive model libraries (functional block, petri-net, or operational) and linking these together. A network editor will soon be available for this (and the models will be displayed in formats similar to those of Figure 6 and 7), but in SMISLE 1.11 the cognitive model editor still has textual interfaces, one for each of the model types. Figure 9 displays the interface of the functional block editor. It provides a number of lists, displaying the building blocks present in the library, those already present in the conceptual model, the free terminals, the connected terminals and the links. The operational and petri-net editor for SMISLE 1.11 look similar but also have a list displaying the places present in the model.

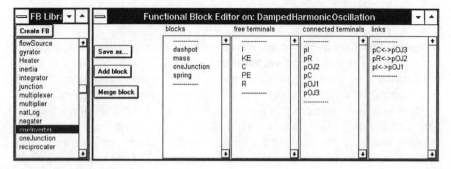

Figure 9 *The Functional block editor*

A building block is added by selecting it in the library, and pressing the 'Add Block' button. Then the terminals of this building block can be inspected, renamed, changed, and linked with a few mouseclicks. In the case of the petri-net based editors links can only be created between a terminal and a place or vice versa, in the functional block editor, terminals can be linked directly.

A functional block model can be compiled into a petri-net model. The compilation process is necessary for creating a runnable model, but it also allows the model to be edited further at the petri-net level. This can be useful to add functionality which the functional block formalism does not provide, such as discrete event simulation (see Section 4.1.1).

5.3   Creating the instructional model

Figure 10 shows the instructional model editor. This editor provides a number of lists which contain the instructional building blocks which already have been selected and instantiated by the author. The author can add an instructional building block by selecting it from the library. Then a *building block editor* can be opened on the building block selected.

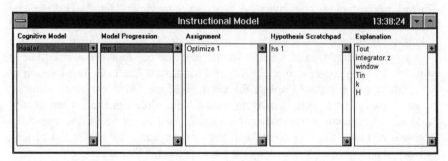

Figure 10 *The instructional model editor*

Figure 11 shows an example of a building block editor for a normal operation assignment which was discussed in Section 4.2.5. The building block editor allows authors to fill in the details of the instructional measure for their particular situation, in the case of the normal operation assignment: an initial state, constraints to hold during the performance of the assignment and a target state to signal successful behaviour.

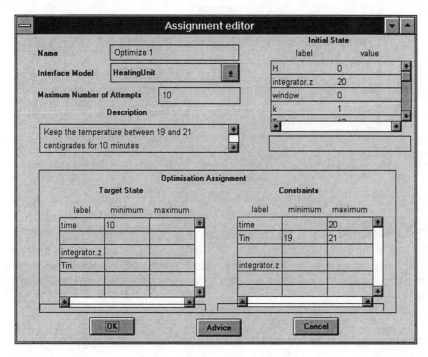

Figure 11 *Example of a dedicated building block editor*

For each type of instructional measure a dedicated building block editor is available. The general lay-out of all these editors is similar but, of course, they differ in the nature of the details to be filled in by the author.

Another task for the author is to specify the conditions under which the learner may select specific instructional measures. For example it may be specified that assignment B can only be selected after assignment A has been completed. A condition editor is available for this task. On this editor, the author can specify the state of instructional measures, which should hold at the moment the instructional measure may be activated, as a logical tree. Figure 12 shows a sequence of actions to define the enabling conditions for an instructional measure.

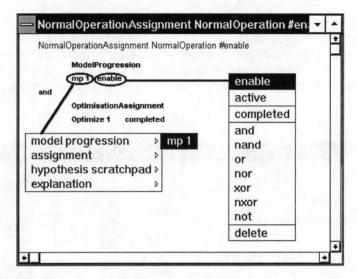

Figure 12 *The editor for creating enabling conditions*

5.4 Creating the learner model

The learner model itself is not created by the author him or herself, but evolves as a function of the behaviour of the learner. The only task for the author is to specify the event types that have to be recorded in the history of the MISLE-learner interaction. The author selects these event types from a complete list that is accessible from the SMISLE main menu.

5.5 Creating the interface model

For creating the interface model, or, more specifically, the interior of the simulation window, the interface editor of the Visualworks™ environment was reused, adapted, and extended. Figure 13 shows the editing screen that the author sees and uses. On the left the library of interface building blocks is displayed, on the right the simulation window that is being created. The author selects interface building blocks from the library and is able to position and size them with the mouse in the simulation window.

After an interface element has been added to the simulation window a *properties editor* can be opened on it in order to fill in the specific details of the building block (see Figure 14). The properties editor is the equivalent of the building block editor for the instructional model. The most important element to be edited in the properties editor is the link to the cognitive model: an interface element represents a variable in

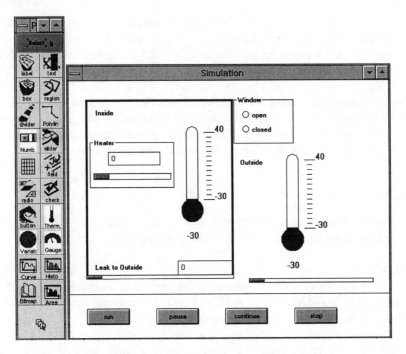

Figure 13 *The interface editor*

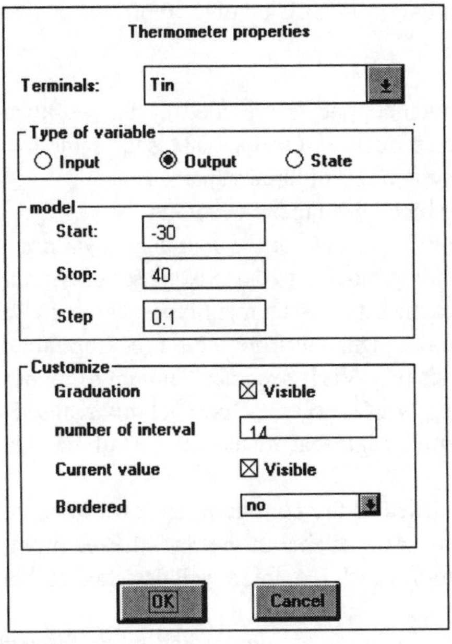

Figure 14 *An example of a properties editor*

the simulation. On the properties editor a list of variables in the cognitive model is automatically available from which the author may select. The properties editor is also used to specify properties like the minimum and maximum value for a slider, the properties of the axes of a graph, etc.

When the simulation window is completed it is installed in the MISLE, which means that the links with the cognitive model are instantiated and the simulation is ready to run. After installation it can immediately be tested, in which case the author sees and is able to interact with the simulation window as the learner will see it.

5.6 Methodology

From the previous sections it can be concluded that building a MISLE with the SMISLE environment is a complex task. This complexity addresses three levels:

- *Task level*
  At this level the author has to decide which general tasks will be performed. A general task is a larger unit of work that has some meaning for the author. It is assumed that the author plans the work of designing a MISLE at this level. A comprehensive task tree is identified that covers a wide range of author concerns. Examples of tasks are: determine low-level learning goals, configure instructional support, determine need for learning environment. Only a subset of these tasks can be carried out with the SMISLE environment, but it is important to represent the notion that building a MISLE involves more issues than those present in the workbench.
- *Configuration level*
  For those tasks which support is provided by the workbench, the author has to deal with a standard sequence of actions that is the same for all types of supported tasks. This sequence consists of three steps:
  ♦ select a building block from the relevant library;
  ♦ instantiate the building block for the domain and learner under consideration;
  ♦ integrate the building block into the existing set of building blocks.
  As an example take the set of assignment types shown in Table 2. The author has to select the required assignment from the set (e.g. optimisation), give 'names' to the abstract variables (e.g. $VarI_1$ becomes 'amount of money') and 'values' to the output variables (e.g. $VarO_1$ becomes 'product mix realised') and finally integrate them with the other elements that are already part of the MISLE.
- *Instrument level*
  The sequence identified at the configuration level must be carried out with the author instruments/tools available in the SMISLE environment. Thus the author has to master this tool, which requires a well designed author interface.

The goal of the methodology is to support and guide the author in mastering this complex task. This is mainly done by considering the entire authoring process as a kind of constrained design activity. The constraints involved are of different types that are linked to the levels described above:

- *Strategic constraints* are derived from 'common practice'. Authors have already been developing simulation systems for a long time and by tapping their expertise heuristics can be generated to steer the less experienced author. An example of such a heuristic is: if the target application is in an operational domain and the required fidelity level is high, work out the interface first before trying to instantiate instructional measures. The rationale for this heuristic is that what can be done with the interface may determine the content of the instructional model to a great extent. It is obvious that constraints of this type are offered to the author as suggestions that can be ignored. In the SMISLE project research is being carried out in order to discover the most salient heuristics.
- *Consistency constraints* that follow from the necessity to keep the MISLE that is being developed consistent. The author can effect changes in one component of a model that will lead to inconsistencies with the state of other models. As an example we can take the author who has decided on three levels of model progression but tries later in the authoring process to define assignments for four different levels. The SMISLE toolkit must check the work of the author for these unintended mistakes. It will give a 'warning' to the author, but will leave the correction to the author because it is conceivable that the author wants to have this inconsistency temporarily.
- *Logical constraints* arising from the dependencies between the models and the building blocks. Examples of these constraints are:
  - ♦ assignments can only be instantiated when a part of the domain model has been defined;
  - ♦ before implementing model progression the progression relations have to be identified in the cognitive model.

The main focus of the authoring methodology is on the constraints. Apart from these constraints the author also has to take into account pedagogical principles for designing educationally sound simulations. These will be most of the time related to specific properties of the domain and the target learners. These constraints are covered by author advice (see Section 5.7).

We have analysed the authoring task and produced initial task decomposition, based on interviews with experienced authors. This will result in a tailored process model for authoring that will act as a high level structure for guiding the work of the author. This process model can be seen as one of the 'top level drivers' of the SMISLE toolkit (see Section 5.1) as well as the 'watchdog' that focuses the constraints mentioned above. The methodology will become apparent to the author partly as a paper document, partly through constraints implemented in the SMISLE toolkit (through 'greying out' unavailable author actions) and partly as messages on the screen.

5.7 Pedagogical advice

The typical author using the SMISLE authoring toolkit is a domain expert who does not necessarily have programming and educational experience. To cope with the latter, the SMISLE toolkit includes an *advice* module. This module provides the author with hints and background information, necessary for making decisions on the choice and instantiation of instructional measures.

The SMISLE advice module consists of four main parts. The first part contains information on each of the individual instructional measures present in the SMISLE libraries. Each measure is explained in detail and specific situations in which the measures can be of use, as well as information necessary for instantiation are given.

The second part of the advice module takes the characteristics of the domain and target learner population as a starting point. The author provides the advice module with information concerning the specific situation (i.e. characteristics of the learners and the domain), on the basis of which the advice module generates suggestions for the selection of instructional measures. Figure 15 shows how the author can enter learner and domain characteristics.

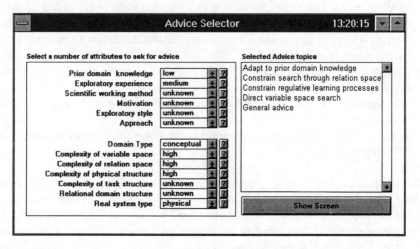

Figure 15 *The advice instructional measures dialogue screen*

The third part contains general background knowledge on discovery learning and simulations as a learning environment. Currently this module has about 150 screens on such topics as: characteristics of simulations, problems that learners encounter in discovery learning, theories of discovery learning, successful simulation projects etc. The rationale for including this module is that authors may want to learn more about the ideas behind SMISLE, both out of interest and for justifying their design decisions.

Finally, the advice module includes a glossary, containing definitions of terms that occur in the SMISLE toolkit. This glossary is accessible both as a separate module and from the positions in the advice module where the glossary terms occur.

Figure 16 presents a screendump from the SMISLE advice module where the author reads advice on a normal operation assignment.

The author has access to advice through a special advice option in the SMISLE main menu, but may also jump quickly to a relevant part of advice from any other part of the authoring process by selecting an 'advice' button.

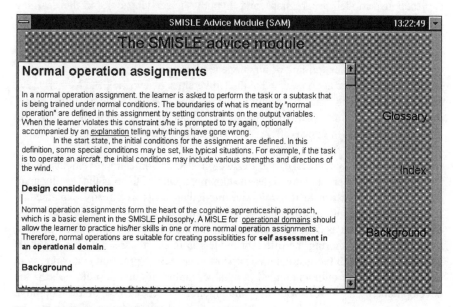

Figure 16 *View on the SMISLE advice module*

6 CURRENT STATUS AND FUTURE DEVELOPMENTS

In this paper we have described integrated simulation learning environments as they can be created with SMISLE 1.11, and the SMISLE toolkit 1.11 itself. As was pointed out, SMISLE 1.11 is an intermediate prototype of the SMISLE toolkit that was released at the end of the project in March 1995. At the moment two types of evaluation study with SMISLE 1.11 are carried out and the results will provide feedback for making improvements in the SMISLE toolkit.

The first type of evaluation studies concerns the authoring toolkit itself. Authors who differ in educational and domain expertise perform the complete authoring cycle with SMISLE 1.11 or are presented partial tasks (such as building the instructional support measures around an existing cognitive model). Data are gathered by logging the author's actions and by an in depth observation (through thinking aloud techniques and interviews) of the authoring process. These data will be used to get indications of unclarities and inconsistencies in the current prototype, and to assess the author's needs in order to decide upon improvements of the toolkit's functionality.

The second type of evaluation is an evaluation of MISLEs. A total of five experiments that basically aim at assessing the effectiveness and efficiency of MISLEs as compared to simulations not embedded in instructional support. Also, an assessment of the effect of the separate SMISLE support measures (assignments, explanations, model progression, and hypothesis scratchpads) on the learning process and resulting knowledge is being made. The domains that are included in this evaluation are three conceptual domains from physics (oscillatory motion, collision and transmission lines) and two operational domains (the start-up procedure of a hydrogen purification unit of an ethylene plant and the modelling of contacting bodies). Experiments are conducted at the Universities of Twente (The Netherlands), Murcia (Spain), and Kiel (Germany), and at Engineering Systems International (France) and Exxon (United Kingdom). Evaluation studies all follow an experimental set-up in which different MISLE arrangements are compared.

Regardless of the outcomes of the evaluation studies some improvements of the SMISLE prototype are already under development. One of them is the development of a graphical interface to the cognitive modelling tools as already explained in Section 5.2. A second improvement is the introduction of a more flexible sequence of authoring actions as defined at the task level described in Section 5.6. At present, the sequence of authoring the different models is fixed, it starts with the cognitive model and ends with the instructional support measures. A pre-pilot evaluation with a limited number of authors pointed out that a number of authors prefer to start the development of a MISLE with the simulation interface instead of the cognitive model. A so-called 'agenda mechanism' will be developed that allows for the introduction of 'dummy' variables in the interface that later on will be replaced by variables from the cognitive model. A third improvement is that we will provide the author with 'author instruments' that will assist the author in performing specific authoring tasks. At the moment such an instrument for analysing the domain for creating different forms of model progression is ready as a prototype and will be tested soon.

REFERENCES

Carlsen, D.D., & Andre, T. (1992). Use of a microcomputer simulation and conceptual change text to overcome students preconceptions about electric circuits. *Journal of Computer-Based Instruction, 19*, 105-109.

Cellier, F.E. (1991). *Continuous System Modeling*. Berlin: Springer-Verlag, 274-282.

Chinn, C.A., & Brewer, W.F. (1993). The role of anomalous data in knowledge acquisition: A theoretical framework and implications for science instruction. *Review of Educational Research, 63*, 1-51.

Collins, A., Brown, J.S., & Newman, S.E. (1989). Cognitive apprenticeship: Teaching the crafts of reading, writing, and mathematics. In L.B. Resnick (Ed.), *Knowing, learning, and instruction: Essays in honor of Robert Glaser.* Hillsdale, NJ: Lawrence Erlbaum.

Dunbar, K. (1993). Concept discovery in a scientific domain. *Cognitive Science, 17*, 397-434.

Faryniarz, J.V., & Lockwood, L.G. (1992). Effectiveness of microcomputer simulations in stimulating environmental problem solving by community college students. *Journal of Research in Science Teaching, 29*, 453-470.

Glaser, R., Raghavan, K., & Schauble, L. (1988). Voltaville, a discovery environment to explore the laws of DC circuits. *Proceedings of the ITS-88* (pp. 61-66). Montreal, Canada.

Grimes, P.W., & Wiley, T.E. (1990). The effectiveness of microcomputer simulations in the principles of economics course. *Computers & Education, 14*, 81-86.

Jong, T. de 1991). Learning and instruction with computer simulations. *Education & Computing, 6*, 217-229.

Jong, T. de, Andel, J. van, Leiblum, M., & Mirande, M. (1992). Computer assisted learning in higher education in the Netherlands, a review of findings. *Computers & Education, 19*, 381-386.

Jong, T. de, Hoog, R. de, & Vries, F. de (1992). Coping with complex environments: The effects of navigation support and a transparent interface on learning with a computer simulation. *International Journal of Man-Machine Studies, 39*, 621-639.

Jong, T. de, Joolingen, W.R. van, Pieters, J.M., Hulst, A. van der, & Hoog, R. de (1992). *Instructional support for simulations: overview, criteria and selection.* DELTA project SMISLE, Deliverable D02. University of Twente, Department of Education.

Jong, T. de, Tait, K., & Joolingen, W.R. van (1992). Authoring for intelligent simulation based instruction: a model based approach. In S.A. Cerri & J. Whiting (Eds.) *Learning Technology in the European Communities* (pp. 619-637). Dordrecht: Kluwer Academic Publishers.

Joolingen, W.R. van (1993). *Understanding and facilitating discovery learning in computer-based simulation environments.* PhD Thesis. Eindhoven: Eindhoven University of Technology.

Joolingen, W.R. van, & Jong, T. de (1991). Supporting hypothesis generation by learners exploring an interactive computer simulation. *Instructional Science, 20*, 389-404.

Joolingen, W.R. van, & Jong, T. de (1992). Modelling domain knowledge for Intelligent Simulation Learning Environments. *Computers & Education, 18*, 29-38.

Joolingen, W.R. van, & Jong, T. de (1993). Exploring a domain through a computer simulation: traversing variable and relation space with the help of a hypothesis scratchpad. In D. Towne, T. de Jong & H. Spada (Eds.) *Simulation-based experiential learning* (pp. 191-206). Berlin: Springer.

Karnopp, D.C., Margolis, D. L., & Rosenberg, R. C. (1990). *System Dynamics: A Unified Approach (2nd. Ed.)*. John Wiley & Sons.

Klahr, D., & Dunbar, K. (1988). Dual space search during scientific reasoning. *Cognitive Science, 12*, 1-48.

Leutner, D. (1993). Guided discovery learning with computer-based simulation games: effects of adaptive and non-adaptive instructional support. *Learning and Instruction, 3*, 113-132.

Njoo, M., & Jong, T. de (1993a). Exploratory learning with a computer simulation for control theory: Learning processes and instructional support. *Journal of Research in Science Teaching, 30*, 821-844.

Njoo, M. & Jong, T. de (1993b). Supporting exploratory learning by offering structured overviews of hypotheses. In D. Towne, T. de Jong & H. Spada (Eds.) *Simulation-based experiential learning* (pp. 207-225). Berlin: Springer.

Petersen, J. L. (1981). *Petri Net Theory and the Modeling of Systems*. Prentice-Hall.

Plötzner, R., & Spada, H. (1992). Analysis-based learning on multiple levels of mental domain representation. In E. de Corte, M. Linn, H. Mandl, & L. Verschaffel (Eds.) *Computer-based learning environments and problem solving* (pp. 103-129). Berlin: Springer.

Reimann, P. (1991). Detecting functional relations in a computerized discovery environment. *Learning and Instruction, 1*, 45-65.

Rivers, R.H., & Vockell, E. (1987). Computer simulations to stimulate scientific problem solving. *Journal of Research in Science Teaching, 24*, 403-415.

Scott, D., Hulst, A. van der, & Hoog, R. de (1992). *The Library Description Language*. DELTA deliverable, Project SMISLE (D2007). Edinburgh: Marconi Simulation.

Shute, V.J. (1991). *A comparison of learning environments: All that glitters ....* Paper presented at the American Educational Research Association (AERA) Annual Meeting, Chicago, USA.

Shute, V.J., & Glaser, R. (1990). A large-scale evaluation of an intelligent discovery world: Smithtown. *Interactive Learning Environments, 1*, 51-77.

Teodoro, V.D. (1992). Direct manipulation of physical concepts in a computerized exploratory laboratory. In E. de Corte, M. Linn, H. Mandl & L. Verschaffel (Eds.), *Computer-based learning environments and problem solving* (NATO ASI series F: Computer and Systems Series) (pp. 445-465). Berlin: Springer.

Wenger, E. (1987). *Artificial intelligence and tutoring systems: Computational and cognitive approaches to the communication of knowledge*. Los Altos, CA: Morgan Kaufmann.

White, B.Y., & Frederiksen, J.R. (1989). Causal models as intelligent learning environments for science and engineering education. *Applied Artificial Intelligence, 3(2-3)*, 83-106.

White, B.Y., & Frederiksen, J.R. (1990). Causal model progressions as a foundation for intelligent learning environments. *Artificial Intelligence, 42,* 99-157.

Acknowledgement: The work presented here is carried out under the DELTA programme of the EC as project D2007. We gratefully acknowledge the contributions of the following, present and former, colleagues from the project: Simon King, Daniel Delmas, Catherine Loprieno, Christian Canella, Jean-Marc Loingtier (Framentec-Cognitech), Anja van de Hulst, Michiel Kuiper, Bert Bredeweg (UvA), Jules Pieters, Janine Swaak, Frank van Doorn (UoT), Ken Horne, Joe Brough (Marconi), Jean-Louis Gregis, Andre Alusse, Christophe Janvier (ESI), Hermann Härtel (IPN), Ernesto Martin (Murcia). SMISLE 1.11 has been implemented by Andre Alusse, Christophe Janvier, Jean-Marc Loingtier, Wouter van Joolingen, and David Scott.

SAM, Simulation And Multimedia

Peter van Rosmalen

Research Institute for Knowledge Systems, Maastricht, The Netherlands

Abstract

In this paper we will present the SAM architecture in which a set of existing and SAM developed tools are offered to create and use advanced simulation-based learning environments. The aim of the SAM project is to specify and develop a modelling, authoring and learning framework based on state-of-the-art software tools. The framework will be completed with specific tools supporting the learner, the author and the modeller. An architecture based on using together a number of existing and specially developed tools has to deal with both a technical and a conceptual integration. SAM will do so by supporting the author in the creation of so-called Instructional Simulation Objects (ISO). ISOs are building blocks that allow for different levels of freedom ranging from fully system guided task exercises to learner controlled experiments. In this way the author can offer the right level of support to the learner at the appropriate time. With the help of a graphical editor the author writes a script both controlling SAM designed functions, e.g. monitoring or exchange of data, and external supplied functions, e.g. running a simulation model or a courseware. To the learner SAM will supply additional tools such as e.g. a Multimedia Notebook. SAM is developed in parallel on 2 platforms, i.e. on 80x86 PCs under Windows 3 and on Macintoshes under System 7. SAM will be evaluated by constructing and using simulations in two different domains: socio-economic and engineering. The model in the socio-economic domain describes the impact of climatic change on the socio-economic and socio-ecological systems of small island states in the Wider Caribbean. The engineering model is a simulation of a spacecraft equipment rack cooling system with a number of experiments in an onboard rack.

1 INTRODUCTION

The importance of simulations is widely appreciated. In many working areas simulations are used to support understanding by allowing for experimenting with different scenarios. Governments are enabled to assess implications of produced policies and to select suitable ones. SENSIM for instance uses simulation to support the planning of public policy for the West-African republic Senegal (Schutzelaars et al, 1994). For similar reasons, also in education and training, simulations are getting more and more popular for acquiring knowledge and skills in an active way.

However to fulfil an instructive role in a satisfactory manner, it is realised that simulations need to be embedded in an instructional environment. This embedding can be done by putting instructional support around the 'untouched' simulation (like

T. de Jong and L. Sarti (eds.), Design and Production of Multimedia and Simulation-based Learning Material, 167-187

a sandwich) or by interweaving the instructional support with the simulation itself (Van Berkum et al, 1991). The first option is only feasible if the learner can be expected to have enough domain knowledge to manage the simulation on his/her own. In most cases the second option must be chosen. This means that the simulation must be adapted by order of the author, who designs the actual support. Adaptation of the simulation requests an active involvement of a modeller, who knows the insides of the specific model. A fruitful dialogue between partners, probably both experts in their own areas of teaching and modelling, is needed.

At the moment there is a wide range of products available such as dedicated simulation environments, multimedia editors, hypertext and computer-based training tools. However, no tools are yet available for supporting the development of an intelligent multimedia simulation with an instructional intention in an integrated way. In Section 2, The SAM Environment, we will give an introduction into the SAM architecture in which a set of existing and SAM developed tools are offered to create and use advanced simulation-based learning environments. In Section 3, Technical Integration, we will elaborate on the technical aspects of this approach.

An architecture based on using together a number of existing and specially developed tools has to deal with both a technical and a conceptual integration. In Section 4, Authoring Support, we will discuss in detail how SAM intends to achieve this by supporting the author in the creation of so-called Instructional Simulation Objects (ISO). In addition we will discuss three other tools that we have planned to supply to the author, i.e. the Instructional Plan (IP) editor, the Concept Network (CN) editor and an editor to create the necessary data for the Monitor.

In Section 5, Learner Tools, we will discuss how users of a simulation-based learning environment can be supported by supplying them with additional tools. We will show one example of a tool we intend to supply in SAM, i.e. a Multimedia Notebook.

In Section 6 we will give an example of a course in population dynamics. In the final Section we will summarise our evaluation approach and discuss our current achievements and plans for the near future.

2 THE SAM ENVIRONMENT

The objective of this section is to introduce the architecture of the SAM authoring, modelling and learning framework. The architecture of SAM can be described from two perspectives, a technical and a conceptual one. The technical (or lower level) architecture describes how we intend to integrate different software packages and modules in one environment. The conceptual (or higher level) architecture describes the functionality of the different software packages or modules and their relations in the SAM environment.

2.1 Technical architecture

In the definition of the SAM architecture we use a bottom-up approach. We start with an integration of existing tools and we gradually add new facilities. This approach makes it possible at an early stage to both have a working environment with a sufficient level of functionality and test the technical integration of different software packages.

The first version of SAM concentrates on tool integration (cf. Figure 1). At development time the possible tools are e.g. a modelling and an authoring package. At both development and runtime the SAM Controller handles the communication and control between the different tools. This communication and control can be used to control e.g. the simulation in the following situations:

- demonstrating how to use the simulation;
- example runs;
- setting up a configuration of the simulation best suited for this learner / learning situation;
- setting up a specific initial state, e.g. for an exercise.

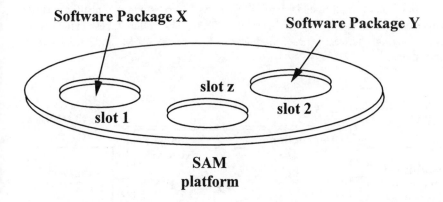

Figure 1 *The SAM slot-based architecture. An author fills the slots of his/her SAM environment by selecting from a list of SAM-compatible applications and SAM-developed modules.*

This SAM component will be generalised (see also Section 3, Technical Integration), so that it can be used for communication and control in general. For instance if one of the learner tools is a Multimedia Notebook, a communication component may be needed between this learner tool and the courseware and simulation. The SAM integration tools are also used for the integration of tools identified at higher level SAM architectures, i.e. including new tools implemented in the SAM project.

It is important to note that an author using the SAM environment first has to define his/her personal SAM environment. The author makes a selection, that is most appropriate to his/her wishes and experience, out of a list of SAM-compatible applications and SAM-developed modules.

2.2 Conceptual architecture

The technical architecture described above is the starting point for the higher level SAM architecture. It allows us to integrate existing and newly defined tools in one environment. There are already a lot of powerful software tools to develop the different components of simulation-based learning environments exist, e.g. authoring and simulation packages and multimedia editors. Our contribution is to add those modules that make these components useful in a simulation-based learning context. The most important modules (cf. Figure 2) we intend to add are the following. An Instructional Plan (IP) module to define the learning space and guide the student through it. A Concept Network (CN) module to enable the author and modeller to specify the model and its role in a course. An Instructional Simulation Object (ISO) module to enable the author to design and execute simulation specific instructional sequences. A Monitor module to watch the use and the behaviour of the simulation and finally additional learner tools to support specific learner requirements. Invisible to the user the SAM Controller takes care of all communication between these modules and between SAM and the external applications.

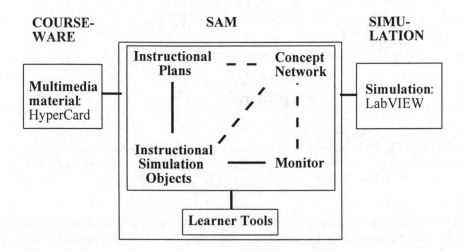

Figure 2 *SAM authoring components selected and developed in one of the SAM prototypes.*

SAM organises the design and development of a course in three layers. External applications and SAM-developed modules contribute to this in the following way.

At the top layer, course and model are defined and the use of the model inside the course. An instructional planner (Wallsgrove, 1991a) tries to optimise the learning process by figuring out what to teach, when and how to teach it. A study advisor (Koehorst, 1992) does a similar job, however it will not make a final conclusion on what, how and when. It merely gives the user an advice of all the current opportune possibilities. The user him/herself may then decide. Both depend on the same information (a.o. information on the learning goals to be achieved and the state of the learner model) and have an equally complex task (i.e. deciding on a large number of knowledge sources, part of which changes dynamically). The Instructional Plan module in SAM is a simplified version of a study advisor. In the instructional plan editor the author describes the learning goals of a course and the instructional plans how to achieve them in terms of instructional objects. The author can specify alternative paths through a course. The learner will, depending on his/her individual profile, gain access to one path. The learner controls his/her progress with the Instructional Plan Browser. The CN-editor is a design tool. It enables the author and modeller to specify the model to be used, its role in the courseware and to prepare the technical integration of the simulation into the course.

At the next layer we specify activities or so-called Instructional Objects (IO), for example an exercise or a demo. A special group of IOs are Instructional Simulation Objects (ISO). An ISO is an IO that integrates the use of a simulation and courseware. With the help of the ISO-editor the author can specify simulation specific instructional sequences such as demo run, task exercise, experiment set-up or free exploration. In the same layer the author specifies the data for the monitor. One of the main objectives of SAM is to enhance simulation-based learning systems with adaptive learning facilities. To enable this a first prerequisite is a Monitor. Monitoring in the context of simulation-based learning environments means recognising patterns and sequences of learner actions and/or state changes of the simulation. We will use an approach similar to projects like MATIC (Wallsgrove, 1991b) and ITSIE (Ravn, 1991), which use an explicit representation (expected behaviour) of learner actions and state-changes. The Monitor classifies the actual learner behaviour by comparing it with this expected behaviour. The outcome can be used to supply e.g. additional feedback to the user.

Finally, at the last layer the simulation and all necessary multimedia material are developed. This will be done in the applications the author and/or modeller finds most appropriate.

In addition to directive (author initiated) support, SAM will supply tools the learner has free access to. One example is the above mentioned Instructional Plan Browser. Other examples are a tool to perform a further analysis on the data supplied by the simulation and a tool to support the student in producing a multimedia report of their learning.

3 TECHNICAL INTEGRATION

The SAM slot-based architecture (cf. Figure 1) is based on the assumption, that it is possible with the current state of the major operating systems to communicate between different applications that run simultaneously.

Dynamic Data Exchange (DDE) (Microsoft Software Development Kit, 1990) of MS-Windows 3 is a protocol for generalised inter-application messaging. It can pass information directly from one application to another. The mechanism is appropriate for sending messages and for passing data. A similar protocol exists on the Macintosh under System 7 (Apple Computer, 1991). It is the AppleEvents standard. It allows any application to activate other applications, to send messages and data to these applications and to handle data arriving from other applications.

To hide for the author the complexity of these protocols and the package dependent technical details, the following two elements will be defined for each slot:

• a slot-related command language used to control the software package from SAM;
• a Control & Communication (C&C) table which contains a translation of the slot-related commands into package-specific commands at runtime and a list of all accessible data in the package.

In the case of a simulation-related slot, the language allows the author to develop short programs used for instance to load a specific model or set some initial parameters. These programs (cf. Figure 3) are translated into package-specific sequences of commands according to the appropriate C&C table and executed by SAM.

4 AUTHORING TOOLS

Ideally the development system of SAM should provide the following types of support:

• user-friendly editors to enter the necessary data;
• context sensitive advice from an instructional design knowledge base;
• provide early feedback during design and implementation phases by means of 'symbolic execution'.

The development system should support the whole life cycle of an instructional simulation. In practice we mainly concentrated on the editors. In particular tools supporting the analysis, design and implementation, especially when information from the analysis and design phases can be re-used in the implementation phase. A largely paper-based methodology will provide the overall framework and glue for author and modeller to work with.

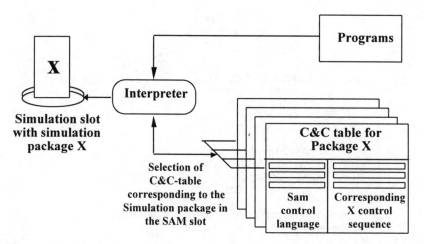

Figure 3 *Runtime interpretation and execution of programs controlling the Simulation Package.*

In the following sections we will discuss four examples of such tools (cf. also Figure 2), i.e. the Instructional Plan (IP) editor, the Concept Network (CN) editor, the Instructional Simulation Object (ISO) editor and the Monitor editor.

4.1 Instructional Plans

The design of a course is a complex task. SAM tries to support this task by decomposing it into manageable sub-tasks, i.e. a course is decomposed into pieces that can be designed more easily. The resulting decomposition can be easily inspected and modified by the author or his/her colleagues. A special representation of the decomposition can be offered to the student as a navigation tool through the course space.

The IP-editor uses Learning Goals, Instructional Plans and Instructional Objects to constitute a course (cf. Figure 4). A course is decomposed in Learning Goals. Each Learning Goal is linked to one or more Instructional Plans which describe different ways to achieve the same Learning Goal. Each of the Instructional Plans in its turn is decomposed into Instructional Objects and/or Learning Goals. A course specification is supposed to be ready when all Learning Goals can be achieved by a set of Instructional Objects.

Learning Goals, Instructional Plans and Instructional Objects can be specialised by attributes. There are two types of attributes. The first type describes the learner, e.g. his/her prerequisite knowledge or preferred learning style. The second can be used to constrain the order, e.g. Learning Goal 1 has to be achieved before Learning Goal 2. The author him/herself defines the attributes of the first type. Together with the attribute the author has to define the valid set of values.

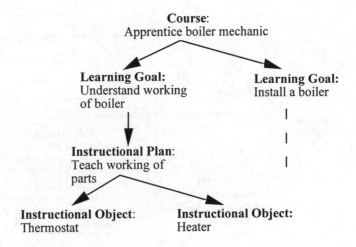

Figure 4 *The course 'Apprentice boiler mechanic' decomposed in Learning Goals, Instructional Plans and Instructional Objects.*

Each student is assigned a Learner Profile. This profile can be an individual or a group profile. It contains the attributes, the author has defined, and a value for each of them. Based on the profile the IP-module compiles an individual course plan. The learner controls the course space with the Instructional Plan Browser (cf. Figure 5). The Instructional Plan Browser displays his/her progress with the status symbols seen, not seen, finished.

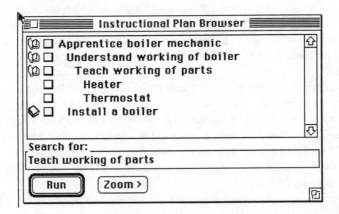

Figure 5 *The Instructional Plan Browser of the course 'Apprentice boiler mechanic'.*

4.2 Concept Network

In SAM we assume that a simulation-based learning environment is developed by at least two different specialists: an author and a modeller. The author is responsible for the overall design and development of the course. The modeller is responsible for the technical specification and the development of a runnable model.

The global design of a model is a collaborative job for author and modeller. The objective is to support the development of a learning environment. Therefore the chosen point of departure is the viewpoint of the author. Author and modeller may have very different viewpoints. The author is mainly interested in what can be learned from the domain and its concepts. The usefulness of a model is determined by its ability to clarify important domain concepts, showing their changes in time in relation with other concepts. These changes must be visualised during a simulation run. Modellers are more interested in an executable model, which is a reliable domain representation. A candidate model for integration must contain the concepts the author wants to teach and a mapping between these concepts and the parameters and/or variables of the model must be possible. In addition the author wants to have easy access to valid initial settings, available operations and such.

The exchange of information can be done by a direct meeting, but also, as we propose, by the creation of Concept Networks (Hensgens et al, 1993). Representations similar to the concept networks have been implemented or are suggested for authors and modellers to support their work (e.g. the PSAUME interface in AAT, 1991). The CN-editor supports the specification of a model and its use in a course. It does this by structuring the necessary author-modeller communication. In addition the CN-editor supports the technical integration of the model in the course.

Specification
A Concept Network is a description of a model and its use inside a course. The author visualises the concepts from the domain of instruction, which he/she wants to show in a simulation by putting these concepts (nodes) and their relations (arcs) in a network. The author can add comments to both nodes and arcs to describe his/her ideas. The complexity of a model can be very high, in which case the author can decide to dose the complexity. The author can define different abstraction levels (cf. Figure 6). These abstraction levels, called views, are sub-networks of the complete network. In his/her turn the modeller is invited to look for the existence or realisation of a model, which fits into these requirements. If this is not possible he/she changes the concept network by editing the network or by giving comments. The CN-editor supports the discussion by giving different visual feedback to proposed, rejected or accepted nodes and arcs. The final network is used by the author to support the technical integration of the model into the course. The modeller uses it as a global specification for a model to be developed or selected.

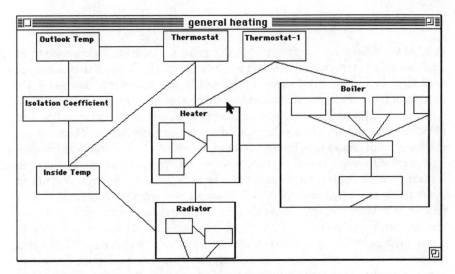

Figure 6 *A concept network of the heating system created with the CN- editor. The boiler is an example of a view. Part of its internal structure is shown inside the node. The complete structure can be seen after a zoom-in action.*

Integration
Once the modeller has developed or selected a model, that fits the specified concept network, the integration can start. The integration has two parts. The first part is the integration of SAM with the runnable model. This consists of linking the nodes of the concept network to the list of variables published by the model. The second part is the integration of the model in the course. This is prepared in the CN-editor and finalised in the ISO-editor. The CN-editor supports the specification of different views on the model. Connected to a view the specification of initial configurations is possible. The author can connect a view and its initial configuration to an ISO. At execution time the chosen view determines what part of the model will be accessible. In this way the author can create different learning contexts or manage the complexity of the model.

4.3   Defining data for the monitor

Monitoring in the context of SAM means recognising sequences of learner actions and/or state changes of the simulation. The monitor process we use, is based on an explicit representation (expected behaviour) of learner actions and state-changes. The author specifies in advance the behaviour he/she is interested in. At runtime the Monitor compares the actual behaviour with the pre-specified behaviour. The author can use the result of the Monitor for example to provide the learner with additional state feedback, recognise a good opportunity to tell the learner something new or provide active task support.

Specification

Expected behaviour (cf. Figure 7) is represented as a combination of tasks (representing possible goals learners might pose themselves in a given context), and plans, which represent the way learners think the task can be accomplished. A plan can be correct and efficient, but also inefficient or even wrong. A plan consists of a set of sub-tasks and a control structure (a block). The control structure (cf. Figure 8) contains Boolean options like 'ordered' and 'optional' and 'before', 'during' and 'after' conditions which have to be fulfilled. The decomposition halts at the time 'posed' primitive events are encountered. An event is the smallest unit, which has a meaning in the concerning domain. (Note: an event can represent an action of the learner on the model but also a state change of the model).

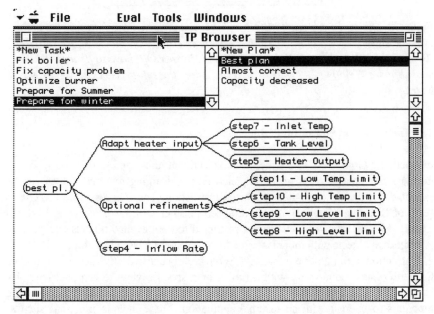

Figure 7 *The TP-browser is the top-level task-plan editor. From here the author can create, edit, delete and find any part of the task-plan hierarchy. In the edit-window one of the three plans ('best plan') for the selected task ('prepare for winter') is shown.*

The use of the Monitor

The specified task-plans are used in the ISOs. An ISO can request the Monitor to start monitoring a number of pre-specified tasks. Based on the assumption that a plan is recognised, the author can specify any appropriate instructional action. At runtime the Monitor informs the ISO, when it recognises a plan of one of the tasks. Subsequently the ISO can execute the specified action.

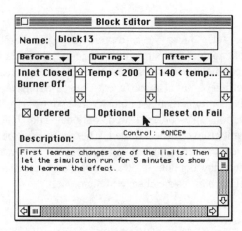

Figure 8 *The block-editor. With a block the author specifies the required control over the sub-tasks of a plan. The sub-tasks under control of 'block13' are 'ordered'. 'Before' the sub-tasks start 'Inlet Closed' and 'Burner Off' have to be true. 'During' the sub-tasks 'Temp < 200' has to be true. 'After' the sub-tasks '140 < temp' has to be true.*

4.4   Instructional Simulation Objects

Instructional Objects (IOs) are the basic educational units used to develop a course. Each IO is a specification of a complete piece of learning material, which can be executed during the computer supported instruction. The IOs resemble the ULMs (Unit of Learning Material) as they are used in other DELTA projects (AAT Final Report, 1991). However they are not restricted to one-levelled objects and provide instructional objects with more (intermediate) levels (MATIC Final Report, 1991).

Instructional Simulation Objects (ISOs) are specialised IOs using simulation. Each ISO has a connection with a model or a specific view to a model (see also Section 4.2, Concept Network). ISOs are defined with structured scripts containing functions to interact with an external simulation. These include functions such as start, stop, init, pause, get-value, set-value etcetera. In addition there are functions that enable communication with the other modules selected in a specific SAM set-up. They include e.g. functions to communicate with the Monitor and functions to invoke IOs. Finally, there are functions to enhance the structure of ISOs. Depending on the type of learning goal and the instructional strategy, ISOs are used in combination with other IOs like introduction, multiple choice, feedback, presentation, motivation and question, to teach the learning goal.

ISOs are subdivided into five basic subgroups, namely: Demo, Task, Hypothesis, Experiment and Exploration. Before discussing the ISO-editor we will give a short description of these subgroups.

The *Demo* using the simulation shows developments and behaviour of the modelled domain in time. The student is able to notice various effects and relationships between different concepts simply by monitoring the ongoing simulation. This makes simulation very useful in any learning environment. The perception and active processing of domain knowledge can be expected to be more efficient in the perspective of the learning objectives than a passive textual description. Apart from this the concerning learning material is often easier to understand, for instance by seeing the development of a complex relation between different concepts instead of reading a (often tedious and abstract) textual description.

In a *Task* the learner is asked to solve a specified problem. The task is used to assess the learner's knowledge or to exercise. The execution of the task is monitored and additional comments (IOs) are given when special situations are encountered. Comments can be used to guide the learner through the problem space, to give appraisal, critics or to clarify found misconceptions. The monitoring is enabled by an explicit representation of the solution processes.

A *Hypothesis* (van Joolingen & de Jong, 1991) is a description of an expected relation between two or more concepts in the domain and it can be formulated in a generic way as an IF-THEN statement. The availability of simulation in the course enables a dynamic and extensive use of hypotheses. The ideal situation would be if the learners could specify their hypothesis interactively, e.g. a question and an answer, run the simulation and thus be able to evaluate it with the found results.

An *Experiment* is a structured way to explore the model and it can be formulated with a generic WHAT-IF statement. The experiment can be used as preceding exercises for hypothesis generation. In an experiment learners specify the experimental concept(s) and their action(s). This must be matched to the initial simulation settings. The simulation is started and the run is used to discover existing effects of the experimental start situation and/or dependencies between different concepts. The experience gained by the learners during experimentation should help with the specification of useful hypotheses.

Exploration gives the learners the opportunity to play around with the simulation. The learners have full control over the model (or over part of the model). The exploration can be divided into two subgroups: free- and guided-exploration. The free-exploration must be done without any active support or guidance. The guided-exploration can give feedback on events of interest, as they are predefined by the author.

So far we concentrated on the editors to specify Demo, Task, and Explore. These three types can be created with the help of two editors. The general set-up of the ISO is created with the ISO-editor. The required details of monitoring can be inserted with the help of the Monitor editor.

The ISO-editor

The ISO-editor provides a complete environment to enable authors to design, edit and test ISOs. The ISO-editor represents an ISO graphically as a flowchart. Nodes in the flowchart represent functions and they are created via the toolbar. The toolbar displays a list of functions and modules. By selecting a function the author creates a node with an instance of this function. Selecting a module activates a sub-palette. From the sub-palette the author can select a function belonging to the module, e.g. load, init and pause for the simulation. A node can be dropped anywhere on the existing flowchart. The dropped node is inserted automatically at the closest valid location in the flowchart. The flowchart is automatically drawn. Next, the author has to enter the information to allow for successful execution of the selected function. This information will vary from simple slot filling, defining the application to be loaded, to the definition of complex branching conditions based on the results of the Monitor. Filling a slot will normally be done by selecting from a list of options or items. E.g. selecting a variable from a list of available variables. This to make the editing process as convenient as possible and to ensure the correctness of the created program as much as possible in advance.

In Figure 9 an example is given of the ISO-editor. To the left the toolbar has been drawn with all available functions and active modules of the used SAM environment. Active means it includes the modules the author has selected to use in the current course. The modules are partly SAM defined tools, i.e. the Monitor (the pig icon) and partly tools based on external applications, i.e. the Simulation (the boiler icon) and the Courseware (the stack icon). Just beneath the toolbar the sub-palette with the functions of the boiler-simulation is shown. The flowchart of the ISO 'inlettempchanged' contains five nodes. First, the simulation is resumed (RESUM) and the Monitor is activated with a number of tasks (INSTA). The learner can now start his/her work. As soon as the Monitor recognises a plan it informs the ISO. In case it is plan 'PL1' a value of the simulation is changed (SET-V), otherwise the ISO invokes an IO.

5 LEARNER TOOLS

Supplementary to the support given to the learner by means of a careful design of the course (e.g. introducing a model from simple to complex) and author initiated guidance based on the use of the Monitor, we also intend to enrich the learning environment with learner tools that are to be at a learners free disposal.

These tools cover (one of) the following needs of the learner:

- To obtain assistance in operating the simulation, courseware, learner tools and in understanding the domain knowledge or skill (help facilities);
- To analyse and explore interim and final results from a simulation. This will be facilitated by exporting information from the simulation and/or courseware application into one or more learner tools. The results of analysing such information in one application may be transferred to another application for further analysis;
- To export information from a learner tool to a simulation (e.g. revised starting conditions) or to the courseware (e.g. to answer a question posed by the courseware).

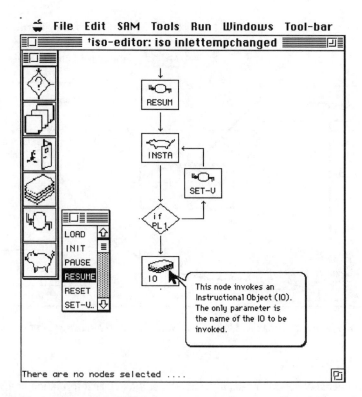

Figure 9 *The window of the ISO-editor, its menu bar, a toolbar and a sub-palette, the flow chart of an ISO and balloon-help.*

To produce a hard copy or multimedia reports as personal records of their learning (note taking) or for formative or summative evaluation of learning (testing).

As an example we will briefly introduce one of the learner tools we are working at, i.e. the Multimedia Notebook (cf. Figure 10). This application can support the learner in the following ways:

- As an aid to short term memory: Either by copying information from the courseware or other applications to be referred to later in a learning session or by keying in their own thoughts for later reference;
- As an aid to long term memory: Copying, changing or creating information usually to be printed or stored on disk for use after the learning session;
- As an aid to understanding: Creating their own representation of the learning material. This could involve text, graphical representations of knowledge, equations, tables, speech or combinations of these formats;
- As an aid to communicating: The Multimedia Notebook is seen as the normal document within which communications will be transmitted to the teacher and other learners.

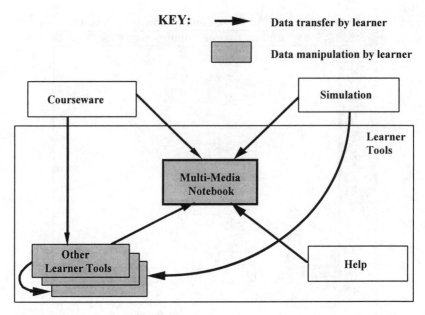

Figure 10 *The position of the Multimedia Notebook in the learner configuration of SAM.*

The Multimedia Notebook needs to be able to pull together information in a variety of forms from the courseware, the simulation, any help facilities and from any other learner tools, including e.g. texts, graphics, numbers, sounds or movies.

6 AN EXAMPLE COURSE IN SAM

SAM will be evaluated by constructing and using simulations in two different domains: socio-economic and engineering. In the socio-economic domain we use a model of an island. The model (Engelen et al, 1993) was developed for UNEP (United Nations Environment Programme) to study the impact of climatic change on the socio-economic and socio-ecological systems of small island states in the Wider Caribbean Region. The model consists of two levels: at one level the socio-economic growth of the island is modelled (macro-scale dynamics), at the other level this growth is distributed over the small cells the island consists of (micro-scale dynamics). The two levels are clearly recognisable in the interface of the island application (cf. Figure 11). All elements of both levels can be made accessible. However, in the course being made we will concentrate on population dynamics, i.e. the social sub-system of the macro-scale dynamics.

The SAM set-up in which the course is built, consists at the moment of the following modules. Authorware (Authorware® Professional™ 2.0) as an authoring

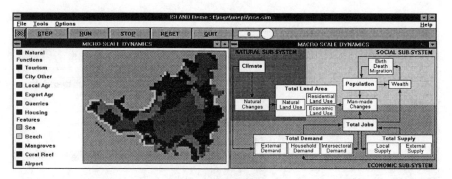

Figure 11 *The interface to the island simulation. At the top is the Control Panel and the menu-bar with which you control the simulation. At the left is the window displaying the micro-scale dynamics, i.e. the land-use on the island and how it evolves in time. At the right is the window depicting a graphical representation of the macro-scale dynamics. It shows the three sub-systems, their variables (as boxes) and the most important loops (as arrows). By clicking the boxes you get access to relevant variables and parameters for that part of the model.*

package, the island model as the simulation, Excel (Microsoft Excel 4.0) as a learner tool (a prediction analyser), the ISO-module to create and run ISOs, and in the background the SAM controller to take care of all communication and control between the modules. The set-up runs on a 80486 PC under MS-windows 3.1.

So far the course contains a theoretical part and an exercise. The theoretical part consists of a sequence of screens explaining the principles of population dynamics applied in the simulation. It was made with Authorware. The exercise aims to test the learner's understanding by asking him/her to make a prediction on the population growth in given circumstances. The exercise was defined with the help of the ISO-editor and it makes use of all the modules in this set-up.

The author defines a script in the ISO-editor to create the exercise. At runtime the script is executed under the control of the learner. The script (cf. Figure 12) contains the following:

- Introduction. In this item the author defines the link to an introduction in Authorware. In the introduction the objective of the exercise is explained and the necessary instructions are given;
- Initialisation. In this block the author defines the initial state of the simulation for this exercise.
- While (Iteration < 20). In this block the simulation is started and for each simulation step (a year) the population is retrieved and displayed in a graph produced by EXCEL;
- Generate Prediction. In this block the Prediction Generator (cf. Figure 13) is activated in which the learner can enter his/her prediction for the next 20 years.

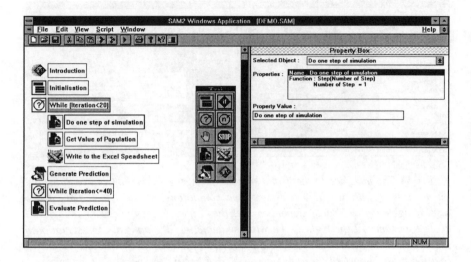

Figure 12 *A script built with the ISO-editor (the MS-windows version). At the left side of the window you see the complete script. At the right you see the editor of the 'Do one step of the simulation'.*

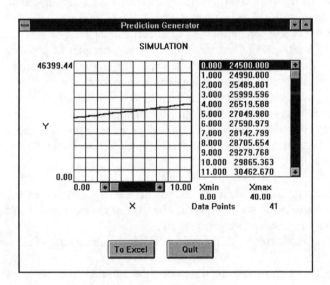

Figure 13 *The Prediction Generator in which the learner gives a prediction on the expected population growth in the next 20 years.*

The learner can do this by direct manipulation in the drawing area or by typing in the numbers;
- While (Iteration < 40). In this block the simulation is resumed and for each simulation step the population is retrieved and displayed in a graph produced by EXCEL. The learner can now compare his/her prediction and the actual simulated values;
- Evaluate Prediction. In this item a macro is activated in EXCEL. The macro compares the prediction with the actual simulated values. Based on the outcome of this comparison additional feedback can be given.

7 CONCLUSIONS AND FUTURE DIRECTIONS

In the first phase of the project we have defined and developed a working version of SAM. The actual implementation shows that it is possible to develop a simulation-based learning environment based on both existing and specially defined software. We offer the developer not only the tools to support the design phase, i.e. the definition of a course, the collaborative design of a model and the definition of individual Instructional Simulation Objects, but we also offer the developer a tool to enlarge the potential use of a simulation in a simulation-based learning environment, i.e. the Monitor. By realising a number of examples of SAM environments, we showed how an author can compose a SAM environment based on his/her own personal preference or experience.

Doing this was possible only because we showed that it is technically feasible to run and use multiple applications simultaneously. We have experienced that the used operating systems (System 7.1 and MS-Windows 3.1) offer the technical possibility to run together multiple applications and dynamically exchange information. However, only very few applications fully support all the necessary features. Therefore we still need a number of ad hoc interventions. Fortunately most of these ad hoc interventions can either be completely hidden or inserted with the help of predefined dialogs.

At the moment a first formative evaluation is made by constructing small courses in two different domains, socio-economic and engineering. Based on our experiences a further evaluation will be carried out within the context of a postgraduate course in Interactive Training Systems. This evaluation will cover the development and the learner perspective.

In the next phase of SAM the objective is to elaborate on the current version. First, we have to standardise and stabilise what we have achieved so far. Second, we intend to elaborate on the functionality and ease of use of the SAM environment. To guide this, there are three categories of inputs. The first source of input is the result of the evaluation of the current version. This should help us to validate our assumptions and, where necessary, adjust our plans. The second is the expertise gained with building the current version. With the help of this expertise we should be capable to indicate what issues are of major concern and to estimate what is realistic to try to achieve. Third, we recognise that our starting assumption, i.e. using existing software packages, is very market dependent. Therefore we have to continuously take into consideration the overall market development. This covers development or changes in general software standards as well as new applications coming to the market due to the efforts of other institutes or companies.

Based on the current results and the above discussed inputs we will make a second version of SAM. The result should be an environment that significantly facilitates the use and development of simulation-based learning environments and that is available to be evaluated or used by a larger audience.

REFERENCES

AAT (1991). *Final Report on Advanced Authoring Tools*. DELTA Project 1010.

Apple Computer, Inc (1991), *System 7 Reference Manual*. Apple Computer, Inc.

Berkum, J.J.A. van, Byard, M.J., & Tait, K. (1991). Formalisation of instructional support in intelligent simulation learning environments. In T. de Jong & K. Tait (Eds.), *Towards formalising the components of an intelligent simulation learning environment*. DELTA Project 1014.

Engelen, G., White, R., & Uljee, I. (1993). Exploratory modelling of socio-economic impacts of climatic change. In: G.A. Maul (Ed.), *Climatic Change in the Intra-Americas Sea*. London: Edward Arnold.

Hensgens, J., Rosmalen, P. van, & Baaren, J. van der (1993). Simulations in Courseware. In *Proceedings of the Seventh International PEG conference 93* (pp. 210-223), Edinburgh: Heriot-Watt University.

Joolingen, W.R. van, & Jong, T. de (1991). *An Hypothesis Scratchpad as a Supportive Instrument in Simulation Learning Environments*. Section 4 of SAFE report SIM/23 under DELTA Contract D1014.

Koehorst, A. (1992). *Gericht leren in een exploratieve omgeving, een case study voor SOLA*. RIKS internal report 92-12-076.

MATIC (1991). *Final Report on Multi-strategy Authoring Toolkit for Intelligent Courseware*. DELTA Project 1009.

Microsoft Software Development Kit: Guide to Programming (1990).

Ravn, F. (October 1991). *ITSIE Monitor Taxonomy*, CRI/ITSIE/016. ESPRIT Project 2615.

Schutzelaars, A., Engelen, G., Uljee, I., & Wargnies, S. (1994). Computer systems that enhance the productivity of public-sector planners. *International Journal for Public Administration, 17 (1)*, 119-153.

Wallsgrove, R. (Ed.) (1991a). *Instructional Planning*. In Final specifications for the MATIC system, MATIC-deliverable 3.8.3.

Wallsgrove, R. (Ed.) (1991b). *Interpretation of complex learner action patterns*. In Final specifications for the MATIC system, MATIC-deliverable 3.8.3.

Acknowledgements: The work described in this paper has been undertaken in DELTA Project D2010 - SAM. The project is partly supported by the C.E.C. under the DELTA programme. DELTA aims to research, develop and provide a series of technology-based flexible training solutions.

SAM is developed by a consortium composed of the following partners:

- Research Institute for Knowledge Systems (NL) (Main Contractor);
- Computer Resources International A/S (DK) (Partner);
  (with Dornier GmbH (G) as associated partner);
- University of Surrey (UK) (Partner);
- INSEAD (FR) (Partner).

The contents of this paper are based on the deliverables:

Rosmalen, P. van (Ed.) (1992). SAM Definition Study. Report to the European Commission - DELTA Project D2010.

Rosmalen, P. van (Ed.) (1992). SAM Design and Specification. Report to the European Commission - DELTA Project D2010.

Rosmalen, P. van (Ed.) (1993). SAM Version 1 Report. Report to the European Commission - DELTA Project D2010.

COLOS: Conceptual Learning Of Science

Hermann Härtel

IPN - Institute for Science Education, University Kiel, Germany

Abstract

The COLOS group was founded in 1988 and today consists of 10 working groups from universities in seven European countries. COLOS stands for 'Conceptual Learning Of Science' and reflects our major goal: to use the potential of modern technology to improve knowledge and understanding of basic concepts in science and technology with a special focus on intuitive and qualitative approaches. A general idea behind the COLOS project was to stimulate the production and use of software for education at university level. Following a bottom-up approach, a group of motivated people from different fields in science and technology were brought together and equipped in such a way that, within a common frame work, different software packages could be developed to meet local needs for teaching and research (Härtel, 1990a; Härtel, 1993). By intensive use of network communication and semi-annual project meetings, the members have moved towards general solutions and cooperative actions. A set of tools to support the production of computer assisted teaching/learning material and a series of software packages on a variety of topics have been developed and will be evaluated during the near future.

1 INTRODUCTION

The exploitation of the didactical potential of modern technology for teaching within COLOS is focused around two topics: tool development and application development.

The tool development is aimed at providing teachers as field experts (with a minimum of programming expertise) access to a programming environment offering a maximum of support with a minimum of restrictions for the implementation of specific ideas in computer assisted teaching/ learning.

To find a balance between these two partly conflicting demands is one of our major concerns. In Section 2 this tool development is outlined in more detail. The second focus is related to application development serving the following goals:

- to increase the visibility of the didactical potential of this technology by demonstrating the state of the art of computer assisted teaching/learning material;
- to aid in actual teaching to provide an increase of efficacy and effectiveness of the learning process;
- to serve as a stimulus and support for individual teachers willing to develop and implement new and fruitful ideas in this field.

189

T. de Jong and L. Sarti (eds.), Design and Production of Multimedia and Simulation-based Learning Material, 189-217
© 1994 *Kluwer Academic Publishers. Printed in the Netherlands.*

The general aspects related to this application development are specified in Section 3. Questions related to evaluation procedures are treated in Section 4 while a list of all COLOS products with a broader description of some typical examples can be found at the end of this paper together with a list of the COLOS sites and contacts addresses.

2 TOOL DEVELOPMENT

Experience shows a great reluctance of many teachers to the use of software in their teaching, especially if it is a foreign, 'out-of-house' product.

As well as the usual conservative structure of the educational sector, the reasons for this reluctance may be seen as follows:

- In general it is a risk to one's professional status to use a complex medium which one does not fully understand. Teachers in their exposed role as experts will not take this risk unnecessarily and therefore they will neither use complex off-the-shelf products nor easily accept tools developed by someone else;
- Teachers have a strong desire to give their presentation a personal look and feel, enabling them to concentrate on the content and on didactics and pedagogy instead of forms and models of presentation;
- Most software has been developed for widely available and less powerful platforms as found today in many schools. The look, feel and functionality of these products reflects these limitations. Teachers may be reluctant to get involved with a still developing medium, waiting for standards to stabilise.

A first decision taken within COLOS to overcome these barriers was to use standards like X and Motif to guarantee a lasting value of investments. Second, it was decided to use advanced workstations (the PC of tomorrow) to provide the possibility for a continuous and smooth adaptation to future technological progress.

The major solution for this problem is the development of tools for teachers to support the production of their own software packages. A major design decision to be taken for such authoring environments is related to the conflicting demands of maximum support and minimal restriction. For the development of the product Xdev, described in Section 4, the decision was taken in favour of minimising restrictions with a trade-off for higher demands on the side of the user. The teacher/author as such a user is expected to be aware of a subset of the C-language and to have acquired some basic knowledge about algorithm and programming. Some principles of Motif, for instance use of widgets and the functionality of callbacks is necessary. Once such basic knowledge has been acquired a maximum support is available for the production of individual simulations. A description of this programs is found in Section 5.

The process of tool development supports the concept 'Model - View - Controller' to organise application development. The 'Model' represents the actual subject matter in the form of simulation algorithms or other descriptions of the topic at hand. The 'View' contains the presentational and interactive software, and the 'Controller' directs the flow of presentations.

For a domain expert authoring courseware the only part of interest is the 'Model'. A major objective of this project is to shield the author, teacher and student from having to write software dealing with the 'View' and the 'Controller' on anything but a superficial level. The existing Motif widgets and a number of generic widgets support automatic generation of 'View' and of 'Controller' software (Krasner & Pope, 1988; Wisskirchen, 1990).

The selection of tools to be developed has mainly been decided by local or individual needs in close consultation with the members concerned and in line with the intended bottom-up approach. These tools can be divided into three categories:

- a programming environment;
- tools for support of graphical design;
- widgets or libraries for special sub-tasks useful within the Motif environment.

New requirements for further tools or widgets are developed mainly by teachers, while learning programming and authoring with Xdev. Such activities are in progress and serve as test bed for the environment as well as a source of new ideas and future requirements.

A second source for additional requirements is growing out of the subgroup of COLOS members concerned with full time programming of complex applications (see next section). From the variety of tasks undertaken and solutions developed within this group and through a permanent exchange and discussion, a list of needs and standard solutions are developed.

3 APPLICATION DEVELOPMENT

3.1 **Goals**

It was stated above that teachers hesitate to use software 'off-the-shelf' and that they should have the possibility of producing their own tailored teaching/learning material. This ideal approach has limits which have to be taken into account.

This period of technological advance offers an increasing spectrum of possibilities for didactics, which at the moment cannot be theoretically predicted and discussed but only explored in form of prototypes and tried out in practice.

There exists a spectrum of topics which due to their complexity of demands for visualisation, interactivity and flow of control cannot be handled by a single person, particularly a non-programmer. Examples of this category are an integrated simulation environment for mechanics, a tool for learning how to design integrated circuits or a package for studying neural nets (see next section). Such programs have to be developed by professional teams and should meet the following demands:

- demonstrate the spectrum of didactical possibilities of the computer as a new medium;
- demonstrate the high degree of interactivity possible with this new technology and its uses in the teaching/learning process for that field;
- offer the highest degree possible for customisation to tailor for local needs and preferences.

With the growing expertise of teachers and the existence of convincing proof for the effectivity and efficacy of these programs in teaching/learning processes, the barrier to acceptance is expected to decrease and more use of these applications in a variety of situations is expected.

The applications developed within COLOS can be roughly divided into two groups:

- applications trying to cover basic concepts in physics - especially mechanics and electricity;
- applications of interest at the conceptual level to engineers and computer scientists like neural nets, seepage, and integrated circuits.

Their specific didactical purpose is manifold and content dependent and will be briefly outlined in the following section.

3.2 Reduction of mathematical overload

Those who are concerned with teaching basic concepts in science, especially physics, criticise the early use of mathematical language and the use of highly abstract terms and constructs at the introductory level.

As many evaluation studies have shown, such teaching falls short of its expectation for many students. The mathematical equations get in the way of any deeper understanding of the physical world (Härtel, 1990b; Krause & Reinders-Logothetidou, 1981).

The advantage of simulations in overcoming these problems is seen as follows. In traditional teaching, explanations and predictions are based on mathematical models like differential equations or a system of such equations in coupled form. Going back to first principles and trying to copy natural processes as closely as possible, provides a more direct approach towards understanding and a substantially reduced demand for mathematical qualification.

It is possible, for instance, to cover a major part of basic mechanics by a numerical solution based on Newton's 2nd and 3rd law in connection with different force laws, both in the form of difference equations. Similar solutions are possible with retardation and transmission effects, covering the field of oscillations and waves.

The replacement of differentials by difference equations and the use of basic principles, often much closer to direct comprehension than definitions in mathematical form, should have an impact on the structure of the curriculum, the selection of topics and finally on the efficiency and effectiveness of the teaching and learning processes.

Such major changes in the curriculum cannot and should not occur fast but have to be carefully monitored. A description of plans within COLOS to deal with this kind of question about implementation and evaluation will be found in Section 4.

3.3 Support for theorising experimental results

The foundation of each scientific course is the real experiment and the collection of measured data to judge the truth or falseness of assumptions. No simulation can replace such a base. However, the didactic value of experiments is often overestimated. What is visible and obvious to the expert within an experimental set-up, is often covered by a complex machinery of devices and connections and can be rather opaque and confusing to the novice. The time scale of an experiment, enforced by laws of nature, and the effort required to repeat it many times, often set further limits to its didactic value.

Computer simulations in close relation to experiments offer an added value in many aspects. The experiment can be schematically reduced to reveal its basic structure, the time scale is under control and can be adapted to individual needs. Alternatives to the real world can be visualised on the screen for direct comparison with the real situation to make the important parameters for determining its unique appearance explicit.

New kinds of experiments, which would take an unreasonable amount of time or effort, are now possible at the click of a mouse and results can be compared with no time delay.

3.4 Support of spatial imagery by 3-dimensional representations.

In teaching physics and technology many explanations and thought experiments are based on the use of spatial imagery.

Before computers, visualisations were normally reduced to two dimensions and often only to 2-dimensional graphs. With the support of modern workstations it is now possible to use the animated 3-dimensional representation whenever topological issues are involved.

Students have differing abilities in applying spatial imagery. However, they are all capable of dealing with structures and moving objects in directly visible 3-dimensional space. Such computer supported 3-dimensional representations can now be used as a tool for beginners, using representations they are comfortable and capable of dealing with. These representations can be transformed, stepwise, to more abstract levels to support the interpretation of abstract representation and more formal thinking.

Use of 3-dimensional images or graphs is based on the assumption that for the majority of students such form of representation is more suitable and fruitful than abstract formalism. The proverb "a picture can say more than 10000 words", often reported to originate from China, summarises this believe. As Larkin and Simon (Larkin & Simon, 1987) have pointed out, there are some provisos. A picture is rather rich in information, especially if it is a moving one. It can put a high cognitive load on the observer and ask for an extended cognitive capacity to organise this flow of incoming information in a constructive way. While equations could be learned by heart with some chance for later comprehension, such method is no longer possible with the presentation of knowledge in visual and animated form.

One of the major aims of the future evaluation studies is to define the values and limits of this approach and to determine the amount of additional support needed by students with different abilities and interests.

3.5 Understanding and dealing with complex systems

Simulations are perfectly suited to support topics like telecommunication, integrated circuits, neural nets and the like. Due to their inherent complexity, these systems have to be modelled in different ways according to perceived needs and purposes. Sub-systems have to be taken as black boxes with input and output to deal with more abstract relations and functionalities.

This complexity is a major barrier to understanding and successful learning, if only print media or static pictures are available. The flexibility of animated computer graphics, controlled by adequate models and adaptable to individual needs, represents a substantial enhancement of teaching and learning in this field.

It is well known that relations or connections between two objects or events are best learned if these two events or objects are presented as close as possible together in space and time.

Computer simulations allow a new and promising approach to put this principle into practice. They allow one to run different modelling procedures and interactive change of important parameters with immediate feedback for the user. This requirement sets the 'teaching simulation' apart from the 'design simulation' where the designer can attend to other tasks while waiting for the results.

Immediate visual feedback is a feature of computer simulations which have already proven their unique didactic value. Their importance will further grow with further advances in hardware and software.

3.6 Exercise and training

In contrast to the teacher-dominated introductory phase, when a new topic is introduced, the following phase of repetition, exercise and training is usually characterised by different needs of different students. Computer assisted learning material is well suited to cope with this problem.

At university level the traditional courses for practical work and exercise are seen as major application fields for this technology. The same basic programs, shown in the lectures and introductory courses, can be used during this practical work, adapted to different levels of student ability and surrounded with a variety of support material like worksheets, guided tours, help files etc.

The development of such support material in close cooperation with the involved teachers is actually of main concern at different COLOS sites. From this experience a collection of typical student reactions, typical questions, typical misconceptions etc. will evolve and serve as base for the development of so-called 'intelligent' training and exercise programs. We see the development of such material, based on practical experience, as a possible and valuable goal.

Today our simulation environments depend on the presence of a teaching person to guide and assist the activities of the students and to prevent them from getting lost and consequently demotivated. The goal for the future is to create proper support for different simulation topics to increase the range and efficacy of independent learner activities.

4 EVALUATION

The COLOS project started from practical needs and a broad base of different field and teaching expertise, striving for common products and standards of quality by continuous discussion and cooperation. In such a bottom-up approach, exploration is the main characteristic of the first phase while critics and questions about common evaluation practice are withhold until a critical mass of ideas and methods have been developed.

Usability tests and case studies as part of an iterative design cycle have been carried out at most COLOS sites in close cooperation between the teaching and programming experts. This and the regular discussions of the developed products at project meetings together with the implementation of a unified programming structure has paved the ground for further integration.

During the coming phase of the project further steps towards a meaningful standardisation of products with common look, feel, and didactical quality will be implemented including the following measures:

External feedback
Feedback from external field experts will be collected, following a common rating scheme and based on a well prepared demonstration.

Tryouts with focus groups
Normally a focus group will consist of a group of up to 10 end-users with a moderator. The moderator guides the group through discussion of an agenda of questions, paced by the group. Often the group will have a working version of the software as a focus. Focus groups are audio/videotaped and the data can be subjected to a variety of analysis techniques. Group techniques have the advantage of allowing new solutions to emerge: group members remind each other of events, encourage

reconstruction, explore gaps in thinking, and overcome the 'not worth mentioning' problem.

Automatic logging of usage data
It is possible to build a data logging facility into the software itself which will record usage data in detail. Errors, response times, keystroke data, hypermedia choices, even mouse movements can be recorded and the data presented in suitably processed form.

Application of learning effectiveness methods
For summative analysis some important questions will be:

- What exactly has been learned?
- How well integrated with other learning is it?
- How durable is the learning?
- Is the learning deep or shallow?
- What effect did the courseware have on motivation to study?

To address these questions, focus groups (of students), questionnaires, self-assessment tests, and both pilot studies and field studies can be considered.

The latter depends strongly on the availability of sufficient working places for larger student groups and the possibility of coordinating the computer assisted learning material with the curriculum and the examination.

At some COLOS sites, where these conditions are fulfilled, such field tests will be carried out and will yield interesting and fruitful information about how well this new media enables us to reach our goal of improving knowledge and understanding of basic concepts in science and technology.

5 LIST OF TOOLS (DEVELOPED OR PROJECTED)

From each of the three categories:

- tools;
- applications developed by programmers;
- applications developed under Xdev;

two selected packages are described in more detail while additional lists provide a survey of all available programs. These list are of course continually changing.

5.1 The development tool 'Xdev' (Murcia)

Global description
Xdev is an authoring system that simplifies the creation of simulation modules. It runs on HP workstations under X windows and Motif.

Xdev has an interface builder and an interpreter based on a subset of C with some extensions. These two elements support the development of a graphical interface as well as the code for the model of the simulation and the response of it to user interactions. The program can run in interpreted mode for the development and testing phase, but faster and independent executables can also be generated. Using dynamic linking, Xdev also provides hooks for the more experienced programmers to include their own functions.

The whole system is extensible for new widgets and libraries, and is site and user customisable. The system is provided with some new widgets devoted to the display of scientific data in 2 and 3 dimensions, as well as new input widgets (Esquembre, Zamarro, & Martin, 1992).

Scope of programming work
Xdev hides most of the programming issues inherent to Unix, X-windows and Motif and lets the user concentrate on the model for the simulation. It is thus very well suited for beginners to this platform. It also speeds up the development of the interface and the assignment of callbacks (or responses to user interactions) and the setting of a periodic process, which makes it useful for expert programmers too.

Target group
Xdev is targeted to teachers of all kinds or science students, who are able to specify their algorithms, equations, models, in a high level computer language, but who are not expert programmers or Unix users. It allows them to access powerful machines and add relatively sophisticated graphical interfaces to their programs.

Available help
Xdev comes with a manual in printed form and has some built-in browsers that help navigating through Motif graphical components or widgets, providing a list and a short description of their resources (customisable internal values) and callbacks (possible responses to user interaction).

Most frequently used widgets are presented in a graphical way in a pick-and-use panel, thus facilitating access. There is also a tutorial to aid in creation of simple programs. A cook-book for individual components and of common interactive situations is being prepared. A set of complete examples, some of them of considerable complexity and of scientific interest is included in the distribution package.

Status
Xdev is now a stable product. It will be subjected to improvements suggested by users. Speed is not a critical issue because executables can be generated at any moment during the development phase, and these show the speed of the final product.

In general, it can be said that the system produces executables that are as fast as those generated by an expert programmer. Right now, the system runs only on

Hewlett Packard series 700 workstations with X11 R4 and Motif 1.1. It is planned to move soon to X11 R5 and Motif 1.2.

Because the system produces executables, the C development software package (which is not included in the standard HP-UX distribution) has to be installed on the system. Figure 1 presents Xdev with all its components.

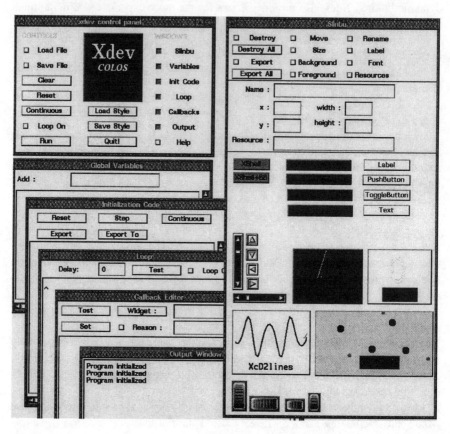

Figure 1 *Xdev displaying all its components*

Evaluation

The program has been used extensively by a small group of teachers and students (both under-graduate and post-graduate) who have a basic knowledge of programming. On average, they were able to produce their first complete program in their own scientific domains in about 3 to 4 weeks (working 1 to 2 hours daily). The teachers who continued developing with Xdev become adapt and work faster. Because they had to concentrate more on their subject than on programming issues, they were very keen to use Xdev, and very pleased with their results.

5.2   The program specification tool 'SoftSpec' (Cambridge)

Global description

SoftSpec is a tool designed to improve communication in a group working cooperatively and perhaps remotely from one another. It is a tool to allow all those interested in the outcome of a software project to specify their requirements in a clear and logical way. The requirements specification document is upgradeable throughout the project and is available in a simple easily readable form to all members of the project.

SoftSpec can also be used to monitor progress on upgrades or maintenance to software. It runs on HP workstations under X windows and Motif. Part of the windows, offered by SoftSpec, are shown in Figure 2.

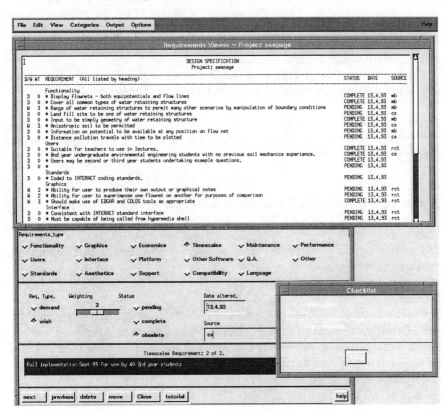

Figure 2 *SoftSpec in use*

Scope of programming work

The work made easier by this product is the work that takes place before programming begins, i.e the production of the requirements specification.

During the requirements specification stage, information must be acquired from the various clients to define the final software product. Frequently there are incompatible requirements in a specification, which often do not become apparent until too late in the project to do much about them. SoftSpec provides clear evidence of conflicting requirements at the start of the project enabling misunderstandings and conflicts to be resolved before programming begins.

The requirements of a software project (tool or application) can be specified as a series of demands and wishes. Demands are requirements which must be met and wishes are requirements which, under ideal circumstances, should be met. Wishes are weighted according to their importance, thus aiding in trade-off between incompatible requirements and in the evaluation of potential solutions.

The requirements are grouped in various category headings such as 'Timescales', 'Educational objectives' - these categories can be altered to suit the requirements of individual projects. Many users can contribute to a project specification, and the software keeps track of who specifies a requirement as well as the status of that requirement (pending, complete or obsolete)

The requirements document can be output as a .tex or .dvi file (easily convertible to postscript) and requirements can be sorted by category or in order of importance.

Target group
Any member of a project team can use SoftSpec to specify software requirements. No programming expertise is required.

Available help
Help on the use of SoftSpec is available on-line within SoftSpec.

Status
The tool is currently functional, but a number of modifications are planned to enhance its overall usability.

Evaluation
SoftSpec is used by students at Cambridge University Engineering Department as part of collaborative design projects where teams of engineering students work to build robots capable of performing a given task. (At least 24 students a year use SoftSpec). It will be used by the INTERACT TLTP project as a project management tool where it will undergo formative evaluation

5.3 List of further tools

The programming tool 'Edgar' (Lyon)
Edgar stands for EDitable Graphics ARea, and is a Motif widget to display, animate and edit graphics. It is particularly well adapted to display moving or self-modifying shapes and to be used as the main display area of graphics editors. (Muller, Mariaux, & Nicolas, 1993a).

The graphic tool 'Pixidor' (Kiel)
Pixidor is a general purpose pixel editor, supporting full scale pixmaps. It closes the
gap left with X11R4 where no such tool is provided. Besides the basic drawing
operations Pixidor offers different block operations and allows to handle a collection
of pixmaps.

Stripchart recorder (Lyon, Berlin)
A Motif widget for recording values given by the simulation as function of time

Graphical data input device (Kiel)
A tool to allow the end user to interact graphically with the system for input of
coordinates within a two dimensional diagram.

Line oriented editor (Lyon)
This application will enable the user to interactively create any graphics made of
lines (i.e. no pixmaps) and to save them for later re-use inside of any application,
provided that application uses an Edgar widget for display.

6 LIST OF DEVELOPED SIMULATIONS

6.1 **The simulation program 'xyZET' (Kiel)**

Global description
The simulation program xyZET offers the possibility of visualising animated objects
in 3d and the simulation of attractive and repulsive forces. All didactically
meaningful parameters are accessible for interactive variation. The program is
intended to support the presentation of concepts during lectures and to form the base
for the arrangement of exercise material to be worked at by individual students
(Härtel, 1993).

Scientific content - important features
The program covers a series of basic concepts of mechanics and electricity which
form part of each introductory course in physics. The main concepts are:

- Kinematics;   Hooks law;
- Kinetic energy;   Gravitation;
- Newton's laws;   Charge, field lines;
- Conservation of momentum;   Coulomb interaction;
- Conservation of energy;   Equipotential surfaces.

Besides the introductory level, some more advanced topics from solid state physics
(lattic symmetry, van der Waals forces) and relativity (relativistic addition of
velocities, retarded potential) are included.

Didactical approach

The standard approach in introductory courses in physics is based on demonstrations of experiments and direct comparison of the results with abstract mathematical expressions. This is accompanied by laboratory work, often not synchronised in sequence and time.

The simulation presented here as a new medium or tool for teaching, offers an intermediate step between real experiments and abstraction. By shifting all the mathematical overload towards the machine, the results can first be presented in visualised form, serving as pre-organiser for the learner to build a knowledge base of qualitative concepts.

The need for mathematical tools and integration of qualitative and quantitative methods for an effective reduction of complexity can be demonstrated convincingly.

Implementation

In its basic form the program presents a cube which can be rotated, zoomed in and out under various perspectives. The simplest use of this 'world' is to load prepared files to present any kind of 3-dimensional object in animation (rotation). Figure 3 shows some examples.

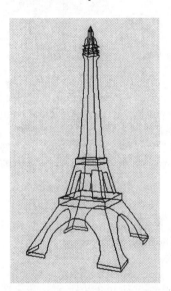 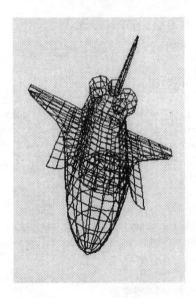

Figure 3 *Objects displayed in 3D for rotation and zooming*

As a more interactive use, small geometrically simple objects can be placed at any position with variable parameters like, coordinates, velocity, mass, charge. Forces of different kind like gravitation, Coulomb, forces of springs of different length (pull, push, both) can be set and monitored. The centre of mass can be indicated as well as the kinetic and potential energy.

This arrangement offers a variety of experiments like inclined throw, pendulum, collision, elastic deformation, vibration, waves and planetarian motion.

The effect of Coulomb attraction and repulsion between particles, enclosed in different parts of the volume, can be shown, together with field lines or equipotential surfaces in animation.

The model used is based on Newton's 2nd law, computing the forces (acceleration) for each particle, using finite differences to find the velocity and the displacement.

A high resolution screen is indispensable to give a satisfying presentation within a '3d-world' in animation. The influence of many particles (many = > 50) is necessary to demonstrate any effect due to bulk material. The computational power needed for this task is offered today only by high powered workstations.

A documentation with a full description of the functionality of the user interface, the didactical principles involved and a list of proposed student activities is being developed and will be available during spring 1994.

Target group
The simulation program should be useful during lectures, mostly on upper secondary and university level in parallel with experiments. It could also be integrated into lab work where additional support material would have to be provided by the teacher. It may serve as an environment for exploration and practice for the motivated individual learner.

Evaluation
Evaluation has been carried out during development in fragmented form and only with small groups. After finishing the documentation the program will be offered to selected teachers for testing. A controlled evaluation study will be carried out during 1994.

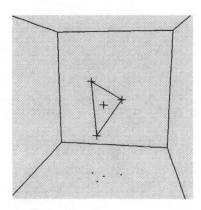 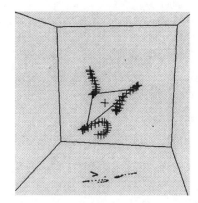

Figure 4 *Motion caused by spring forces with centre of mass at rest*

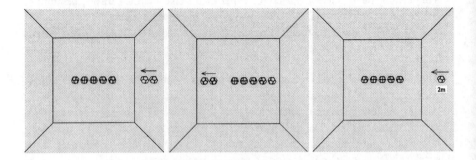

Figure 5 *Collision of two balls same velocity - Collision of one ball doubled mass*

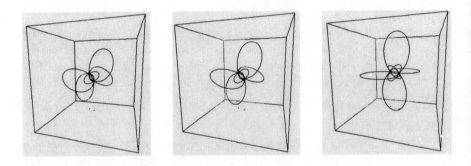

Figure 6 *Dipole and field lines in motion*

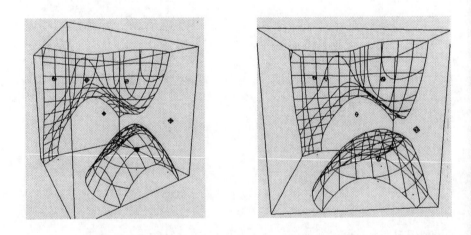

Figure 7 *Surface of equipotential (3 positive and 3 negative charge carriers)*

6.2 The simulation program 'INNE' (Milan)

Global description

The application INNE - Interactive Neural Network Environment - is a neural network simulation environment for UNIX workstations. Its aim is to provide a tool for modelling and experimenting neural networks: it allows the user to interactively design, train and test neural networks and to visualise their behaviour. The net editor allows the user to deal with large networks and to define their structure graphically. Different neural models are available to define the network behaviour.

Scientific content

Neural networks are computational models that perform computation via a densely connected net of very simple processing elements. This idea is an abstraction based on the behaviour of biological nerve cells. The application provides the background to master with this paradigm of computation; it covers three basic models of neural computation: back-propagation networks, Boltzmann machines and Hopfield networks.

The back-propagation is one of the most popular neural network paradigms, and it is used successfully in many applications that require pattern-matching: after a supervised learning phase to establish the connections weights, the network responds to an input pattern by producing the corresponding output pattern.

The Boltzmann machine (see Figure 8 for an example) can be used to solve combinatorial problems by approximation: it implements a probabilistic optimisation algorithm, called simulated annealing, able to avoid locally optimal solutions. A learning algorithm allows to use this model also for classification problems, even though to this purpose the back-propagation learning algorithm is more efficient.

The Hopfield model can be seen as a particular case of the more general Boltzmann machine; it is able to find the locally optimal solution nearest to the starting solution. It performs a gradient descent method, which is the deterministic version of the Boltzmann machine simulated annealing.

Didactical approach

The standard didactical approach to this subject is mathematical: different models are introduced, formally analysed and some very simple examples are shown. In contrast, the emphasis of this application is on experimenting and visualising. This last feature and the ease of interaction are the main difference comparing to other simulators. Learning session and computational processes can be stopped any time to allow users to modify the network interactively (Alberti, Marelli, & Sabadini, 1993). Figure 9 shows the control panel offered to the user.

During learning phase and simulation, statistics are graphically displayed so that processes can be easily monitored. The most important educational aspect of the application is the possibility of exploring different models and different activation modes for the same model in a simple way and comparing them with each other.

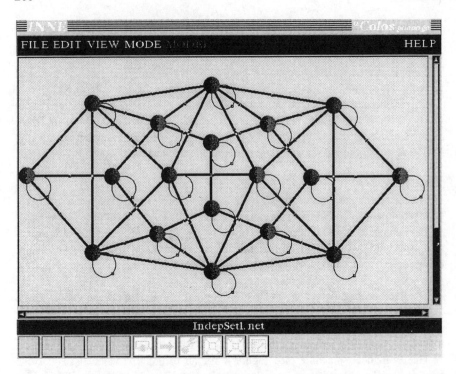

Figure 8 *Example of a Boltzmann machine. The net solves the problem of finding the greatest subset of nodes, which are not connected with each other.*

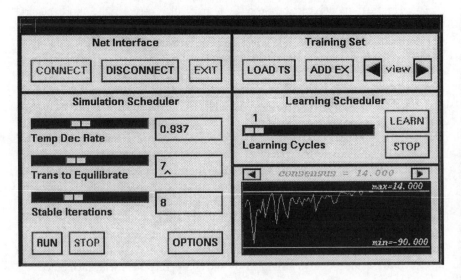

Figure 9 *The Boltzmann machine control panel*

Implementation
The application consists of several modules: a simulator kernel, the main part of the application, that manages the net internal representation and the memory, written in C so that it is portable, the graphic user interface with the graphical net editor, the modules of the different neural models, and some tools, such as a text editor, and an example editor to edit easily the training set files.

The net editor is a very powerful tool to design neural networks, that typically consist of thousands of elements. Figure 10 shows a modest example. Every implemented neural model has its simulation panel; a panel can be connected to the net and it is used by the user to drive the computation processes, and by the application to display simulation reports. Two original cooling schedules for the Boltzmann machine are implemented. This application requires high level workstation both because of the computation complexity and of the visualisation for educational aims.

Target group
The application is intended for students of computer science interested in neural computing. It covers topics usually introduced in university courses on neural computing. It can be used by students directly or by teachers in classrooms to show effectively different neural models. Students can explore the topic and implement in the environment significant neural networks to carry on projects that teachers can ask them to do.

Evaluation
The environment has been only informally tested by scattered group of teachers and students, while it was under development. It will be used in a course offered at the Cybernetics Department, as soon as it will be robust enough for the didactic laboratory.

6.3   List of further applications

The simulation program 'BRAKE / HEATFLOW' (Berlin)
This program simulation simulates the flow of heat in a cubic volume divided into prismatic elements with one of three possible shapes. It visualises the temperature behaviour of a disc brake as a function of distance and time.

The simulation program ' DACOTA' (Berlin)
An active interface, representing a RS232 connection between two devices, is presented to the end-user, offering different possibilities for change of parameters and visualising the functionality of this interface.

The simulation program 'SEEPAGE' (Cambridge)
SEEPAGE is a simulation application which allows the user to explore the migration of ground water through water retaining structures. The program does this by generating flownets for a series of commonly occurring geotechnical problems.

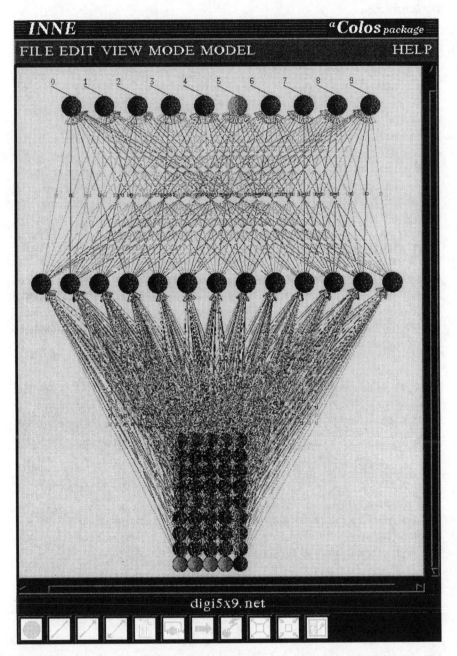

Figure 10 *Example of a net trained by the back error propagation algorithm. The net recognises hand written digits: the input pattern is provided in the bottom node matrix and the output nodes are labelled on top.*

Integrated Circuits - VHDLEDIT/VHDLSIM (Delft)
The application VHDLEDIT/VHDLSIM allows the creation and simulation in pseudo real time of digital circuits. It uses a small sub_set of the hardware description language VHDL to describe the circuits and allows the creation and simulation of a lot of (basic) digital circuits. Pulse generators are available to provide continuous input_stimuli to the circuits and stripchart recorders and number_displays to show results. The status of the ports is also shown in the circuit.

The simulation program 'Phasor' (Edinburgh)
Phasor is a set of applications which enable the user to interactively build up an understanding of phasors and their uses in a wide range of electrical engineering areas. The presentation links the phasor and the time domain picture dynamically, allowing parameter changes to be explored. The use of multiple phasors allows both frequency and time domain illustrations to be displayed and ultimately complex frequency signals to be introduced (Close, Conner, & Linnett, 1993).

The simulation program 'TeEl' - Transmission Line (Kiel)
This program simulates the transmission of voltage and current steps or continuous changes along a one dimensional double line, based on numerical solutions of the telegraph equations. All relevant parameters can be changed interactively, allowing for a broad spectrum of phenomena to be studied (dc, ac, high frequency) (Härtel & Martin, 1993).

The simulation program 'rectif' (Lyon)
'rectif' is a program to study the single-phase bridge rectifier. The switches may be either diodes or thyristors and the load may adopt several different configurations. The resulting waveforms are animated while time flows and to follow any input parameter interactively modified by the end-user (Muller, Mariaux, & Nicolas, 1993b).

The simulation program 'mField' (Lyon)
'mField' is an application to study how to generate a rotating field inside the airgap of a rotating machine. The field may be generated using either one, two or three inducting currents, and the phase of these currents may be adjusted to result either in a pulsing or a rotating field.

The simulation program 'Circuits' (Lyon)
Circuit is a microworld to study electrical circuits. The circuit can be interactively entered, stored on file, simulated and the simulation results may be graphically displayed and animated versus time or parameter change .

The simulation program 'MICROWAVES' (Lyon)
'mWave' is a microworld to study the microwave distribution in a waveguide, which may be either of rectangular or circular cross- section (Muller, Mariaux, & Nicolas, 1993c).

The simulation Program AUTOMATA (Milan)
AUTOMATA is a learning package for modelling automata and experimenting with grammars.

The simulation program SimCatS (Oxford)
A simulation of catalysis on surfaces is being developed, through which the user will be able to both study the molecular basis of catalytic reactions, and investigate the experimental consequences of changes in the chemical and physical parameters of the species involved.

The simulation program 'elCur1-5' (Palo Alto)
elCur1-5 is a set of applications which allow the user to observe delayed interaction of electrons in conductors and to study the associated phenomena. The presentation consists of controllable dynamic graphics displays which provide means for interactive variation of relevant parameters.

The simulation program 'TREEDEMO' (Paris)
This application supports the teaching of recursivity and binary trees concepts. It allows the user to visualise recursive tree traversal algorithms with a graphical representation of the data structure and the stack evolution.

The simulation program 'POTENTIAL' (Paris)
This application allows visualisation of trajectories of particles in a central field.

The simulation program 'MAXWELL'S DEMON' (Paris)
This application demonstrates the dynamic statistical distribution of the velocities of colliding particles in an adiabatic container (Perrin, Constanciel, & Bonnair, 1993).

7   APPLICATIONS DEVELOPED BY NON-PROGRAMMING EXPERTS USING XDEV

7.1   The simulation program 'WAVES' (Murcia)

Global description
The WAVES program is intended to support the presentation of concepts about waves during lectures. It has been developed with Xdev.

The application introduces the basic concepts of the topic providing an efficient tool to simulate different situations. A main window appears when the application is running with a display where waves under a string will be shown. A toggle button calls a control panel from which a wide variety of features can be selected and changed (see Figures 11 and 12).

Scientific content - important features
WAVES can show the propagation of a perturbation, the dynamics of the propagation along a string, the superposition of travelling waves of opposite

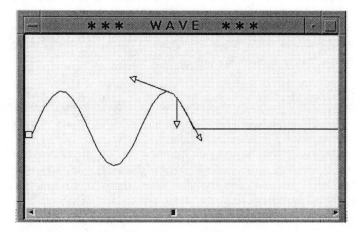

Figure 11 *Display window of the simulation program 'Waves'*

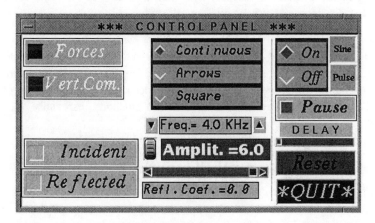

Figure 12 *Control panel for 'Waves' offered to the user*

direction, reflection at the end of a string with different reflection coefficients and standing waves.

The topic is important for introductory courses and first university level. It should be of special interest for those students who do not have a deeper knowledge of mathematics but need to acquire a qualitative understanding about waves, e.g. students of life science.

Didactical approach
The standard approach to this topic is to introduce definitions and to use mathematics to describe the phenomenon.

Waves are a classic topic where animation is an important feature in the teaching process. Using the simulation program WAVES, teachers can use a dynamic medium to teach a dynamic phenomenon. Additionally, they have the opportunity to explain these concepts without any mathematical overload. This program will be implemented within an Electronic Book about this topic.

Implementation
The model used in the simulation is based on a fundamental feature of waves: the perturbation in one point at an instant is equal to the perturbation one instant before in the preceding point.

To show three different displays with animation and modification in real time the parameters of the model makes use of high speed machines with outstanding graphic capabilities. These features are regarded as essential to achieve an adequate appearance of the simulation.

An on-line text describing the main aspects of the program is available.

Target group
The application is useful to teachers who want to introduce the basic concept of waves. It can support exercise material for self study.

Evaluation
An evaluation will be performed by some teachers and smaller groups of students. A chapter of an Electronic Book, written for this application, will be used. It is expected that the introduction of a qualitative understanding of basic concepts will support the later introduction of mathematical methods, especially the wave equation.

7.2   The simulation program 'PARTICLES' (Murcia)

Global description
The application, 'Particles' allows the simulation of the dynamics of particles which can interact through different forces and/or by external fields.

'Particles' is an application developed with the COLOS development tool Xdev. It was originally developed in 2-dimensions and it is now also implemented in 3-dimensions. It takes many ideas from the 'xyZET' application from Kiel.

Scientific content - important features
The application allows the design of different experiments covering several concepts in mechanics and electricity at an introductory level:

- Kinematics (velocity and acceleration);
- Dynamics (Hooks law, gravitation);
- Energy concepts (potential and kinetic, conservation);
- Coulomb interactions;
- Magnetic force on moving charges.

Besides the already implemented interactions and external fields, the user, if an Xdev expert, can access hooks in the source program to add additional interactions or external fields. This make the application into a more general environment where the teacher can design his/her own class to cover a specific topic of interest.

Didactical approach.
The standard approach to cover the above mentioned topics can be found in any general physics text book, where the student can find everything related to the mathematical description of forces and closed form solutions to different problems. Sometimes experimental work is available to show the behaviour of very simple systems.

With this application, an introduction to the basic concepts can be made, which hides much of the mathematical load usually involved when teaching those concepts. The graphical animation also allows a deeper understanding of those concepts, preparing the student for a much easier introduction to the mathematics behind the formal approach. The behaviour of complex systems, difficult to be dealt with in terms of an analytical approach, can also be shown.

Implementation
This program has been developed with Xdev with extensive use of the XcWorld or Xc3DWorld Widgets.

The application shows two different panels. The first (Figure 13) presents the simulation, the second is used as a control panel where the user interactively defines the kind of interactions or external fields acting on the particles (Figure 14). The velocities and accelerations for all the particles can be graphically displayed.

The particles are mouse sensitive for moving and changing of velocity. A strip-chart recorder has been implemented to show different quantities (energies, positions), allowing the students to link the visualisation on the screen to standard graphical representations found in text books.

A numerical finite difference algorithm has been implemented to integrate Newton's second law: The force on a particle is first computed in terms of the present interactions and external fields. Then the new velocity is computed in terms of the acceleration and old velocity. Now the new position is computed in terms of the velocity and old position. This process is iteratively applied to all particles.

With a high powered workstation, the number of particles that can be involved in a simulation with no appreciable loss of speed is around 100. This is enough to get an idea of the behaviour of complex systems. For instance, the electrostatic behaviour of a conductor with fixed positive ions and free moving electrons can be easily shown.

No additional help, besides a self-explaining user interface design has been implemented.

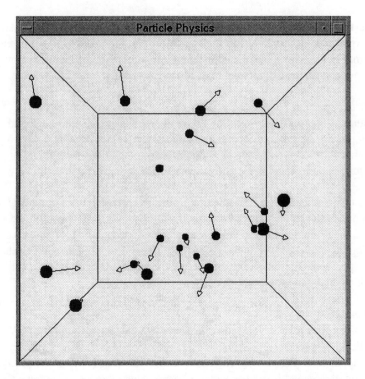

Figure 13 *Display window from "Particles" with indication of velocity*

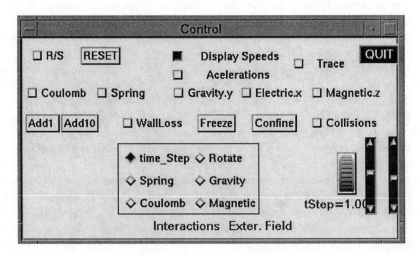

Figure 14 *Control panel of 'Particles'*

Target group
'Particles' is intended to be used for three different purposes:

- As an environment for learning basic physics concepts at an introductory level, guided by a teacher or in a self-supporting way. For this last possibility, some additional support material should be provided by the teacher (parallel experiments, assignments, etc.);
- As example for Xdev users where a novice user of this authoring system can find many suggestions for solving his/her own design problems;
- As a general environment where the Xdev-expert teacher can design his/her own classes, by modifying or adding interactions or external fields needed to show the particular phenomena under study.

Evaluation
Evaluation has been carried out only in the second modality mentioned above (see Section 4). This application was one of the first made with Xdev and has been taken as an example for different teachers to design their own software using Xdev.

It will be used during the present university course (introductory level), as support for teaching basic concepts in mechanics: velocity, acceleration, momentum and energy conservation. This will be done in combination with the Electronic Book application.

7.3 List of further programs developed under Xdev

The simulation program 'CYCLOTRON' (Murcia)
The trace of a charge carrier within a cyclotron is simulated. Various parameters can be altered.

The simulation program 'PARTICLE PHYSICS IN TWO DIMENSIONS' (Murcia)
The program allows the simulation of interaction between particles due to a variety of forces. Some topics that can be covered within this application are: Newton's Laws, planetary motion, Coulomb interaction, the concept of metal (electrostatic behaviour), cyclotronic movement, etc.

The simulation program 'DIELECTRICS' (Murcia)
Two applications have been developed concerning the basic polarisation mechanisms of dielectrics: electronic and polar (distortion and orientation).

8 MEMBERS OF COLOS

Site, contact person and address

Berlin   Klaus Rebensburg, PRZ, TU-Berlin Sekr. MA073
                  Strasse des 17. Juni, D-10623 Berlin

Cambridge	Ruth Thomas, Dept. of Engineering, Cambridge University
	Trumpington St., CB2 1PZ, England
Delft	Joop Liedorp, Dept. of Electr. Eng. Delft University of Technology
	Mekelweg 4, NL-2628 CD Delft
Edinburgh	Alex Close, Dept. of Comp. and Elec. Eng.
	Riccarton, Edinburgh EH14 4AS, Scotland
Kiel	Hermann Härtel, IPN
	Olshausenstr. 62, D-24098 Kiel
Lyon	Alain Nicolas, CEGELY, Ecole Central de Lyon
	BP 163, F- 69131 ECULLY - Cedex
Milano	Maria Alberta Alberti, DSI, Universita' degli Studi di Milano
	Via Comelico 39, I-20135 Milano
Murcia	Jose-Miguel Zamarro, Dpto. FISICA, Universidad de Murcia
	Apartado de Correos 4021, E-30071 Espinardo, Murcia
Oxford	Hugh Cartwright, Physical Chemistry Laboratory
	South Parks Road, OXFORD, OX1 3QZ England
Palo Alto	Zvonko Fazarinc, Hewlett-Packar Laboratories
	1501 Page Mill Road, Mailstop 3L, Palo Alto, CA 94304, USA
Paris	Georges Alquie, Universite P & M Curie
	casier: 203, 4 place Jussieu, F-75252 Paris Cedex 05

REFERENCES

Alberti, M.A., Marelli, P., & Sabadini, N. (1993). Automata and NeuralWorks: learning environments for automata theory and neural nets. In: N. Estes & M. Thomas (Eds.), *Rethinking the Roles of Technology in Education.* Morgan Printing, Austin - TX, Proc. of the Tenth ICTE '93. Cambridge USA: MIT.

Close, A.M., Conner, H.M., & Linnett, L.M. (1993). Teaching Signal Concepts in Electrical Engineering. *Proceedings of the 'International Conference on Computer Based Learning'* CBLIS 93 (pp. 603 - 612). Wien.

Esquembre, F., Zamarro, J.M., & Martin, E. (1992). Authoring tool under UNIX/X-windows/ Motif oriented to program development for simulation of physics phenomena'. *Computers in Physics, 6, 4.*

Härtel, H. (1990a). Interactive Learning Programs for UNIX-Machines. First results of the COLOS project. In: Norrie, D.H. & Six, H.W. (Eds.). *Lecture Notes in Computer Science, 438.* Computer Assisted Learning, Springer Verlag.

Härtel, H. (1990b). *Learning and Understanding Concepts in Physics.* IRL Report No. IRL90/0017, Palo Alto.

Härtel, H. (1993). Computergraphik als Zwischenschritt zur Abstraktion. Beitrag zur Hauptversammlung der MNU. In: Lichtfeld, M. (Ed.) *Ideen für den Physikunterricht* (pp. 191-201). Berlin: MNU.

Härtel, H., & Martin, E. (1993). New path for teaching electricity. *Proceedings of the 'International Conference on Computer Based Learning'* CBLIS 93 (pp. 275 - 284). Wien.

Krasner, G.E. & Pope, S.T. (1988). A Cookbook for Using the Model-View-Controller User Interface Paradigm in Smalltalk-80. *Journal of Object-Oriented Programming, 1* (3), 26-49.

Krause, F. & Reinders-Logothetidou, A. (1981). *Kenntnisse und Fähigkeiten naturwissenschaftlich orientierter Studienanfänger in Physik und Mathematik. Die Ergebnisse des bundesweiten Studieneingangstests Physik 1978.* Universität Bonn.

Larkin, J.H. & Simon, H.A. (1987). Why a diagram is (sometimes) worth ten thousand words. *Cognitive Science, 11,* 65-99.

Muller, D., Mariaux, L., & Nicolas, A. (1993a). A Motif Widget to Display, Animate and Edit Graphics', submitted to the Oopsla conference (*Object-Oriented Programming Systems, Languages and Applications).* Washington D.C.

Muller, D., Mariaux, L., & Nicolas, A. (1993b). *A computer aided education environment used in teaching the single-phase bridge rectifier.* EAEEIE conference. Prague, Czech Republic.

Muller, D., Mariaux, L., & Nicolas, A. (1993c). *A C.A.E. package for an intuitive approach to microwaves.* Compumag conference. Miami, Florida.

Perrin, H., Constanciel, R., & Bonnair, R. (1993). Developing simulation software for teaching physics at the university level with the X-Window system. *Proceedings of the 'International Conference on Computer Based Learning'* CBLIS 93 (pp. 302 - 309). Wien.

Wisskirchen, P. (1990). *Object-Oriented Graphics.* Berlin: Springer Verlag.

Acknowledgement: The COLOS project has been continuously supported by Hewlett-Packard, and, for a two years period, by the COMETT programme of the European Commission under project number 88/3/1800-D1. In writing this paper I received valuable input from my COLOS colleagues, who I also acknowledge for their contributions to the different COLOS tools and applications.

Towards a Common Training Architecture for FDL: Description and Definition

Wil A. Verreck & Hilda G. Weges

Centre for Educational Technology and Innovation Research (OTIC),
Open University, The Netherlands

Abstract

The DELTA project Common Training Architecture (CTA) is concerned with the harmonisation of technologies that (will be able to) support flexible and distance learning (FDL) and training in a wide sense. Integration of systems and applications suffer from the lack of appropriate standards, the variety of standards that do not interwork correctly, the fact that systems, tools, and applications do not comply to existing standards, etc. It all amounts to technological issues like interoperability, portability and ease of use. The proposals and recommendations to be developed by the CTA start from the consideration of the benefits and support to the various actors in education, learning and training situations. The end-user, say student or trainee, therefore needs special emphasis, but at the same time the embedding in 'enterprise' objectives needs to be recognised as important. The latter directs attention to issues of development and authoring, production and delivery. This paper gives a survey of the CTA objectives and the approach that has been developed. It describes the intermediate results, especially that on the development of the framework on educational dimensions and some basic scenarios that contain the requirements for architectural solutions.

1 INTRODUCTION

This article describes the intermediate results of the work 'Scenarios and Architectures for European Education and Training' that has been done in the CTA-project. The broader context of the objectives and approach in the project is described in Section 2. In this article we describe the results along two lines. First, the work related to the framing of training scenarios, that is considered the starting point in the approach. Second, we outline the work on development of architectures and technical options, that is still under way.

The work on scenarios takes its starting point in the results of previous and ongoing DELTA projects, as the project concerns a major objective of the total programme. It is envisaged to extend it with experiences from outside DELTA, even during the project's life cycle. The main goal is to develop a framework for educational and training dimensions and aspects, that may be used to develop a set of scenarios covering the major trends in technology-based learning in the near

T. de Jong and L. Sarti (eds.), Design and Production of Multimedia and Simulation-based Learning Material, 219-243

future. Both the framework of learning and training aspects and the basic scenarios are described in Section 3.

The work on architecture development started by examining alternative architectures which may apply to European technology based learning. In order to cover a series of interrelated perspectives on a technology-based training systems, it starts with the viewpoint originating from enterprise modelling as one of a set of viewpoints. It arrives finally in the description of a general architecture, that contains the technical meta-models to be further detailed in the ongoing work. The enterprise model, the meta-models and the main services which can be extracted from these models are described Section 4.

As this article gives an intermediate survey of particularly the work in the first project year, the final section will outline the future work, that even extends into a second project, the CTA-II project on demonstration and validation.

Most of the contents of this article has already been described in some of the CTA-deliverables. Further detailed information can be found in Zorkoczy (1992); Collins, Pratt, Schmutz, Verreck, and Van Bruggen (1993); Collins and Pratt (1993); Verreck (1993a and 1993b); and Verreck, Weges, Van Bruggen, Ray, and Collins (1993).

2 A COMMON APPROACH TO DEVELOPING THE CTA

2.1 Introduction

A main objective of the DELTA programme is: 'To harmonise technologies, systems and infrastructures, and their adaptation to optimally convey learning services Europe-wide'. To the base of it is the recognition that technology-supported education, learning and training (for short referred to as ELT) is characterised by fragmentation and 'islands' of implementation, both the development and production approaches as well as the delivery and presentation of courses, training, etcetera. This inhibits the benefits of scale, the cost-reduction that technology-support may give, the access by various main actors, including students, to new opportunities that meet changing demands for flexible and distance learning, in fact the development of the ELT market.

One way is to opt for a more open systems approach built upon agreed standards. A major constraint to this is the fact that technology for ELT is a subset of technologies used in a wide range of applications. Technologies that may develop into standardisation processes quite independent from the specific ELT requirements, as long as these have not been well-defined and then may become a driving force too. Altogether the process has to be built also on growing consensus amongst the main actors in the fields of ELT. The CTA project aims to contribute to these objectives, and therefore conceived of a development process that is in main lines similar to the one of standards development:

• development of a common understanding;

- development of common frameworks;
- specification of functional requirements;
- development of technical options and standards profiles;
- development of validation and conformance testing methods;
- dissemination of results.

This article will mainly deal with the first two issues. The CTA addresses in particular three areas of tremendous importance to the harmonisation issues: Open Communication Interface (OCI), Common Information Space (CIS, previously called multimedia databases), and Common User Interface (CUI). They are basic to the issues of interoperability, portability, reuse, and ease of use that are other ways to express the needs for harmonisation.

2.2 Description of the common approach

The basis of the common approach taken within CTA has been to use the evolving work on Open Distributed Processing (ISO/IEC 10746), in conjunction with other techniques. The ODP Reference Model is attractive, because it describes five viewpoints or levels on the object system: enterprise, information, computational, engineering, and technological. The object system in this context may be considered any ELT system.

One part of the approach is to ensure that the business level considerations, with the stakeholders identified with their needs, are detailed in what could be stated as a 'top down' approach. It is to be supplemented by a 'bottom up' approach, that takes account of the technology constraints which exist in the real world.

The first part of the approach leads us to base the work on architecture modelling techniques. It describes the ELT business within an architectural framework, using a standard modelling technique and process. The enterprise, information and computational viewpoints of a distance learning environment, or ELT system, may be referred to as the ELT Enterprise Model.

The second part of the approach means adequate recognition of the practicalities of what currently exists and is likely to exist in the near future. It is to derive the architectural framework from existing and emerging system architectures in support of functions (or services) needed in a distance learning environment.

A unifying force is that the perspectives which are expressed in the enterprise have an interest in the strength of the selected qualities predicted by appropriate engineering models.

The derived architectural framework is aimed to accommodate all the actors, characteristics and situations which currently exist and be flexible such that new ELT situations are also able to be accommodated given that significant changes are expected to evolve. The framework is also aimed to provide the ability to identify relationships (and discontinuities) whilst providing a (logical) hierarchy of co-operating and balanced components and subsystems.

An overriding aspect of the approach is to derive a process which can be followed by different target user groups in an area which is very complex. The significant work is to show how a range of pedagogic aspects can be related to technology solutions.

2.3 The framework of models

The CTA comprises a number of models with appropriate specifications across a spectrum of business, training, and technological issues. We outline the models, with some indication of their relationships in Figure 1, as the Common Training Architecture Framework. This diagram describes the architecture at the highest level.

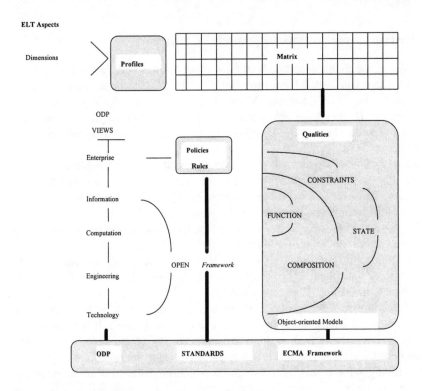

Figure 1 *The CTA Framework*

This figure can be read as follows:

- *ELT Aspects* are the essential input to the process. They are produced as the output from the consideration of scenario profiles and enterprise modelling work;
- *ODP Views* are the overall modelling approach because of their relevance through the five viewpoints;

- *Policies and Rules* are used in the context of the OPEN*framework* systems architecture to assist in the task of describing how external constraints, for example legislation, management practices, processes and standards should be applied. Some of these may be mandatory, whilst others will be discretionary;
- *OPENframework* is an architecture which enterprises can use to create information systems which meet their business requirements;
- *Qualities* are described in OPENframework as the value system used by enterprises concerned with behavioural requirements of information systems. Attention to the qualities of availability, usability, performance, security and potential for change are required if the system provided is to achieve the behaviour the enterprise needs;
- *Object Oriented Models* are used in the building of various models to express differing facets of the needs of the enterprise and the technology solution being proposed;
- *ECMA Framework:* the ECMA Software Engineering Environment Reference Model is used to express the services which are required from the technology components to meet the needs of the ELT expression for the enterprise. These services are a fundamental component of the CTA;
- *Standards* are the fundamental output from the CTA in the sense that many standards per se will be recommended, but also the overall approach described by the CTA is a standard itself;
- *The matrix* is the transformation or mapping mechanism used in various ways at differing times. The matrices are used ultimately to relate abstract items such as enterprise models to technology components.

The users of the CTA may be organisations in the context of their business activities whilst a project will build an instantiation to test a situation in a real world setting. An organization or project aiming to exploit the CTA should therefore decide which specifications and models described in the framework are most relevant to its situation.

2.4 A modelling approach

The modelling approach is illustrated in Figure 2. This figure also shows a process on how the modelling approach should be used. Figure 2 should be seen as a simpler form of Figure 1.

Implementation or operation of the architecture is documented as a *process* stating how the specifications and models are produced and used. In producing these specifications and models projects will also be able to demonstrate how they conform to the architecture.

The business need with ELT aspects identified as well as the IT systems supporting it, should be modelled using different models, the ELT *Enterprise* Model and the ELT *Engineering* Model and a set of *services*.

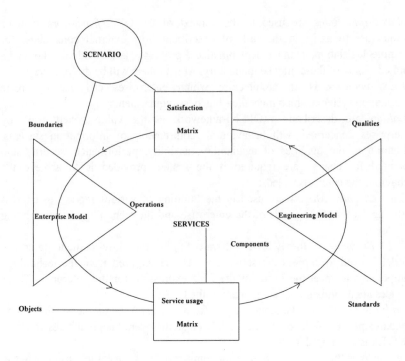

Figure 2 *The selected modelling approach*

The ELT Enterprise Model, ideally, should be created by a person with ELT knowledge and using top-down systems analysis techniques. It incorporates the enterprise view and the information view following the ISO ODP standard.

The ELT Engineering Model, ideally, should be created by a person with knowledge of IT system design and operation. It incorporates the engineering view and the technology view of the ISO ODP standard.

The set of services links the two models. It represents the computational view of the ISO ODP standard.

Following this approach, illustrated in Figure 2, the following steps are needed:

- *Identification of ELT scenario:*
From the available scenarios select the one most appropriate to the needs of the organization or project under consideration.

The scenario descriptions have been chosen to provide an adequate set of details to enable ELT aspects to be properly taken into account in making this early decision. If there is no suitable scenario then an enterprise model should be produced, so that ELT needs are identified.

The essential output from the enterprise model should be the list of ELT aspects valued as to the needs of the organization or project concerned.

From the scenario analysis and enterprise model the list of ELT attributes is then used as the basis for completing statements of the desirable 'qualities' against the ELT needs. This work results in the production of the Satisfaction Matrix.

- *Definition of services:*

In order to propose how an IT system could be a solution to the ELT system requirements as expressed in the Enterprise model the relationship between abstract models and technology objects needs to be derived.

To promote maximum convergence between the Enterprise and Engineering models, CTA defines a set of *services* which encapsulate the desired functionality and operations most appropriate to the ELT needs. The Enterprise model should express the needs of such services to support the ELT situation, and the Engineering model should express the provision of such services through components.

The services are shown as the essential link between the Enterprise and Engineering models. They perform the function of conversion between the abstract ELT expressions and technology components. The services provide the software environment required for open distributed processing in a flexible and distance learning environment. They are ordered in groups each with a common area of concern, such as the management of multimedia objects, open communications and common user interfaces, and are user interface services, information management services, distribution application services, networking services (interconnection as well as inter working services), system management services, and the platform.

The descriptions of the Services also define the standards to which they conform now and those to which they are most likely to be targeted to conform to in the future.

- *Selection of ELT Engineering Model:*

The Engineering Model defines the Services in detail, identifies the components in hardware and software terms, proposes configurations with a means of determining dependencies and versions, and describes the standards which should be followed.

Another major task of the Engineering Model is to provide a means to convert between the services as well as the qualities expressed in the 'satisfaction matrix' and technology solutions (or components).

In order to complete the process and ensure adequate relationships have been described, it is recommended that a set of matrices is used: satisfaction matrix, service usage matrix, service to technology matrix, ELT to technology matrix.

3 TOWARDS AN ELT FRAMEWORK AND SOME BASIC SCENARIOS

The basic models and scenarios within CTA are based, as mentioned above, on a framework of education, learning and training dimensions or aspects. By using this framework it becomes possible to describe ELT scenarios in a more or less standardized way.

The first section outlines the dimensions that were considered important for description of technology-based learning and training configurations. The emphasise on the ELT situation arises from the consideration that this provides the most specific starting point for getting the requirements of the training enterprise activities in place, as far as they are different from general business activities.

The second section describes a set of ELT configurations in an abstract way. They are called scenarios, although the use of this term has some ambiguity in this context, because the dynamics remain somewhat implicit. Four of these scenarios are directly concerning an ELT situation, the other two emphasise the development and authoring issues and the production and delivery issues and are indirectly related to the ELT situation. The argument is that any technology strategy deployment will in some way change the borders between the various activities, for example by changing access rights, information exchange, re-use of materials, etcetera, between the actors and new processes and services may develop.

3.1 A framework of ELT dimensions and aspects

Main constituting elements of every ELT configuration that may be the subject for technology support are:

- tasks related to the ELT goals that have to be performed by actors (students, tutors, managers, etcetera);
- materials to be used by the execution of tasks of various actors, in particular students;
- support services to the actors, again especially referring to the students' tasks;
- a technological infrastructure that enables the work and communication flows.

Processes of data transfer (i.e. learning materials) by different kinds of representation forms (media) and processes of communication between different actors are basic to every ELT task situation. The detailed analysis of information flows and communications will lead to the points of application for consensus-building on harmonisation and agreements on standards that may improve efficiency, effectiveness, quality, etc.

The dimensions for the description of the ELT settings are an intermediate abstraction, based on an analysis of many empirical situations available from DELTA projects and elsewhere (Verreck, 1993b, page 131-132).

The following eight dimensions are considered relevant for the objectives of the CTA; the first two of them being of a more general nature, the others more directly of importance in ELT situations:

- Learner Environment and Age Range;
- ELT Task;

- Learning Support Actors and Roles;
- Learning - Work Transfer;
- Learning Material Flexibility;
- Communication Services;
- Presentation Systems.

These dimensions are clarified and illustrated below.

3.1.1 *Learner environment and age range*

There is a wide age range of potential learners and their backgrounds, ranging from poorly educated to highly trained professionals. For example there is the conventional or traditional range of learners in various forms of education. Target groups for the CTA are mainly from university and higher education. They are in the age range of 18 to 25.

Potential learners can also be found in work related situations ranging from 18 to 60 years of age. Other spectra can be taken into account in the socio-economic environment, now prevailing in Europe. A target group may be the unemployed, that also covers the age range of 18 to 60.

Another one relates specifically to women, as far as they timely and/or partly are not employed due to motherhood. The age range may then be divided in for example 23 to 30, and 40 to 60.

Many other more detailed examples could be mentioned The rate of change with which some people are employed and then unemployed is increasing rather than decreasing.

The learner environment is more directly relevant to the CTA issues, as they are related to the general flexible distance learning concerns of the DELTA programme. It may be specified in several ways. Four main learner environments can be used for the learning process:

- Home;
- Educational institute;
- Education/Training Centre;
- Work.

Also mixed forms are possible. For example when practicals take place in a study centre and student has to study the printed course materials at home.

3.1.2 *ELT task*

A basic constituting element of an ELT situation is a task or series of tasks to be executed by one or more learner simultaneously, either in collaboration or independently. The task is provided by some means, either persons or systems, and there is as well in a similar way support (additional resources) available.

The first dimension classifies learning tasks with respect to the characteristic: *the number of learners involved in a specific task setting*. This is a quite important element in the design of any ELT scenario. As soon as, for example, large numbers are involved there are strong constraints on the degree of possible interactions with learning support actors or with fellow students. The explicit design of the degree of interactivity has to be considered as a main task requirement.

The following positions on this dimension may be distinguished. Type names are given for ease of reference.

- Student/Trainee: 1;
- Minimal Group: 2;
- Work Group: 5;
- Project Group: 10;
- Small Class: 20;
- Class: 40;
- Large Class: 60;
- Audience: 100;
- Large Audience: > 200.

3.1.3 Learning support actors and roles

This aspect relates to the different services available to the learner by way of an actor or role in the ELT scenario. The involvement of different roles may differ as to the phases of the learning / training cycle through which the individual passes, such as orientation, preparation, learning, assessment and transfer.

A weak ordering of different actors/roles available to the student in assisting with his ELT is possible as to the degree of involvement in the learning task itself. For example: *administrator, manager, mentor, tutor, or teacher.*

A general framework on roles and functions, also applicable to ELT scenarios, is the CCITT draft standards recommendation for Audio-Visual Interactive (AVI) Services (October 1992). The purpose of the CCITT recommendation is to define and describe, from the user's point of view, the general features and attributes of the AVI Services, regardless of the network environment where the service might be provided. AVI Services concern facilities to fulfil the requirements of users that are involved in creating, exchanging, modifying, managing and executing AVI applications. Several types of users have access to the AVI Service with different rights given to them. The information life cycle varies according to the type of application and can have different value on a scale from short to long.

The users of the AVI service may have several roles:
- Author,
- Information Manager,

- Preparer and
- Retriever,

enabling them to deal with the families of functions:

- Editing;
- Information Management;
- Execution.

The recommendation gives more details on the needs of the four categories of roles according to the families of functions.

3.1.4 *Learning - work transfer*

The amount of fit between the ELT task and the work situation is an important issue for business-oriented ELT (as is another objective of DELTA). The possibilities for transfer of the training to the work situation are for example very important as far as technologies are used in ELT that are similar or the same to those in the work situation.

A weak order of positions, again with types indication for ease of reference, on this dimension is:

- Instruction: for a specific task execution on the workplace;
- Training: for knowledge and skills necessary for specific tasks on workplace or not;
- Courses: for knowledge and skills generally useful for tasks not on work place;
- Education: for preparation to higher qualification and/or function;
- Development: for personal and or organisational purposes.

3.1.5 *Learning material flexibility*

The flexibility of use or re-use of (parts of) learning material requires inevitably support by technology. Various actors in the scenario are involved: authors and developers, as well as learning support actors and even learners may have choices. This makes clear that this dimension is at the cross-roads between various subsystems in the ELT 'business' system: authoring, development, production, delivery, usage, etc.

The flexibility aspect is important for learning situations that may become feasible in the near future, in which ELT tasks require the students to retrieve and 'assemble' their learning materials ('products'), tailored to their learning needs, knowledge state, etc.

To specify a dimension for this aspect, a reference can be made to logistic issues in manufacturing of goods and components. It uses a well-known classification from these production environments based on where the location in the development-production-delivery processes is of the so-called customer-order-de coupling point. It may serve as a reference for the flexibility issue as described in this place.

The order of aspects proposed here is one of increasing availability to adapt the learning material to one's demands, and uses the type names from the reference source.

- Made-to-Stock: the learning material is available in total and cannot be adapted itself to the learner's demands;
- Assembled-to-Order: the learning material is available on a well-defined and engineered parts basis and can be put together from these parts to adapt to learner's demands;
- Make-to-Order: the learning material is constructed from parts as well as add-ons to adapt to learner's demands;
- Engineer-to-Order: the learning material is designed and constructed to meet specifically the learner's demands;
- Selling Capacity: the learning material is not directly available, but the expertise is and may be questioned directly.

3.1.6 *Communication services*

Communication services are a major part of any ELT scenario that is technology supported. Three groups of services are distinguished in order of increasing direct communication needs. CTA deliverable 4 provides much more detail.

- Remote Access to Multimedia Information: Remote access is the interactive filing, retrieval and processing of information stored on remote computing systems and made accessible to clients via a server. Remote access may involve the same types of objects as deferred time communications, however, the information is supplied to the client on demand within a short response time.
- Deferred Time Communications: This is the non-interactive exchange of information and it does not depend on the concurrent presence of the communication partners at their communication terminal. The method of communication may be electronic mail, file transfer, a bulletin board or deferred time computer Conferencing.
- Real Time Communications: With real time communication we mean any transport of data from a source to a sink (or target) with time constraints. Several of the functions are to be provided via servers (e.g. any conferencing). The forms of communication may be one or a combination of the following: replay of stored multimedia objects, real time audio conferencing, slide shows, screen sharing, real time video conferencing, etc.

3.1.7 Presentation Systems

This aspect concerns the hardware and software available to the learner, and the costs involved. In fact several dimensions might be taken into account here:

- Capital Costs. This factor for using technology to deliver distance training is variable and increases significantly using a basic PC, MPC, + moving video, + ISDN and/or + Satellite;
- Delivery Systems. A range of media exists depending on the media chosen to deliver the material, such as PC, Video VHS, Television, Conferencing, Classroom, etc;
- Existing Desktop Systems. Another consideration is that many people in all sizes of organization will have existing desktop systems in use. It is likely that any new service must be able to integrate and co-exist with the current business applications.

3.2 Scenarios for education and training

This section deals with scenarios for ELT. The general meaning of a *scenario* is a sequence of events, showing interactions, information exchanges, etc. By developing a scenario one gets a feeling of the main objects, processes, resources, and their interdependencies in a particular existing or future situation. A scenario can thus be conceived as an internally consistent vision about a situation to come. It is important to get hold of the most relevant variables in the scenarios that one builds.

One step further in the CTA approach is the development of models based on the scenarios. *Models* are abstract descriptions of the real world, simple representations of more complex forms, processes and functions of phenomena and ideas. Their purpose is to facilitate understanding and enhance prediction. They consist of a form (verbal, analogue, mathematical) and a content. For some if the work on modelling we refer to CTA deliverables 4 and 6.

Before we start with the description of scenarios in use by the CTA, we have a short view on some well-known general pedagogical situations that are in use or will become so by technology support.

3.2.1 General pedagogical situations in a distance education scenario

The most commonly known pedagogical situation is the one of one teacher in a classroom delivering a training course to several students. It is characterized by oneness of place, time and topics but also by high directivity from teacher and low creativity from students except during questions/answers sessions where interactivity is at its maximum.

Several other situations are also well-known. The first situation is a group situation, in which some group task or assignment exists.

The second situation we all bear in mind is also a group situation called tutoring. In this case, the tutor is much more there to help students who are progressing at their own speed during exercises or experimentation's in a laboratory for example.

The third situation is an individual situation where the student is learning by reading a book, watching TV or doing his homework.

All of these situations can be transposed to technology-supported learning including distance learning due to geographical fragmentation of public and lack of teachers or experts. But all the situations can be properly implemented only if the technical solutions are first cost effective and second well accepted by users. Those two points are in fact leading to the definition of architectures and usage scenarios for distance education and training with the creation of models able to evolve with technics and prices for each pedagogical situation.

The various situations may have to be combined during a long training course, and it is clear that there is no way to totally replace the classical learning by distance learning.

The most common technology-supported pedagogic situations in existence now may be called:

- Virtual Classroom Situation;
- Distance Tutoring Situation;
- Self-learning Situation;
- Distance Education Situation.

What is called a *Virtual Classroom* is when a teacher is delivering a training course to a group of students, that is in fact constituted of several groups geographically separated but linked by communications systems giving to anybody the impression they all are in the same classroom.

In the *Distance Tutoring Situation*, students are working individually or in small groups more or less geographically separated and a tutor is able to survey what they do and can help them on request.

What differentiates a *Self-Learning Situation* from a tutored one, is that there is no human help during the training session, but both situations potentially use the same types of terminals, networks and resources. Another difference with tutoring is that the remote stations can be connected onto the network only during the searching phase and during the transfer phase. In that case every student or group of students works self-paced as long as necessary without cost constraint coming from communications.

Based on the previous descriptions of situations we can combine them in order to get a complete, coherent and cost effective educational system. The challenge of tele-training is not a technical one but lays in assembling existing or emerging technologies and the economics of tele training depends mainly on the organization of the use of technologies among the training process. In this *Distance Education Scenario*, for better return on investment, each classroom has been designed in order to operate as normal classroom or as virtual classroom. During self-training sessions, as for tutoring sessions (local or distant) the computers of the students have access to on line local or distant libraries of training material of various types; text files, video sequences.

3.2.2 Basic scenarios and models for distance education and training

A series of six scenarios is proposed, that may be considered basic ones for flexible distance education and training, that is they are intended to cover most of the existing situations, and those that are envisaged in innovative R&D projects such as in the DELTA programme. In fact, they are mainly based on current DELTA projects, and it quite evident that other scenarios and models may exist or can be developed. On the other hand many of those will match to a large extent these scenarios. It is also evident that the scenarios may be mixed in implementations of them.

To put it in another way: the scenarios are constructs, having considered empirical scenarios from several projects but not exactly reflecting them. They are provided with a label for easy reference. Enterprise modelling aspects for the basic scenarios are difficult to describe independent from the enterprise context, and sufficient detailed empirical data were not available for most of the projects' scenarios.

Four scenarios are directed at ELT situations, one is concerned with collaborative authoring and one with production and delivery. The latter two are included, because it is conjectured that technology developments will shift boundaries between available services in these scenarios and the more strict ELT ones. Major obstacles to more flexibility and interchanges in the moment are e.g. access and copyrights.

• *Professional expertise update scenario*
The scenario is especially aiming at professionals, that is persons with a reasonable high level of initial education and training, who already have had some work experience.

They need not be working solely as specialists in their domain, but may also be involved in multidisciplinary business activities, or in core business activities, like development of new products or contacts with clients within or outside the company. They usually have a relatively high salary. The number of them within the company is, also relative to other employees restricted, but it may also be the case that the company consists mainly of such professionals, like in a consulting enterprise.

They need regularly updating of their knowledge and skills in their specific domain and in new domains for their tasks. Needs for training arise from the launch of new products, start of the development of new products or opening up new markets, business reorganisations and mergers, or usual staff development programs. A common element in it is that the needs are related to the (new) tasks and/or positions that are given to them.

Updating of their expertise by training has for the most part to be done in a relatively short period of time, because of demands from the ongoing work, and group work (virtual or real) as well as individual work is usually part of the training setting. It also means that there are some fixations on time and place in the ELT setting, and one or more teacher/tutor support actors are involved.

• *Professional expertise demand scenario*

The scenario concerns especially professionals, that is persons with a reasonable high level of initial education and training, who already have had some work experience.

They work alone or in small teams on projects and problems, that especially require their domain expertise and at the same time a reasonable acquaintance with knowledge and skills from other disciplines in cases of multidisciplinary teams. They usually have a relatively high income, as employee in an enterprise, or as independent professional. In the former case the number of colleagues with similar expertise within the company is relatively low, but it may also be the case that the company consists mainly of such professionals, like in a development or consulting enterprise. In the latter case, there usually exist collaboration 'networks' with colleagues elsewhere for peer consulting and the like.

A common element is that they are engaged in strongly project-oriented or problem-directed activities. This is a main reason for their training need: they have to solve problems for which they may not have the all the knowledge and skills at their disposal, but know that this may reside with colleagues elsewhere. Availability of them may be directly and personal or indirectly by a remote resource base.

The expertise usually is needed urgently in the ongoing work, that is there is a serious time constraint. The training setting may contain some group conferencing (virtual or real), but the main characteristic is independent and individual work in an as flexible way as possible. Scheduling of the training opportunities is of minor importance, and the involvement of one or more teacher/tutor support actors is also less.

• *Employees training scenario*

The scenario aims at employees in a company, that have work experience and a level of education that may be regarded medium-level.

Their jobs are part of operational business activities in primary processes or in support departments, and their is not much multidisciplinarity involved. They have an average salary in the enterprise. A relatively large number of employees in the enterprise belongs to this category.

As regards the specific training needs they can be divided into many groups, each of considerable size, depending upon specific responsibilities in the business. Besides, there are common training needs to be fulfilled time and again, because of enterprise-wide policies. They need regularly updating of their knowledge and skills for performing their tasks and jobs, arising from by new enterprise policies, the launch of new products and services, as well as business reorganisations and mergers.

Updating of their knowledge and skills has to proceed in a well-organised time frame and manageable as to interferences with day to day operations. There is usually no specific task-related argument to have the training within a short period of time, organization of training by shifts is sometimes a feasible option. Constraints on time and place in the ELT setting are caused by practical and cultural considerations. There are one or more teacher/tutor support actors involved, as well as training managers and training resource centres.

- *Open distance education institute telematic services*

This is the scenario for an institute that develops and delivers education to students at a distance, who usually engage in a more long-term relationship with the institute, that is a programme of study consisting of many courses.

A study and work environment is available with a number of tools that support the students in their contacts with the institute, tutors, fellow students, etc. Telecommunication services are a significant component of the scenario, and available for remote, deferred and real-rime interactions, besides more traditional means of delivery. Another part of the services is to support resource-based ELT, and may entail connections to distributed repositories elsewhere.

Various groups of students or clients may be distinguished, and part of the services may also be available to potential students or former students, more or less public. In the latter case the 'work' environment is more restricted.

- *Distributed production and delivery scenario*

This scenario focuses on development, production and delivery of learning materials in a way that is appropriate to fast changing demands on contents, types of formats, supporting services, etc. from the education and training settings itself.
A summary of the main objectives from different perspectives in this scenario:
   - exchange and handling of data on training demand and supply;
   - collaboration on development and production;
   - tailoring learning materials to different circumstances, e.i. languages, versions;
   - delivery of training on demand;
   - browsing, pick and mix by several actors to meet tailoring requirements;
   - distributed printing on demand;
   - inclusion of other distribution devices.

The main functionality and services, as well as the boundaries and limitations of the system can be described as an integrated co-production support environment.
   - Integrated: support of wide range of activities, consistent , and shared information;
   - Co-production: support of development and production, but also requirements, design, etc.;
   - Support: different levels from data integrity control, etc. to knowledge-based techniques;
   - Environment: managerial aspects as well as technical aspects.

- *Distributed collaborative authoring scenario*

This scenario, as stated before, focuses on collaborative authoring of learning materials or computer-based training materials. The scenario is based on the collaboration of multiple actors, and the distribution of the development process over several workplaces. The development is addressed to advanced multimedia courseware and other learning materials, on such a large scale that quality and efficiency are main commitments.

The ELT aspects do not apply to this scenarios, but we envisage that this scenario itself may be attached to all of the other scenarios. That may happen when ELT actors and settings get access to tools and data that are also used by authors and course developers.

4 ARCHITECTURE DEVELOPMENT FOR THE CTA

An *architecture* is defined as a framework for functional components, embracing application of standards, rules, conventions, and processes (in which there is human involvement). This supports the integration of a wide range of (information technology based) products and services, enabling them to be used effectively within an enterprise.

In order to model the role of computing mechanisms it is necessary to model the world in which they operate. In other words, both the Education, Learning and Training situation (that is a real world system including the learners, tutors, etc.), and the support systems (the machinery which supports ELT), should be modelled. Ideally, one makes abstracts at both of these scopes, since the former gives purpose to the latter, and the latter supports the former.

The architecture development also provides the methodology, or process, by which organisations and/or projects can use the CTA. It is recommended that the methodology of the CTA be considered as a set of processes. This is believed to be familiar to many organisations who are using process as a means of describing their businesses.

4.1 Modelling techniques

A number of models and/or approaches are used to describe in structured ways the logical and physical technologies. We give a brief survey of them.

Open Distributed Processing Reference Model is a system projection model to describe the enterprise, informational, computational, engineering, technology views of the system, all in object oriented terms.

The *ECMA CASEE Reference Model* is becoming widely accepted in Software Engineering fields. This model is used as a framework to describe the services which are of importance to the CTA.

The *OPENframework* model is used, because the ECMA Reference Model has some limitations when it is re-used to describe situations for which it was not designed, e.g. general information systems architectures and business models.

Object Oriented modelling techniques (Rumbaugh, et al., 1991) will be used to detail the various views, like in the ODP-RM.

Measurement models also need to be considered and a methodology recommended if at all possible. Possible contenders, areas for consideration include:

Service Level Agreements; Systems, Communication, Processor and Storage Benchmarks, NSTL Laboratory Methodology; Application Programs, Success Factors and Process Maturity Assessment.

Physical models. There is a need to consider which of the physical models has relevance to the CTA work and how the resulting architecture may be represented and supported by existing models wherever possible. Examples which should be considered further include: Client/ Server Model, a Personal/ Departmental/ Corporate Model, ISO 7-Layer Model and Audio and Video Functions Model.

4.2 Meta-models

Each type of model is detailed in terms of the characteristic attributes which form the model: the Meta-Model. For each attribute several examples are given to illustrate the concept of the attribute:

1. A Scenario, expressed in ELT terms;
2. An Enterprise model, expressed in terms of
   - Objects (Actors, Agents, Artefacts);
   - Operations (Methods, Actions, Processes, functions);
   - Boundaries (Scheme, obligations, permissions, states).
3. An Engineering model, expressed in terms of
   - Components (Logical and physical units, Configurations, Dependencies, versions);
   - Qualities (Performance, Availability, Reliability);
   - Standards (Policies, Protocols, Interfaces).
4. Services, which are provided by Engineering Components, and which are used to provide Enterprise operations to meet the needs of the chosen scenario;
5. Matrices, which record and summarize how results of the models, such as predicted and required qualities, compare.

The Concept of a 'Service' needs to be clarified on a more detailed level. The CTA is characterized as a set of services. A service may be regarded as a package of related functionalities and could be composed at any level of detail. Thus we may refer at a gross level to the provision of a 'Training Service', or at a detailed level refer to a 'Data Storage Service'. CTA uses the term at the Engineering level to characterize the basic functions which can be used to construct ELT systems.

The Scenarios have been described above. The next sections describe in broad lines the Enterprise Model, the Engineering Model and the Services. For further details we refer to the CTA deliverables with the remark that the latter are subject of further work in the project, that falls out of the scope of this article.

4.2.1 *The Enterprise Model*

The Meta Model - of a CTA conformant system - distinguishes and defines:

- the components (the objects) which may form a system;
- he dynamic activity of the objects, either individually (i.e. the methods in the objects), or collectively (which characterises the overall activity of the system);
- the boundaries which must be observed during operation, (i.e. the constraints), including the states permitted during operation of a system, and the external interface to the system.

CTA will use these types to classify all aspects of relevance, from the training enterprise down to technology. In more detail these types can be amplified in the terms of Objects, Operations and Boundaries.

Objects
Objects are produced or consumed by a system. They are also used to construct a system conforming to CTA. The Meta Model classifies the various types of objects encompassed in CTA. Examples are learning material, tutors/mentors time, learner's time, personal information, navigation structures (relationships, links), tools, physical resources, software or hardware components.

The Enterprise Model will be formed from the following types of object:

- Actors;
- Public Information;
- Personal information;
- Domain (of knowledge);
- Course Content;
- Course Structure;
- Instruction (Unit of Learning Material);
- Multi Media composition (in units of media);
- Media Layout (In space and time);
- Administrative information (resources, timetable);
- Business model (finance, plans).

Operations
The Meta model classifies the various operations by the type of activity in the Enterprise. The following types of Enterprise operations are distinguished:

- Communicating (e.g. with a tutor or within learning group);
- Sequencing   (e.g. presenting learning material);
- Distributing   (e.g. locating material);
- Assessing   (e.g. of achievement);
- Recording   (e.g. the use of services or material);
- Managing   (e.g. making decisions on policy).

4.2.2 *The Engineering Model*

In the Engineering Model each service (engineering object) contains the methods which are relevant to internal working of that service. The Meta-model focuses attention on the collective activity of services, and distinguishes models of activity which enable deduction of 'qualities'. In other words, the interworking of selected services will determine each quality, and the types of model of the services are distinguished in the Meta-model.

The Meta-model therefore distinguishes the following types of models of service interworking:

- Performance;
- Usability;
- Availability;
- Security;
- Potential for change.

These models predict the 'Qualities' obtained by using the services in combination.

Boundaries

Boundaries define the constraints to be obeyed in a system conforming to the CTA. These need clearly stating to reduce ambiguity in the detailed design. There are three main sub-types of boundaries: policies, external interfaces and standards.

- Policies. These are determined by the Enterprise management, in order to ensure the efficient production and delivery of high quality (and lawful) training. They will however limit the degrees of freedom with which the goals of the Enterprise can be achieved.
  The CTA policy is that Enterprises should use the services defined in the CTA where appropriate. That is the 'services' should be used to show the relationship between the engineering and enterprise models;
- External interfaces define the boundary usable by an external system. This may be in terms of types of messages permitted or expected;
- Standards are fundamental to CTA. This subtype includes all relevant standards. They are all external to the CTA and referred to as relevant. They are detailed in the Engineering model.

4.2.3 *Services*

The next level of detail of the Meta-Model is a description of types and services. They are provided in an initial listing. Both of these lists will evolve as detailed study is made of these topics.

Each service is described in general terms:

- the data and methods contained within the service (viewed as an object);

- the methods contained within the service;
- the external boundaries and standards to which the service object conforms.

The services provide the software environment required for distributed processing in a heterogeneous multi vendor network. The services are ordered in groups each with a common area of concern, such as Data management, Remote communication or User Interface. This is illustrated in Figure 3.

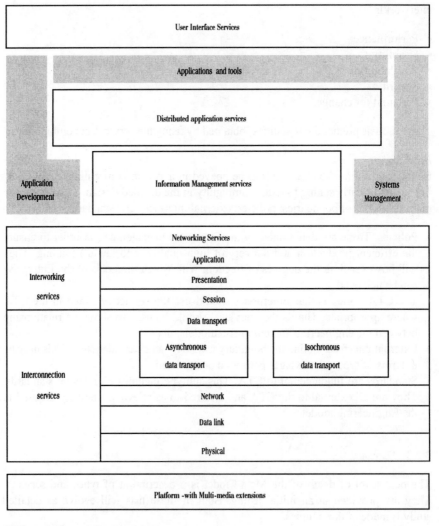

Figure 3 *The services groups*

A list of services is distinguished that formed and divided among the three technical areas OCI, CIS and CUI as a provisional input for their work:

- Information Management services:
  Metadata service;
  Data Storage and Persistence service;
  Document structuring service;
  Data Transaction service;
  Backup/Archive service;
  Derivation service;
  Distribution and Location service.
- System Management Services:
  Fault Management;
  Performance Management;
  Platform Service.
- Distributed Application services:
  Name service, Directory;
  Access Control and Security service.
- Interworking services:
  Application communication, (File transfer, Mail);
  Remote Procedure Call;
  Distributed Stream Management.
- Interconnection services:
  - The Transport Layer;
    Isochronous Data Transport;
    Asynchronous Data Transport.
  - The Network Layer;
    Telecommunications services;
    Broadcast services.
  - The Physical Layer.
- User Interface Services:
  Presentation/Interaction Service;
  User Interface data Service;
  Dialog Service;
  Profile Service;
  User Assistance Service.
- Miscellaneous group:
  Session Service;
  Application Interface Service;
  Applications;
  Application Development service;
  Accounting Services.

5 FUTURE CTA WORK

This article has presented a survey of part of the work in the CTA project. On the base of this, the three areas Open Communications Interface, Common Information Space and Common User Interface have been taken up the work along three steps.

Step 1 is a detailed requirements analysis of the various scenarios. Step 2 is the development of a sub-architecture for the domain, specifying the technical options and technical profiles and standards available or needed. Step 3 is the development of validation procedures by which any project scenario may be tested as to its conformance to the recommended profiles.

The result of the CTA project will be a handbook that may be used to develop scenarios and technical solutions that take into account the recommended technical profiles.

The next step is to demonstrate and validate the recommendations and profiles in practice. This is outside the scope of the CTA project, but in the meantime a subsequent project is approved to do the work: the CTA-II Demonstration and Validation project. This project is collaborating with a number of current DELTA projects and other projects to this ends, as these have developed systems for technology-based ELT support. A series of support services will be available to these projects.

The final result of the CTA-II project are twofold. First, an update of the handbook, including high-confidence configurations, that is having met some approval in practice. Second, the design of an integrated information base that supports ELT system integrators by providing details on existing products and components.

Again, one step further would be the development of a certification service that may provide certificates to enterprises and projects that meet standards recommendations. Similar services are well-known in general software engineering and system integration practice, and their are many companies and institutes that provide them. The development of these services to the field of technology-supported flexible distance learning is even outside the scope of the CTA-II project, but it is the envisaged final result of the CTA approach that has been taken.

REFERENCES

Main references, especially to CTA deliverables are listed here. More detailed references are available in the CTA deliverables themselves, and will be available in the CTA Handbook Series, that is to appear to the end of 1994, as a first edition.

Collins, J.R., & Pratt, J. (1993). *The Meta-models for the Common Training Architecture* (Deliverable 5). CTA - Common Training Architecture, Delta D2023.

Collins, J.R., Pratt, J.M., Schmutz, H., Verreck, W.A., & Bruggen, J. van (1993). *Education and Training Enterprise Models* (Deliverable 2). CTA - Common Training Architecture, Delta D2023.

ICL (1993). *OPENframework System.* Architecture Series. London: Prentice Hall.

ISO/IEC 10746, *Basic Reference Model of open Distributed Processing*, RM-ODP.

Rumbaugh, J., Blaha, M., Premerli, W., Eddy, F., & Lorensen, W. (1991). *Object-Oriented Modeling and Design.* Englewood Cliffs, N.J.: Prentice Hall.

Verreck, W.A. (eds.) (1993a). *A Framework for Education and Training Models and Scenarios* (Deliverable 3). CTA - Common Training Architecture, Delta D2023.

Verreck, W.A. (eds.) (1993b). *Description and Definition* (Deliverable 6). CTA - Common Training Architecture, Delta D2023.

Verreck, W.A., Weges, H.G., Bruggen, J. van, Ray, D., & Collins, J. (1993). *Models and Scenarios for Education and Training* (Deliverable 4). CTA - Common Training Architecture, Delta D2023.

Zorkoczy, P. (eds.) (1992). *CTA Booklet* (Deliverable 1). CTA - Common Training Architecture, Delta D2023.

Acknowledgements: Acknowledgements are given to the partners in the CTA project. The presentation in this article is the responsibility of the authors mentioned. The partners involved are: Peter Zorkoczy (EPOS International, Switzerland), John Collins and John Pratt (Peritas/ICL), Hermann Schmutz (IBM - European Network Center, Germany), Harald Mispelkamp and Ulrich Kohler (Dornier, Germany), Mario Capurso (Tecnopolis Csata, Italy), Dominique Ray (CITCOM, France), Joseph Fromont (CCETT, France), Augusto Chioccariello (CNR-Istituto per le Technologie Didattiche, Italy), Norbert Benamou (SELISA, France), Chris Hornung (FhG - Institut für Graphische Datenverarbeitung, Germany), Graeme Oswald (MARI Computer Systems, UK).

Author Index

Subject Index

List of Addresses

This list of addresses contains the addresses of the first authors and the editors

Professor Philip Barker
Interactive Systems Research Group
Human-Computer Interaction Laboratory
School of Computing and Mathematics
University of Teesside
United Kingdom
Email: Philip.Barker@teesside.ac.uk

Dr. Norbert Benamou
SELISA
17 Avenue du Parc
F-91380 Chilly-Mazarin
France
Email: norbert.benamou@sp1.y-net.fr

Mr. Peter Busch
Danish Technological Institute
Teknologiparken
DK-8000 Aarhus C.
Denmark

Professor Monique Grandbastien
C.R.I.N
Bâtiment LORIA
Campus Scientifique
BP 239
54506 VANDOEUVRE Cedex
France
Email: monique.grandbastien@loria.fr

Dr. Hermann Härtel
IPN
Olshausenstraße 62
24098 Kiel
Germany
Email: haertel@cul-ipn.uni-kiel.de

Dr. Ton de Jong
Faculty of Educational Science and
Technology
University of Twente
PO Box 217
7500 AE Enschede
The Netherlands
Email: jong@edte.utwente.nl

Dr. Harald Mispelkamp
Dornier GmbH
An der Bundesstraße 31
D-7990 Friedrichshafen
Germany
Email: Harald.Mispelkamp@eurokom.ie

Mr. Peter van Rosmalen
Research Institute for Knowledge Systems
PO Box 463
6200 AL Maastricht
The Netherlands
Email: rosmalen@riks.nl

Dr. Luigi Sarti
Istituto per le Tecnologie Didattiche
Consiglio Nazionale delle Ricerche
via De Marini, 6
Torre Di Francia
16149 GENOVA
Italy
Email: sarti@itd.ge.cnr.it

Mr. Kenneth Tait
Computer Based learning Unit
The University of Leeds
Leeds LS2 9JT
United Kingdom
Email: ken@cbl.leeds.ac.uk

Dr. Antonio Ulloa
Tecnoplois CSATA Novus Ortus
Str. Prov. Casamsassima km. 3
70010 Valenzano
Italy
Email: ulloa@vm.csata.it

Dr. Wil Verreck
Open University
Centre for Educational Technology and
Innovation Research (OTIC)
Valkenburgerweg 167
6419 AT Heerlen
The Netherlands
Email: oicwav@ouh.nl or hiw@ouh.nl